A COLLECTION OF NEW RECIPES FROM
THE ICONIC SAN FRANCISCO RESTAURANT

Seasons of Greens

KATIE REICHER, EXECUTIVE CHEF

PHOTOGRAPHY BY **ERIN SCOTT**

weldon**owen**

TO MY MOTHER & GRANDMOTHERS
who taught me to love food, work hard, and be kind

& TO MY HUSBAND, JESSE
who inspires me always

CONTENTS

INTRODUCTION 10

A VEGETARIAN PANTRY 15

HOW TO USE THIS BOOK 22

KITCHEN LARDER

Quick Kimchi 29

Pickled Mustard Seeds 29

Standard Pickles 32

Sweet Pickles 32

Compound Butters 32

Garlic Confit 33

Chili Crisp 35

Aioli 35

Vegan Aioli 36

Cashew Cream 36

Macadamia Nut "Ricotta" 37

Vegetable Stock 39

Porcini Jus 39

Creole Broth 40

SPREADS & SAUCES

Green Goddess Hummus 44

Chimichurri 47

Roasted Carrot Hummus 48

Eggplant Caponata 49

Peperonata 50

Whipped Garlic Ricotta 52

Sun-dried Tomato Harissa 53

Mint Pesto 55

Rhubarb Muhammara 56

Peanut Hoisin Sauce 57

Grilled Romesco Sauce 58

Roasted Cherry Tomato Sauce 59

SNACKS & THINGS TO SHARE

Fried Baby Artichokes 62

Slow Roasted Chile–Orange Pecans 65

Grilled Baby Fava Beans 66

Goat Cheese–Stuffed Cherry Bomb Chiles 67

Burrata Toasts with Balsamic Cherries 69

Smashed Cannellini Bean Toasts 70

Savory Johnny Cakes with Marinated Tomatoes . . . 71

Corn & Asiago Arancini 75

Fresh Spring Rolls with Sweet Potato 76

Chanterelle Shumai with Mirin Sauce 79

Nettle & Goat Cheese Filo Rolls 82

SOUPS & SALADS

Summer's Bounty Salad 86

Roasted Pepper Panzanella 89

Fava Bean & Green Garlic Fattoush 90

Roasted Cabbage & Farro Salad 91

Celery & Peanut Noodle Salad 92

Strawberry Tatsoi Salad 95

Kale & Apple Salad 96

Baby Lettuces with Snap Peas &
Extra-Herby Ranch 97

Avocado & Citrus Salad with Chimichurri 98

Escarole & Potato Salad 101

Couscous & Baby Artichoke Salad...............103

Creole Pumpkin & Collard Greens Soup..........104

Turmeric Chickpea Soup 106

Roasted Eggplant & Pepper Soup................107

Spring Minestrone 109

Creamy Corn Chowder 110

Black Lentil Mulligatawny 111

Coral Lentil Dal................................112

Portobello Tamarind Soup 114

Butternut Squash Soup.........................115

Kimchi Noodle Soup 117

Pozole Verde 118

Heirloom Tomato & Stone Fruit Gazpacho 121

DOUGHS & SAVORY PASTRIES

Spinach & Ricotta Dumplings.................... 124

Caramelized Mushroom & Onion Pasta 127

Honeynut Squash Gnocchi with Brown Butter 128

Fetuccine with Herb-Marinated Tomatoes
& Burrata 130

Escarole & Fagioli Pasta 131

Linguine with Cauliflower & Chard............... 132

Basic Cut Pasta 134

Pappardelle with Peperonata & Shell Beans.......135

Pierogi with Peas & Feta........................ 137

Basic Flaky Pastry 139

Corn & Poblano Empanadas......................140

Ethiopian Cabbage & Potato Puffs................143

Brussels Sprouts, Caramelized Shallot
& Taleggio Galette.............................145

VEGETABLE SIDES, BEANS & GRAINS

Yuca "Fries" with Beet Slaw 148

Gigante Beans with Mint Pesto & Barley 151

Grilled Cabbage with Makrut Lime Sambal........ 152

Sautéed Pea Tendrils with Calabrian Chile 153

Grilled Zucchini with Mint Pesto.................. 158

Grilled Sweet Potatoes with
Tahini Garlic Cashew Cream.....................159

Stewed Romano Beans in Arrabiata.............. 161

Grilled Peppers with Herby Corn Salsa............162

Masala Roasted Winter Squash...................165

Blistered Shishito Peppers.......................166

Mayocoba Beans with Urfa Biber 167

Steamed Brussels Sprouts with "Cali" Kosho......168

Asparagus with Cannellini Beans, Creamy Tarragon
Vinaigrette & Pickled Mustard Seeds 171

Berbere Spiced Lentils 172

Creamy Garlic & Herb Polenta 173

Roasted Potatoes with Dill & Garlic...............174

MAIN COURSES

Spring Vegetable Piccata........................178

Wild Mushrooms "Au Poivre"..................... 181

Autumn Vegetable Jambalaya 182

Wild Rice–Stuffed Portobellos 183

Lemongrass Tofu & Asparagus Stir-Fry............186

Chipotle & Lime Grilled Tofu 187

Shepherd's Pie 188

Manicotti with Broccoli & Béchamel 190

Chiles Rellenos. 193

Sunchoke Koftas in Curry 194

Spring Yellow Curry. 197

Moussaka. 198

Root Vegetable Biryani 200

Tofu & Vegetable Brochettes with Chimichurri . . . 203

Saffron Goat Cheese Risotto 204

Grits with Creamy Creole-Style Mushrooms 207

Stuffed Eggplants with Couscous. 208

Aloo Saag Pot Pie 209

DESSERTS

Sesame–Brown Sugar Cookies 212

Cranberry Pistachio Almond Shortbread. 215

Ginger Parsnip Oatmeal Cookies 216

Graham Crackers 217

Raspberry–White Chocolate Pound Cake 218

Rye Cake with Apricot Preserves 220

Maple Black Walnut Baklava. 223

Mocha Roulade with Hazelnut-Mocha
Whipped Cream. 225

Peaches & Coconut Frangipane Tart 227

Blueberry Lavender Cake with
Cream Cheese Frosting 230

Chevre Cheesecake with Fresh Berries 233

Vanilla-Poached Apple Cake. 234

Vegan Lemon Mousse with Cherry Compote. 237

Makrut Lime Granita 238

Coconut Tapioca. 239

Strawberry Rhubarb Squares 240

Fig Preserves Tart with Pistachio Crust 242

Almond Cardamom Persimmon Pudding. 243

ESSAYS

What Does It Mean to Preserve
a San Francisco Legacy? 12

The Deep Fryer Debate. 34

A Word on Artichokes 64

A Word on Nettles. 83

Microclimates & Seasonality 129

Green Gulch Farm. 155

Sustainable Greens 184

Black Walnuts & Native Plants. 224

ACKNOWLEDGMENTS 244

INDEX 246

Introduction

My very first encounter with Greens pretty much sealed the deal for the rest of my career, although, at the time, I didn't know it. What I found when I first walked through the black walnut doors was a palatial beauty, with floor-to-ceiling windows stretching across the far wall, a giant redwood masterpiece embracing guests as they sipped on lattes and noshed on hummus with tomato jam and olives, and a smiling staff welcoming me inside. When I walked in, I asked for Chef Somerville, who, I quickly learned, prefers to go by Annie. Annie introduced the restaurant to me as though she were welcoming me to her home.

We walked through the dining room together, meeting server Sadie and busser Manny along the way, heads turning as Annie in her white chef's coat glided through. I saw our private dining room, met Maria in her closet-of-an-office, passed the guest bathrooms and entered the loading dock, which is where, Annie told me, I would enter the building during my working days. The annex kitchen was the next stop, where I met our pastry team and learned where the door to the wine cellar is. And finally, we went into the main kitchen. Backlit by more floor to ceiling windows, I saw, in one moment, all of the daily commotion that is lunch service. Sergio and Carlos, both line cooks, and brothers, were on the line assembling more plates than I could count. Todd was placing orders, and the rest of the team, who I had yet to meet, were all working together like honeybees. Instantly I was hooked.

I learned in my first few years that, to Greens, vegetables are a celebration of many things: the seasons, the land, the farmers, the presence of rain

and water, and the people at Greens who come in to work every day to carefully prepare these vegetables for our guests to enjoy. We are ever inspired by the extraordinary land that is right outside our dining room windows, and our ever-changing menus reflect that. Driven by Zen values imparted by our connection with the San Francisco Zen Center, plus our long history of female chefs, the company culture at Greens fosters mindfulness and care in all that we do. There is a unique spirit in the kitchen and dining room that our guests, both new and returning, can feel. Even as we pass our forty-fifth year, through a pandemic and all, the dynamic and energy of Greens are more alive than ever.

Over the past few years, we have seen many changes. We started to alter our menus more often, mindfully changing each item after about two months in order to keep things fresh, hyper-seasonal, and interesting to our many returning guests. Our Greens to Go concept was retired in 2020 after our pandemic closure, when we pivoted to offering takeout from our main menu for the first time. The Greens to Go counter itself was finally removed in early 2024, making space for a beautiful new entryway. We have made new friendships and maintained others for decades, like with our own farm, Green Gulch. We have collaborated with other chefs, vintners, and artisans, while giving back to the nonprofits that stand for food justice and equality, like Foodwise, the same nonprofit that runs the farmers' market that we have been attending for years. And perhaps most significantly, we have expanded the diversity and inclusiveness of our menu, taking inspiration from places like Ethiopia, Korea, Singapore, Ukraine, Iran, Hungary, and Brazil—all while fostering the heart and soul of our unique cuisine.

In these pages, you'll find a host of new recipes that detail our expanded horizons, from roasted carrot hummus with harissa sauce (the first recipe I ever developed for Greens) to yuzu kosho–slathered Brussels sprouts to aloo saag pot pie to Creole-style mushrooms and grits. Some recipes in this book can be quickly assembled for a weeknight dinner, while others

are best saved for the weekends. Part of the beauty of these recipes is their adaptability—if it's springtime, consider switching garlic cloves for green garlic, its more tender, funkier spring version. If your local farmers' market has a particularly irresistible heirloom pepper available, use that in place of a more common bell variety. Perhaps you are gluten free or vegan and would like to change barley to brown rice or omit some cheese? I encourage you to do just that. While these recipes are intentional and delicious as written, they also serve as a blueprint for adaptation.

Another wonderful feature of these recipes is that they are labeled for the seasons. Some recipes might list more than one season, and others may be great year-round. Regardless of the season listed, if you can find a fruit or vegetable at your local farmers' market, consider it in season and use it with delight. Around here, asparagus wakes up and pops out of the earth in February, so don't be deterred from using asparagus because the calendar says that it technically isn't yet spring. If it's at the market, it's in season wherever you are.

At Greens, our goal is this: Make delicious food with the bounty around us. I hope these recipes inspire you and nourish you. And I hope that as you follow these recipes, you are reminded of the farmers, the land, the seasons, and the people at Greens who make our restaurant the special and timeless place that it is, and hopefully always will be.

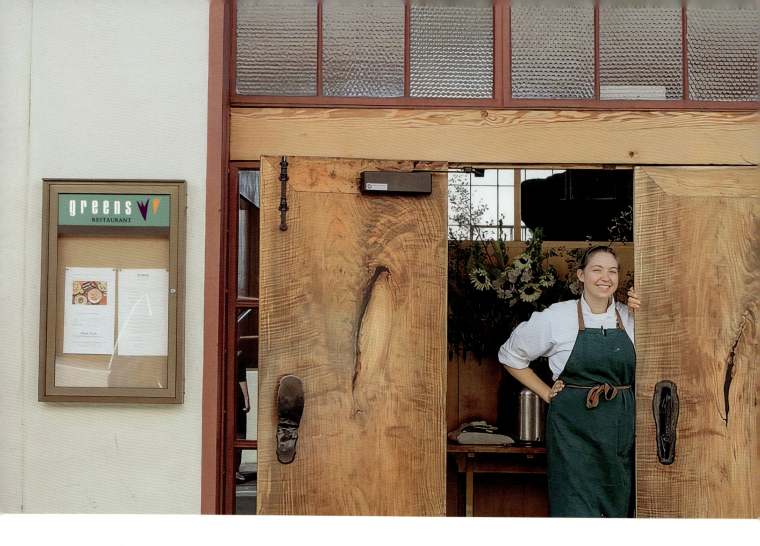

What Does It Mean to Preserve a San Francisco Legacy?

On February 26th, 2024, Greens Restaurant was added to the Legacy Business Registry of San Francisco. This program was created in order to celebrate "longstanding, community-serving establishments" and acknowledge these businesses as part of the "soul of the city." In other words, it's the city's way of acknowledging that it wouldn't quite be the same without us, along with more than 400 other businesses that have also been added to the program. But what does our legacy really mean to the average San Franciscan, and how do we maintain this legacy, and more importantly, build upon it in the years to come?

At the surface, Greens is known for its contributions to modern-day vegetarian cuisine, its incredible bay views, and iconic dining room. Most also know that we've been women-led since our inception by the San Francisco Zen Center. But I would argue that the legacy itself can't be pinpointed to any one thing or any one idea. It isn't a thing that can be touched, tasted, or looked at. The legacy, the significance, of Greens is subjective and is built by our collective experiences. It might be someone's routine of coming to brunch on Sundays, ordering the Pinnacle Scramble and talking with their favorite server. It could be an annual trip for an anniversary or birthday. Perhaps it's one's memory of how they felt the first time they walked into the restaurant and saw the view or tried the cuisine, which has celebrated farmers and seasonal vegetables for 45 years. The point is, the legacy of Greens is something that feels and looks different to everyone who has ever walked through our black walnut doors.

To preserve the legacy is to not only understand the restaurant and its history, but to love it and cherish it and allow it to grow. A longtime server recently said to me that welcoming guests into Greens feels more like welcoming guests to your home. To the employees, Greens is something of a family affair, since most of us here measure our time worked in years or decades. I'm not sure if it's because we have always been women-led or because of our close ties to the Zen Center, but the work environment at Greens is one that makes people stick around. I can humbly admit that I have never once made our Black Bean Chili because the same man, Edgar, has been making it for almost 40 years. Yet, despite having routines and menu mainstays, we work hard to keep Greens as pristine and cherished in 2025 as it was in 1979.

Greens has undergone some of the biggest changes in its 45-year life span in the years following the pandemic. Shutdowns and regulation changes meant constant pivots and adaptations that allowed us a unique opportunity to reevaluate some of our systems and routines, while also asking ourselves what this meant for the restaurant as a whole. Some changes were more difficult to make than others; while we were able to bring our bread production in-house during this time, it also meant that the days of free bread and slow-roasted almonds were over. And while Greens to Go was a beloved lunchtime staple, the rise of delivery apps, the closing of Fort Mason's San Francisco Art Institute, and our newly founded takeaway program made the counter obsolete. We made up for this closure by offering our pastries on the takeout menus and adding a second sandwich to the lunch and brunch menus, but still the empty counter was a melancholic symbol of change.

But not all changes were as unpleasant and sunsetting as Greens to Go. We reignited our long-standing relationships with our farmers and made space for new, like-minded makers, like Shared Cultures. We redesigned the menu and are excited to change it

much more often than before, weaving legacy recipes alongside new ones that celebrate the epic cuisine that has evolved over decades. We are inspired by our world cuisine and celebrate it with other incredibly talented chefs in our community through our Greens Guest Chef Series: A Global Celebration of Vegetables. We feel that all cuisines and life experiences can be expressed through Greens' cuisine, and we share this sentiment through our seasonal menus and collaborations.

Preserving our legacy often feels like we're holding on to a big bunch of balloons. We hold on to the bunch and care for it so it doesn't float away. We add new balloons to the bunch along the way, add air to the older balloons that need new life, and gently retire those that just can't float anymore. Some hands let go of the bunch while new hands grab on. We build on our legacy as a community every day; it is intangible, yet we all feel it and cherish it. The induction to the Legacy Business Registry is an acknowledgment of this effort, and we look forward to growing our legacy for years to come.

A Vegetarian Pantry

There are a few things to consider when building a vegetarian pantry. Whether you're including more vegetables into your diet or staving off animal products completely, creating a strong pantry will help you build flavors for all of your meals. Vegetables take a bit of a lighter touch, and often need help from fats, ferments, and acids like vinegars and citrus to create well-rounded flavors. Luckily, many of us have most of these ingredients on hand already, like soy sauce, apple cider vinegar, olive oil, and fermented chile sauces like sriracha or sambal.

PROTEINS

One of the first questions that any vegetarian gets from an omnivore is "how do you get enough protein?" The answer is simple: Plant protein is everywhere. While it's true that soy products like tofu and tempeh are great, hearty sources, you don't have to live off of tofu or processed or cultivated meats to enjoy a plant-based lifestyle. Legumes, nuts, mushrooms, whole grains, broccoli, and dark leafy greens are also full of protein for a balanced diet. If you eat animal products, dairy and eggs are also wonderful options. So, in short, if you're eating a wide range of vegetables, you needn't worry about how much protein you are getting.

FATS

You may notice, as you flip through this book, that the recipes don't skimp on the fat. Don't be alarmed by the quantities. Building flavor in a vegetable world means adding the necessary fat to bring out flavor, because vegetables on their own hardly have any at all. Because of this, it's important to choose the right type of fat for the recipe you're making. At Greens, we keep it relatively simple:

ALL-PURPOSE OIL The fat that we use for 95% of our cooking is Sciabica Family 90/10 California olive oil. This is an oil that is 90% refined olive oil and 10% extra-virgin olive oil. We love this oil because it has a mild, buttery flavor that is great in raw applications like hummus and vinaigrettes and is also great for sautéing and roasting.

Olive oil is also produced locally in California and is one of the healthiest oils you can use. If you choose to work with a different oil, some great options for an all-purpose oil include "light" olive oil, avocado oil, and grapeseed oil. You can also mix a small amount of extra-virgin olive oil into a light oil to give it some more character. Any recipe that calls for light olive oil in this book can be substituted for any of these options.

EXTRA-VIRGIN OLIVE OIL We reserve extra-virgin olive oil for garnishing only, since it has such a strong flavor compared to our all-purpose oil. Sometimes we will use a mix of extra-virgin oil and our light oil for some recipes, but as a general rule, this oil is not meant for cooking.

BUTTER Because most of our menu is vegan possible, we cook most food with olive oil. When we do use butter, it's typically for things that can't be made vegan, like our piccata sauce (see Spring Vegetable Piccata on page 178) or in pastries. We prefer to use unsalted butter and season it ourselves, but you are welcome to use either salted or unsalted butter for any recipe in this book. While we don't typically use vegan butter at Greens, you can use it in place of dairy-based butter.

FRYING OIL The most cost-effective frying oil is canola or vegetable oil. We use canola oil only for deep frying and occasionally in our pastries. If you would like to avoid canola oil, you may substitute another high-heat-tolerant oil such as grapeseed.

SALTS

Salt is another necessary ingredient for building flavor in food. Salt comes in various forms and can vary in "saltiness" depending on how the salt was produced. There are several forms of salt that we use at Greens that will come in handy throughout this book.

DIAMOND CRYSTAL KOSHER SALT In this book, every recipe that simply states "salt" is referring to Diamond Crystal Kosher Salt. By volume, this is one of the least salty varieties, which is ideal for making minor seasoning adjustments to your food. This also means that the recipes may appear to call for a lot of it.

If you are using a different brand of kosher salt, such as Morton's, or another type of salt, like table salt or fine sea salt, start with less and add more to taste. You can always add more as you need it.

MALDON SEA SALT Another type of salt that is listed in this book is Maldon sea salt. This salt is a flaky variety of salt that is good for topping over finished items, like ripe summer tomatoes in a panzanella salad (page 89). While flaky sea salt is more expensive than kosher salt, a little goes a long way. One small box will last for months, and your food will surely benefit from that little sprinkle.

SOY SAUCE Soy sauce is a fermented product that is a significant source of salt in many recipes. Oftentimes, soy sauce alone isn't enough to make a dish overly salty, but it will have an effect on how much kosher salt you will need. If you are salt-sensitive, you may use the soy sauce in the recipe and then add kosher salt to taste. For those with soy allergies, any of your favorite substitutes, like coconut aminos or Shared Cultures lentil quinoa shoyu, will work.

MISO Miso is by far one of the most underrated ingredients to use in vegetarian cooking. Fermented foods are rich with umami, or savoriness. Miso is very versatile and easy to use once you get in the habit of adding it to your dishes. We throw miso in sauces, vinaigrettes, braises, and even mix it with butter (page 32) to then put in our pastas. Miso has a salty-sweet flavor and provides a lot of substance and depth to dishes, which is what makes it so special to our cuisine. Our absolute favorite miso brand is Shared Cultures, a small-batch miso maker based in San Francisco.

PANTRY STAPLES

Keeping a well-stocked pantry can be useful in building more flavor in your food and is also a great way to use flavors and ingredients that are out of their usual season.

SUN-DRIED TOMATOES Unlike fresh tomatoes, sun-dried tomatoes have a deep, raisin-like flavor that is a great accompaniment to chiles and heartier flavors.

Look for sun-dried tomatoes that are jarred in oil. For the recipes in this book, drain the oil before using. If you happen to find just the plain dry tomatoes, soak them in hot water for at least 20 minutes before using. Drain the water before using.

VINEGARS There are so many wonderful kinds of vinegar that make dishes stand out. It's OK if you don't have every kind of vinegar to make recipes in this book. Most light-colored vinegars, such as Champagne, white wine, apple cider, etc. can be substituted for one another. Similarly, dark vinegars, like balsamic, sherry, and red wine, can be interchanged as well.

BALSAMIC VS. GOLDEN BALSAMIC VS. AGED BALSAMIC Some recipes specify a type of balsamic to use, and it's important to note that these balsamics should NOT be substituted with one another. Simple "balsamic" vinegar is relatively tart and liquidy, and better to use in sauces and things that need acidity. Golden balsamic, or white balsamic, is sweeter and lighter than regular balsamic and is used in lighter dishes that require a touch of sweetness and not too much acid. Aged balsamic is thicker and somewhat syrupy in consistency and often has less acidity. Aged balsamic is not meant for cooking and should be used as a finishing touch to completed dishes. Good aged balsamic will be on the more expensive side, but it's worth the splurge for a better-quality product.

PANKO BREAD CRUMBS These Japanese-style bread crumbs have larger flakes for a more textured end result, which is ideal for topping pastas and crispy fried dishes, like Corn & Asiago Arancini (page 75). It's best not to substitute panko for other kinds of bread crumbs, unless you are substituting for a gluten-free variety of panko.

COOKING WINE They say that the wine you cook with should be good enough to drink, but I find this to be superfluous. Boxed wine, cheap bottled wine, and wine that you left on your counter for a couple of days are all perfectly fine for cooking. I use boxed wine in my own kitchen at home, because the bagged wine is not subject to oxidation, so I never worry about having good wine on hand. Just be sure to use dry varieties.

DRIED & CANNED CHILES Dried chiles are a great tool for building flavor. Throwing a dried arbol chile in a pickling liquid or a pot of stew can dramatically change the flavor. Chipotle chiles in adobo are a canned variety of preserved jalapeño peppers. Use these peppers in things like marinades, like in the Chipotle & Lime Grilled Tofu on page 187.

CANNED TOMATOES & COCONUT MILK Apart from chipotle chiles, these are pretty much the only kind of canned item that we ever use at Greens. Keep them on hand for several of the recipes in this book.

JARRED CAPERS You either love them or you hate them, and my goal is to get you to love them. Jarred capers in a brine are quicker to prepare and don't require rinsing. This is my go-to variety. Salted capers feel a bit more luxurious but require thorough rinsing before using. Whichever you choose, make sure that you are using just the capers—drain off any brine and rinse off any salt.

OLIVES As a former olive hater, I can tell you that the variety of olive that you use matters. Green olives are milder and more citrusy—a good "beginner" olive, if you ask me. The recipes that call for green olives need an olive that is buttery and mild. Black olives like kalamata pack a salty punch and are often placed in recipes to give a small pop of flavor, something a green olive won't quite do. It's best to avoid substituting in this case. If you don't love olives, feel free to leave them out.

HONEY VS. AGAVE NECTAR Honey and agave nectar can be considered interchangeable in this book. Both are liquid sugars that are ideal for adding to vinaigrettes and things that don't need cooking. Beware of substituting granulated sugar in raw recipes, as you may get a grainy texture, and definitely do not substitute agave nectar or honey in recipes that call for granulated sugar, especially when baking, as it may negatively affect the texture of the final product.

DRY PASTA While this book has a recipe for fresh pasta, it isn't always practical to make, especially on weeknights. It's always a good idea to have some dry pasta on hand in a pinch.

FLOUR The flour used in this book is all-purpose flour. For some recipes, a cup-for-cup gluten-free flour alternative can be used instead. Check each recipe for notes on substituting gluten-free flour. Note that the gluten-free versions of these recipes were tested using Bob's Red Mill all-purpose gluten-free flour and other varieties of gluten-free flour may result in a different final product.

SUGAR When granulated sugar is listed in a recipe, you may use either regular white sugar or evaporated cane sugar as a vegan alternative. Do not substitute a liquid sugar like agave nectar.

BEANS & LENTILS Beans and lentils are best when cooked from dry. They last forever and make a delicious broth when cooked. For cleaning and cooking instructions, see page 22. In a pinch, canned substitutions will also work. Canned beans should be rinsed before use.

....

IN THE FRIDGE

In addition to the pantry, stocking your refrigerator with the following items is essential to making the recipes in this book.

EGGS At Greens, we use eggs. There are many recipes in this book that do not call for eggs or that have vegan substitutions, such as the Vegan Aioli on page 36. Note that the recipes that call for eggs have not been tested with vegan egg substitutions and may not yield the same results if substituted.

MILK When milk is listed in a recipe, it refers to whole cow milk. Check each recipe for notes for acceptable plant-based substitutes. Some recipes will specify plant-based milks anyway, like the wonderful vegan Vanilla-Poached Apple Cake (page 234).

CHEESES The cheeses listed in this book refer to dairy-based products. Recipes that call for cheese have not been tested with vegan cheese substitutions. Hard cheeses for grating like pecorino and Parmesan can be substituted with other hard cheeses as desired.

How to Use This Book

The cuisine of Greens is farm-driven, and world inspired. There are always more recipes to write, more cuisines and regions to explore, and new people to work with and learn from. Within these pages, you will find recipes from around the world for every season and everything in between. Many of these recipes are those that have been on the menu in the last 4 to 5 years, and others are developed for this book only. As you flip through the recipes in this book, there are a few things to keep in mind.

SEASONALITY

One of the most important lessons that I've learned from working at Greens for the last 10 years is that the seasons are ever changing. I don't just mean from spring to summer and fall to winter. I am talking about the small changes that affect a farmer's output on a daily basis. In the Bay Area, we are lucky to have asparagus pop up in the delta sometimes as early as Valentine's Day. But other years, we wait and wait and wait until almost April. The weather makes a huge impact on when produce becomes available, and it can even affect size and flavor of the produce, too. So when do you really know when something is in season? The foolproof method is shopping at your local farmers' market. Whatever you see at the market, consider it to be in season and use it gleefully.

BASIC COOKING PROCEDURES

BEANS & LENTILS

Beans and lentils greatly benefit from being made from dry, but they take some time and planning. If you've never made beans from scratch, I highly recommend setting aside some time to soak your beans the night before and enjoy a peaceful hour or so of simmering the following day. The loveliest part of cooking your beans from scratch is that the flavor is malleable. I particularly love throwing half an onion, some garlic cloves, and a few fresh bay leaves into my beans for most applications, but you can switch this up depending on the recipe you're making, or simply keep them a blank slate, too.

The one caveat to beans is that cooking times vary based on the bean. Black beans from the supermarket may not cook at the same speed as Rancho Gordo's black beans. Factors such as how fresh the beans are, the specific variety, and how they were grown will all affect how your beans cook. Lentils are a bit easier—they don't require soaking and generally cook in 20 to 40 minutes. But for everything else, there is a general process to get perfect beans, every time.

STEP 1 Rinse your beans and remove any debris, stones, broken beans, and any floating bits.

STEP 2 Soak your beans using clean, cold water for at least 8 hours, or preferably overnight. For every cup of beans, use at least 2 cups of water. The beans should be fully submerged in a large container that will allow for the beans to properly soak. The beans will roughly double in size overnight, so be sure to use a container that will hold them all. If you're short on time, you can boil the water, pour it over the beans, and let them sit for about an hour at room temperature, but think of this for "emergencies only."

STEP 3 Drain the soaked beans and add them to a pot. Completely submerge the beans with clean cold water. Hard or dry aromatics can be added at this time, such as dried chiles, bay leaves, or large chunks of onion.

STEP 4 Cook the beans at a simmer, stirring occasionally and adding more water as needed. Most beans will take anywhere from 30 minutes to 2 hours to cook. The beans are done when they are soft and creamy all the way through. If they feel chalky, crumbly, or have a gap in the middle of the bean, keep cooking. Soft aromatics, like herbs, should be added 20 to 30 minutes before the beans finish cooking.

STEP 5 Once the beans are cooked, remove from the heat and add salt. Adding a handful of salt at the end of cooking is preferred so the beans cook evenly, and the skins remain soft. Allow the beans to sit on the stove with the flame off for at least 10 minutes to allow them to absorb the salt.

STEP 6 Cool your beans in their cooking liquid! The bean broth is liquid gold. This protein-rich powerhouse is a great way to thicken soups and purées.

GRAINS

You can get a little more granular when cooking grains (pardon the pun). While cooking times will vary here as well, they won't vary as much as with bean cookery. If you're buying local, feel free to ask the farmers about cooking times for their specific grains. Otherwise, checking on them in the last few minutes of cooking will let you know whether or not your grains need more time. Use the table below for guidance on cooking a variety of different types of grains.

NUTS & SEEDS

You'll often find that recipes in this book call for toasted seeds or nuts. At Greens, we toast our nuts and seeds to a gentle golden brown. A good guideline is to use a still or conventional oven oven at 325°F (160°C) for about 10 to 15 minutes, stirring the nuts or seeds halfway through to ensure they all brown evenly. Don't rush this process—using a hotter oven for less time will only burn the outsides of the nuts and leave you with raw interiors. A slower oven allows for the nuts to toast gently and evenly, as the oils in nuts are volatile and will burn quickly at higher temperatures.

GRAIN	COOKING METHOD
WHITE RICE	Put the rice in a colander and rinse well under cold water until the water turns from cloudy to clear. This may take a few rinses. Once rinsed, put the rice in a saucepan and add 1½ cups (360 ml) of clean cold water per every 1 cup (200 g) of rice. Heat the rice over high heat until it comes to a boil, then reduce to a slow simmer and cover the pot. Cook the rice for 12 minutes, then remove from the heat. Keep the lid on the pot for another 5 to 10 minutes to allow it to steam, then fluff with a fork.
BROWN RICE	Put the rice in a saucepan and add 2 cups (480 ml) of clean cold water per every 1 cup (200 g) of rice. Heat the rice over high heat until it comes to a boil, then reduce to a slow simmer and cover the pot. Cook the rice for 35 to 45 minutes, then remove from the heat. Keep the lid on the pot for another 5 to 10 minutes to allow it to steam, then fluff with a fork.
QUINOA	In a saucepan, bring 1 cup (240 ml) of water to a boil for every 1 cup (180 g) of quinoa. Add a pinch of salt and the quinoa and reduce the heat to low. Cover the pot and cook for 15 to 18 minutes, then allow to steam for another 5 minutes.
FARRO	Bring a large pot of water to a boil. Cook the farro like you would pasta. This process can take anywhere between 15 minutes to over an hour, depending on what kind you have. Once the farro is plump, tender, and chewy, it's ready. Strain the grains well.
MOROCCAN COUSCOUS *A pasta that cooks like a grain.*	Bring 1 cup (240 ml) of water per every 1 cup (180 g) of couscous to a boil. Remove the saucepan from heat . Add the couscous and shake the pan to evenly distribute. Immediately cover with a tight-fitting lid and let sit undisturbed for 10 to 15 minutes, then fluff with a fork.
WILD RICE	Bring a large pot of water to a boil. Add the wild rice and reduce the heat to a strong simmer. Cook the grains until they open up and are just tender and chewy, between 30 to 45 minutes. Drain the grains well through a colander.

COOKING METHODS

PURÉEING

Puréeing pops up quite a bit throughout this book. Not all puréeing tools will create the same result.

For the finest, creamiest purées, use a high-powered blender, such as a Vitamix. It's certainly an investment, but a worthy one. This is the only way to truly get ultra-creamy cashew creams, and it will make a difference with some salsas and soups.

Immersion blenders are a wonderful tool to have on hand for quickly puréeing soups and salsas. It will definitely not blend as finely as a blender, so expect to have some texture if you're using one of these. Sometimes it's desirable to have some texture, like in the Heirloom Tomato & Stone Fruit Gazpacho (page 121).

Food processors often create the coarsest texture of them all but are also ideal for keeping things cool and preventing them from breaking. Aioli is best made in the food processor for this reason, along with hummus and dip recipes that beg for a little texture. If you like your hummus ultra-creamy and smooth, you can use a blender instead, but you'll likely need to add a little more water or bean broth to loosen it up so that it can properly blend.

ROASTING & PEELING PEPPERS

Homemade roasted red peppers or poblanos are a worthy investment of your time. They have a fresh flavor that a jarred pepper simply can't beat.

First, it's important to completely char your peppers. It's best to do this directly on the grates over a gas burner. If you don't have a gas range, you can also do this under the broiler, on the grill, or in the oven at the highest setting.

Turn the peppers every few minutes so that they blacken on all sides. As soon as they're done blackening, place the peppers in a just-large-enough container so that they are snug, then cover tightly with plastic wrap or a lid for 15 to 20 minutes.

After this time, the peppers should have cooked through and wilted, and the steam will have loosened the skins. Use a clean tea towel to gently rub off the skins. For the Chiles Rellenos (page 193), keep the stem intact and only remove the seeds. For all other recipes, remove the stem and seeds and cut according to the recipe instructions.

JUICING CITRUS

Every recipe in this book that calls for citrus juice should be freshly squeezed. It doesn't take much—you can use your hands and be careful with the seeds or use a handheld squeezer. The difference between concentrated juice and fresh will be palpable. Luckily, citrus lasts for a very long time if kept in the refrigerator, so you can always have some on hand for these recipes.

VEGETABLE PREPARATIONS

Vegetables in this book should be washed thoroughly before use. Scrub root vegetables especially well to remove dirt that clings to them. Herbs don't need to be washed necessarily, unless you can feel sand on the leaves, then gently wash in a water bath.

TO PEEL OR NOT TO PEEL?

I don't believe that vegetables always need to be peeled. The peels of vegetables are wonderfully nutritious, so as long as they are washed well, the skins can stay (if they're edible). Sometimes peeling is mentioned for stylistic or textural reasons, like for the Honeynut Squash Gnocchi with Brown Butter (page 128), but for things like purées, soups, or sauces, you can skip this step if you would prefer to keep your veggies skin-on.

V - Vegan | VP - Vegan Possible

GF - Gluten Free | GFP - Gluten-Free Possible

DF - Dairy Free | DFP - Dairy-Free Possible

NF - Nut Free | NFP - Nut-Free Possible

SF - Soy Free | SFP - Soy-Free Possible

KITCHEN LARDER

Building a kitchen larder is like getting geared up to go out in the snow. You can skip a few steps and maybe go out without gloves, but you'll probably be cold and end up wishing you brought them along. In this section, think of the following recipes as a guide to greatness. These base recipes are a collection of best practices that will give your dishes that "restaurant-level" quality that you'd get at Greens. Many can be made ahead of time and stored so you always have incredible flavors at your fingertips. Of course, you can always make substitutes for these recipes as needed, but if you have the time, why not give them the full Greens treatment?

QUICK KIMCHI

V | GF | DF | NF | SFP

This easy kimchi can be made and eaten on the same day; no fermentation required. Unconventional ingredients like gochujang and miso help immediately deepen the flavor of this kimchi without having to wait for it to ferment. Substituting fermented gochujang for the traditional gochugaru chile flakes is also helpful in building deep umami flavors in this vegan kimchi.

YIELDS ABOUT 4 CUPS (600 G)

1 small to medium napa cabbage (about 1 pound/450 g)

1 tablespoon salt

4 scallions, cut into 1-inch (2.5-cm) segments

¼ cup (25 g) finely grated carrot

¼ cup (25 g) finely grated daikon radish

2 tablespoons onion, coarsely grated

1 clove garlic, grated finely

1 teaspoon finely grated fresh ginger

¼ cup gochujang (such as Mother-in-Law's)

1 tablespoon miso (plain white miso or a specialty miso such as Shared Cultures black garlic or morel miso)

1 teaspoon seaweed powder, such as kelp or dulse

2 teaspoons sugar

¼ teaspoon mushroom umami powder (optional)

Cut the cabbage in half lengthwise and rinse under cold running water. Then, cut each half in half lengthwise to create 4 wedges. Cut across each wedge in 2-inch (5-cm) segments to create somewhat uniform cabbage rectangles. Add the cabbage to a large bowl and add the salt. Massage the salt into the cabbage by tossing and mixing thoroughly. Allow the cabbage to sit for at least 20 minutes, or up to 1 hour.

In a clean bowl combine the scallions, carrot, daikon, onion, garlic, ginger, and optional umami powder with the gochujang, miso, seaweed powder, and sugar and mix well.

When the cabbage has sat for at least 20 minutes, use your hands or a clean tea towel to wring the water out of the cabbage. Squeeze mightily and make sure the cabbage is mostly dry. Add it to the bowl with the vegetables and mix thoroughly to combine; it is best to use your hands to really massage everything together.

This kimchi is ready to eat immediately after mixing, but it improves with time in the refrigerator. Pack it tightly into a container and place in the refrigerator for up to 1 month. This kimchi will be at its peak for up to 1 week. After that, the kimchi may become overly strong.

PICKLED MUSTARD SEEDS

V | GF | DF | NF | SF

Pickled Mustard Seeds are absolutely delightful. As a mustard-hater myself (I know), I am pleased to announce that these are not at all sharp or mustard-like at all. Instead, pickled mustard seeds lend a sweet, tangy pop to anything you put them on. This ingredient is one of our best-kept secrets, as it is a surprising flavor and texture that you can't easily achieve without making them yourself. Try them tossed in a lovely fall salad (page 91).

YIELDS ⅓ CUP (75 G)

½ cup (120 ml) water

¼ (60 ml) cup golden balsamic vinegar

¼ (50 g) cup sugar

¼ (50 g) cup yellow mustard seeds

1 teaspoon salt

Add all of the ingredients together in a small saucepan. Bring to a slow simmer over medium-low heat, stirring occasionally. Continue cooking the mustard seeds until most of the liquid has evaporated and the remaining liquid starts to become syrupy, and forms many small bubbles, about 30 minutes. Do not rush this process! The mustard seeds will become plump and will burst like caviar after simmering for a while. The mustard seeds should not be cooked dry or else the sugar will burn and get sticky.

Once the liquid is syrupy, remove from the heat and allow to cool to room temperature, stirring occasionally as it cools. Store in the refrigerator until ready to use.

CABBAGE

For too long, cabbage has been the supporting character that does a lot of the work and gets none of the credit. It's an incredibly versatile vegetable that deserves the spotlight. Cabbage is excellent marinated and grilled or roasted because its many layers absorb flavor and distribute it as it cooks.

STANDARD PICKLES

V | GF | DF | NF | SF

Pickles are ubiquitous on the Greens menu because they have a superpower: creating balance. Pickles are tart! Whenever I think my dish might be missing something, I know that I can usually turn to a pickle to create harmony. This standard pickle brine is as simple as it gets, and it works for nearly everything: onions, carrots, peppers, strawberries even!

YIELDS 4 CUPS (560 G)

BRINE

1 cup (240 ml) Champagne vinegar (or other light-colored, neutral vinegar such as white wine vinegar or apple cider vinegar)

2 cups (480 ml) water

2 tablespoons sugar or agave nectar

1 tablespoon salt

1 tablespoon pickling spice (optional)

4 cups (560 g) of fruit or vegetables, for pickling

Combine all the brine ingredients together in a small saucepot. Bring to a boil over medium-high heat, then allow to simmer for 5 minutes.

While the pickling brine is simmering, prepare your fruit or vegetable to be pickled. Pack the vegetables in a glass jar or food-grade plastic container. When the pickling brine is finished simmering, pour the brine over the vegetables. Cover with a bit of parchment paper to keep the vegetables submerged in the brine.

Allow to cool to room temperature before storing in the refrigerator for up to a week.

STANDARD SWEET PICKLES

V | GF | DF | NF | SF

While the standard pickling brine is great for most things, sometimes a sweet pickle is desired. I like to use this pickle brine for things like dried currants, unripe green strawberries, or papaya salad. This type of pickle is great alongside spicy foods. It'll be a crisp, refreshing accompaniment.

YIELDS 4 CUPS (560 G)

BRINE

1 cup (240 ml) Champagne vinegar (or other light-colored, neutral vinegar such as white wine vinegar or apple cider vinegar)

1 cup (240 ml) water

2 teaspoons salt

1 cup (200 g) sugar

4 cups of fruit or vegetables for pickling

Combine all the brine ingredients together in a small saucepot. Bring to a boil over medium-high heat, then allow to simmer for 5 minutes.

While the pickling brine is simmering, prepare your fruit or vegetable to be pickled. Pack the vegetables in a glass jar or food-grade plastic container. When the pickling brine is finished simmering, pour the brine over the vegetables. Cover with a bit of parchment paper to keep the vegetables submerged in the brine.

Allow to cool to room temperature before storing in the refrigerator for up to a week.

COMPOUND BUTTERS

V | GF | DFP | NF | SFP

These Compound Butters are a huge time-saver and flavor booster. I nearly always have at least two or three different flavored butters floating around in my refrigerator or freezer, which I use in nearly everything I make. While these butters are used in recipes throughout this book, consider using them during your laziest moments, or when you have little time or ingredients but still want to impart a great amount of flavor. My go-to non-recipe is to melt a couple of tablespoons on some angel hair pasta, although these butters can be thoughtfully substituted for regular butter almost anywhere.

EACH RECIPE MAKES 1 LOG

HERB BUTTER

1 pound (450 g) unsalted butter, softened

1 bunch parsley, stems removed

1 bunch sage leaves

1 bunch thyme, stems removed

1 bunch marjoram leaves

1½ teaspoons salt

Working with one type of herb at a time, bunch the parsley and sage leaves together tightly and slice into a thin chiffonade. Then, turn the leaves 90 degrees and slice thinly the opposite way to create a fine mince. Try to slice (not chop) as thinly as possible the first time around, so the leaves do not oxidize. A chopping motion will damage the leaves, and they will brown more quickly.

Mix the finely minced herbs, salt, and butter together until fully combined. Refrigerate for up to a week or freeze in logs for up to 3 months.

To create a log, lay the butter in a 2-inch-thick row along a sheet of parchment paper. Fold the parchment paper over the butter, leaving about a 4-inch (10-cm) overhang. Use a pastry scraper or a flat spatula to push the butter back toward the folded edge, which will round out the butter evenly. Then, roll the butter forward to wrap the parchment over itself.

LEMON BUTTER

1 pound (4 sticks/450 g) unsalted butter, softened

4 lemons, zested and juiced

4 teaspoons salt

Combine all the ingredients together in a bowl and mix until fully combined. Be sure to chop the lemon zest finely and remove any seeds that may fall out of the lemons when juicing. The juice may take some time to incorporate into the butter by hand, but it will come together with some elbow grease and patience. A food processor may be used to speed up the process. Follow the instructions above to roll into a log and store in the refrigerator or freezer.

MISO BUTTER

1 pound (4 sticks/450 g) unsalted butter, softened

1 cup (275 g) miso (such as Shared Cultures)

Mix the butter and miso together until they are fully combined. Follow the instructions to the left to roll into a log and store in the refrigerator or freezer.

GARLIC CONFIT

V | GF | DF | NF | SF

Garlic Confit is my favorite condiment and is something that will change your life for the better. It's a completely hands-off recipe if you use pre-peeled garlic cloves, and the result is a luscious garlic oil and wonderfully soft, buttery garlic cloves that can be used on anything.

YIELDS 2 CUPS (640 G)

3 cups garlic cloves, peeled and left whole

2 cups extra-virgin or refined olive oil

To make on the stove top, combine the garlic and oil together in a small saucepot. Bring to a simmer over medium-low heat, stirring occasionally. Once the garlic starts to bubble, adjust the heat if necessary to make sure that the garlic simmers very slowly and only small bubbles appear around the cloves. The garlic should start to float at first and then turn a pale golden brown after about 45 minutes. The cloves should be very soft and can easily be mashed with the back of a spoon.

To make in the oven, preheat to 350°F (180°C). Combine the garlic and oil in a small oven-safe crock with a tight-fitting lid. Bake in the oven for about 1 hour, or until the cloves have browned and softened completely. Store in the refrigerator for up to a week. It can be frozen for up to 3 months.

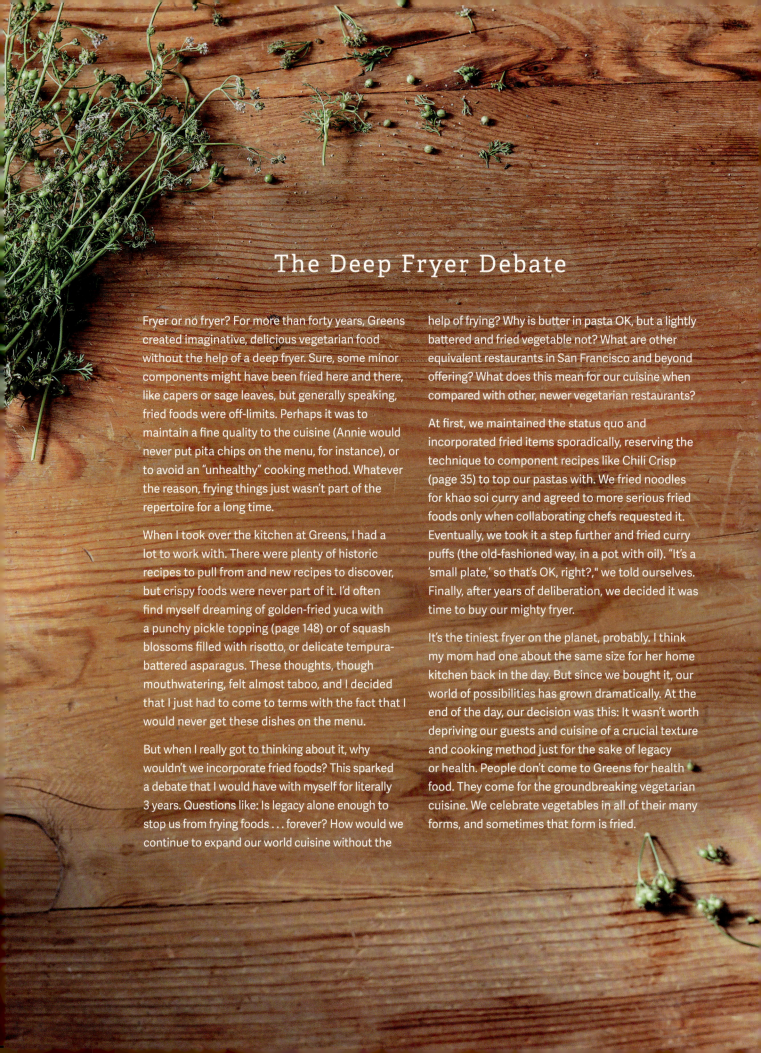

The Deep Fryer Debate

Fryer or no fryer? For more than forty years, Greens created imaginative, delicious vegetarian food without the help of a deep fryer. Sure, some minor components might have been fried here and there, like capers or sage leaves, but generally speaking, fried foods were off-limits. Perhaps it was to maintain a fine quality to the cuisine (Annie would never put pita chips on the menu, for instance), or to avoid an "unhealthy" cooking method. Whatever the reason, frying things just wasn't part of the repertoire for a long time.

When I took over the kitchen at Greens, I had a lot to work with. There were plenty of historic recipes to pull from and new recipes to discover, but crispy foods were never part of it. I'd often find myself dreaming of golden-fried yuca with a punchy pickle topping (page 148) or of squash blossoms filled with risotto, or delicate tempura-battered asparagus. These thoughts, though mouthwatering, felt almost taboo, and I decided that I just had to come to terms with the fact that I would never get these dishes on the menu.

But when I really got to thinking about it, why wouldn't we incorporate fried foods? This sparked a debate that I would have with myself for literally 3 years. Questions like: Is legacy alone enough to stop us from frying foods . . . forever? How would we continue to expand our world cuisine without the help of frying? Why is butter in pasta OK, but a lightly battered and fried vegetable not? What are other equivalent restaurants in San Francisco and beyond offering? What does this mean for our cuisine when compared with other, newer vegetarian restaurants?

At first, we maintained the status quo and incorporated fried items sporadically, reserving the technique to component recipes like Chili Crisp (page 35) to top our pastas with. We fried noodles for khao soi curry and agreed to more serious fried foods only when collaborating chefs requested it. Eventually, we took it a step further and fried curry puffs (the old-fashioned way, in a pot with oil). "It's a 'small plate,' so that's OK, right?," we told ourselves. Finally, after years of deliberation, we decided it was time to buy our mighty fryer.

It's the tiniest fryer on the planet, probably. I think my mom had one about the same size for her home kitchen back in the day. But since we bought it, our world of possibilities has grown dramatically. At the end of the day, our decision was this: It wasn't worth depriving our guests and cuisine of a crucial texture and cooking method just for the sake of legacy or health. People don't come to Greens for health food. They come for the groundbreaking vegetarian cuisine. We celebrate vegetables in all of their many forms, and sometimes that form is fried.

CHILI CRISP

V | GF | DF | NF | SF

Chili Crisp is all the rage right now—though it is not a new condiment. Made famous in the '80s, chili crisp has been a favorite of many for decades and is now making a resurgence in mainstream restaurants. This recipe is a bit more advanced than most in this book—mostly because it involves some heat control and a good eye. Heating the oil from the beginning over a medium-low flame will help with this temperature control—it just takes some patience. Adjust the spiciness in this recipe by adding or reducing the amount of chile flakes.

YIELDS 1¼ CUPS (280 G)

1 cup (240 ml) canola or other neutral, high-heat oil

1 cup very finely minced shallots

¼ cup very finely minced garlic

2 tablespoons paprika

1 tablespoon brown sugar

1½ teaspoons chile flakes

1½ teaspoons seaweed powder, such as kelp or dulse

1½ teaspoons mushroom umami powder (optional)

1 teaspoon salt

Add the oil to a small but deep saucepan over medium-low heat. The oil should be about ¾ inch (2 cm) in depth and still allow about 3 to 4 inches (7.5 to 10 cm) of headspace for the oil to expand when the wet ingredients are added. Any shallower, and the oil may overflow.

Heat until the oil has reached 340°F (170°C). If not using a thermometer, test the oil by adding a single piece of shallot. The shallot should drop to the bottom of the oil for just a moment, then immediately rise to the surface and bubble. If not, allow the oil to continue heating.

Once the oil is at temperature, add all of the shallots to the oil at once. They will bubble up high and sputter— this is why a high-walled pot is important. Cook the shallots in the oil, stirring frequently, until the large bubbles have subsided. Continue cooking, stirring occasionally, until the shallots around the edges of the pot start to turn golden brown. This should take about 15 minutes or more. Do not raise the heat of the oil or the shallots will burn before they get crisp. Once the shallots on the edges start to brown, stir constantly until all of the shallots are an even, deep golden brown.

Once golden, strain the shallots from the oil with a fine-mesh strainer or spider and spread on a tray to cool. The shallots will crisp up as they cool. Be sure to remove all of the shallots from the oil, or the remaining bits will burn. Immediately return the oil to the stove and add the garlic. Repeat the frying process with the garlic. Once golden brown, remove the garlic from the oil and add to the tray with the shallots to cool. Remove the oil from the heat and allow it to sit for 15 minutes.

In a medium, heat-safe bowl, add the paprika, brown sugar, chile flakes, seaweed powder, umami powder (if using), and salt. Pour the warm oil over the spices and mix well. Allow to cool completely. Once cool, add the reserved shallots and garlic to the oil. Do not add the shallots and garlic to the warm oil or they will not remain crispy. Store the chili crisp in a sealed container at room temperature for up to 1 month.

....

AIOLI

GF | DF | NF | SF

This Aioli is a straightforward recipe that will come in handy for several recipes in this book. Homemade Aioli is always preferred over store-bought, but be sure to use the best ingredients, particularly the oil, for the best flavor and texture.

YIELDS 1 CUP (230 G)

1 large egg yolk

1½ teaspoons Champagne vinegar, or other light-colored vinegar such as apple cider

¾ teaspoon cold water

¼ teaspoon Dijon mustard (optional)

1¼ teaspoons salt

1 cup (240 ml) refined olive oil or other neutral oil such as grapeseed or avocado

CONTINUES

To make by hand, add the egg, vinegar, water, mustard, and salt together in a medium bowl. Whisk together to combine. Then, slowly whisk in the oil, a few tablespoons at a time, making sure that the oil completely incorporates into the egg yolk mixture each time before adding more. Adjust the seasonings to taste. The Aioli will last 1 to 2 days in the refrigerator, or up to 1 week if using pasteurized egg yolks.

To make, add all of the ingredients gradually, using a food processor or immersion blender, and blend until thick. Adjust the seasonings to taste.

VARIATIONS

MISO AIOLI: Incorporate 2 tablespoons of your favorite miso to the egg and vinegar mixture before adding the oil and omit the salt.

LEMON CHIVE AIOLI: Replace the Champagne vinegar and cold water with 1 tablespoon plus 1 teaspoon fresh lemon juice. After emulsifying, fold in 1 teaspoon lemon zest and 2 tablespoons chopped fresh chives.

....

VEGAN AIOLI

V | GF | DF | NF

This Vegan Aioli is delicious, and it avoids using processed ingredients and emulsifiers. This recipe can be substituted in for any recipe that calls for Aioli.

YIELDS 1 CUP (230 G)

½ block (5 ounces /140 g) firm tofu, such as Hodo, or 5 ounces of any firm tofu, crumbled

¼ cup (60 ml) refined olive oil or other neutral oil such as grapeseed or avocado

2 tablespoons Champagne vinegar or other light-colored vinegar such as apple cider

¼ teaspoon Dijon mustard (optional)

1 teaspoon salt

Cold water

Combine all the ingredients in a blender pitcher, starting with 2 tablespoons water, and blend until

very smooth. Depending on the firmness of the tofu, you may need to add more water to reach a smooth, shiny consistency.

VARIATIONS

VEGAN MISO AIOLI: Incorporate 2 tablespoons of your favorite miso, omit the salt, and then blend together until smooth.

VEGAN LEMON CHIVE AIOLI: Replace the Champagne vinegar with ¼ cup (60 ml) fresh lemon juice. After emulsifying, fold in 1 teaspoon lemon zest and 2 tablespoons chopped fresh chives.

....

CASHEW CREAM

V | GF | DF | SF

This recipe for Cashew Cream is incredibly simple, but it requires a high-powered blender and a little finesse. But, in 30 minutes, you can have a lusciously creamy and smooth no-cow cream that is useful in veganizing many of the recipes in this book.

YIELDS 3 CUPS (345 G)

2 cups (230 g) cashews

2 cups (480 ml) water + more when blending

¾ teaspoon salt

Combine the cashews and water in a small saucepan. Bring to a boil over high heat, then reduce to a simmer. Allow the cashews to cook for about 20 minutes. You may see a purplish foam forming around the edges of the pot—that's OK.

Once the cashews have cooked, place them in a blender pitcher with their cooking liquid and the salt. In order to blend properly, the water level in the blender should be about equal to the cashews. If there is not enough water, add more until the cashews and water are about the same level. Do not add too much water or the cashew cream will be too thin.

Start to blend the cashews on low speed to break them up to small bits, then slowly increase the speed until the cashew cream is blending on high. If the cream gets stuck at any point during blending, use a tamper to tamp down the cream so that it blends smoothly. If you don't have a tamper, you can turn off the blender, mix the contents with a rubber spatula, and continue to blend until it creates the vortex (and stops getting stuck). Once the cream is silky smooth, it is ready to use. Remove from the blender and store in the refrigerator for up to 3 days. Place plastic wrap directly on the cashew cream or it will form a film while cooling.

VARIATIONS

TAHINI GARLIC CASHEW CREAM: Add ¼ cup (65 g) tahini, 2 tablespoons Garlic Confit (page 33), and 2 tablespoons fresh lemon juice to the blender when blending.

TURMERIC GINGER CASHEW CREAM: Add 1 tablespoon ground turmeric and 2 tablespoons freshly grated ginger to the blender when blending.

CILANTRO-LIME CREMA: Add ¼ cup (60 ml) lime juice and blend. Then fold in ¼ cup (10 g) chopped fresh cilantro.

....

MACADAMIA NUT "RICOTTA"
V | GF | DF | SF

Macadamia Nut "Ricotta" is one of those condiments that we keep around at Greens when we sell cheesy menu items with a vegan substitution. This ricotta will be particularly handy when making a vegan version of the Pappardelle with Peperonata & Shell Beans (page 135) or Fetuccine with Herb-Marinated Tomatoes & Burrata (page 130).

YIELDS 2 CUPS (460 G)

1 cup (115 g) macadamia nuts
2 cups (480 ml) cool water
⅓ cup (80 ml) light olive oil or other neutral oil
1 tablespoon fresh lemon juice
¼ teaspoon lemon zest
1 teaspoon nutritional yeast (optional)
½ teaspoon salt

Combine the macadamia nuts and water in a container with a lid. Refrigerate overnight to soak. Alternatively, combine the macadamia nuts and water together in a small saucepan and simmer for about 20 minutes to soften the nuts.

Once the nuts have soaked, drain from their soaking or cooking liquid, reserving the liquid for later. Add the nuts, olive oil, lemon juice and zest, nutritional yeast (if using), and salt to a blender pitcher. Add ¼ cup (60 g) of the reserved liquid to start.

Blend on high speed, using a tamper to tamp down the nuts until a thick, very lightly textured purée is made. If your blender does not have a tamper, stop the blender every now and then to mix up the contents with a spatula and continue to blend until this consistency is reached. If the nuts are having a hard time blending, add more soaking water, a little at a time, until it blends. The "ricotta" will never become as smooth as a cashew cream, so don't be afraid of overblending.

VEGETABLE STOCK

V | GF | DF | NF | SF

This Vegetable Stock is our go-to recipe, and because you don't have to peel the onions or carrots, it's a great way to reduce waste. We go through a ton of vegetables every day and we often save our carrot peels and onion trim for this recipe. You can save your vegetable trim in a gallon-sized freezer bag and add scraps to it until the bag is full. Just be sure they're washed well beforehand. Then, it's as simple as throwing them into a pot with some herbs and spices.

YIELDS 6 CUPS (1.5 L)

1 large onion with the peel

2 ribs celery

2 to 3 carrots

1 bulb garlic

¼ bunch parsley

¼ bunch thyme

½ teaspoon whole black peppercorns

2 bay leaves

2 quarts (2 l) cool water

Start by preparing the vegetables. Thoroughly wash the onion, celery, carrots, and garlic bulb to wash away any dirt from the peels and skins. Do not peel! Onion skins are wonderful for coloring vegetable stock to make a deep, rich golden-colored stock. As long as they're washed, onion skins are a great way to add flavor and color.

Slice the onion in half, and then slice each half as thinly as possible, yielding about 2 heaping cups of onion. Slice the celery ribs crosswise as thinly as possible, yielding about 1 cup. Finally, slice the carrots into thin coins, yielding about 1½ cups. Cut the garlic bulb in half crosswise to expose the cloves.

Place the prepared vegetables in a large stockpot. Add the parsley, thyme, peppercorns, bay leaves, and cool water to the pot. Place over high heat and bring to a boil. Once boiling, reduce the heat to low

and slowly simmer for about 45 minutes to 1 hour, or until the vegetables are extremely tender and can be mashed easily with the back of a spoon. Remove from the heat.

Strain the stock by pouring through a fine-mesh strainer set over another large stockpot. Use the back of a spoon or ladle to press on the vegetables that fall into the strainer and extract the liquid caught inside. Discard the vegetables once the liquid has been extracted and repeat the process until all of the stock has been strained. Store for 3 to 4 days in the fridge, or up to 3 months in the freezer

VARIATIONS

ASIAN: Omit the thyme, parsley, and bay leaves. Add 1 cup (140 g) cubed daikon, ¼ head napa cabbage, and one 2-inch (5-cm) piece of kombu (or 1 teaspoon kelp powder).

CORN: Add 2 to 3 corncobs, kernels removed and saved for another use.

....

PORCINI JUS

V | GF | DF | NF | SF

This stock is incredibly funky and rich, and it's what we use for practically everything that would normally call for a demiglace or a brown stock. This porcini stock is thicker than your average stock, and if you thicken it further with a little cornstarch, it makes for an excellent gravy on its own. We love it especially around the holidays; it's what we serve alongside our mushroom terrines and wellingtons for Thanksgiving and Christmas.

YIELDS 4 CUPS (1 L)

Olive oil

¼ cup (60 g) tomato paste

1 cup (240 ml) dry red wine

1 gallon (4 l) water

4 ounces (115 g) dried porcini mushrooms (abou 5 cups)

CONTINUES

¼ cup (30 g) garlic cloves

4 bay leaves

1 teaspoon black peppercorns

2 large onions, each cut into 8 wedges

2 large carrots, cut into 1-inch (2.5-cm) chunks

½ bunch thyme

¼ bunch parsley

Heat a large heavy-bottomed stockpot over medium-high heat. Add a small glug of olive oil and add the tomato paste. Cook the tomato paste for 3 to 5 minutes to start caramelizing it. Add the red wine and reduce by half, about 5 minutes.

Once the wine has reduced, add the water, dried porcinis, garlic cloves, bay leaves, and black peppercorns. Bring to a boil and then reduce the heat to a very slow simmer. Simmer for 1 hour.

After an hour, add the remaining ingredients and cook for another 45 minutes, or until the stock is thick, rich, and funky. The carrots should be very soft.

Remove from the heat and strain into a clean container using a fine-mesh strainer. Press on the vegetables in the strainer to be sure to extract all of the liquid. Discard the vegetable solids and allow the stock to cool. The stock will keep for up to 3 to 4 days in the refrigerator and up to 3 months in the freezer.

CREOLE BROTH
V | GF | DF | NF | SF

This recipe came about while we were developing the Autumn Vegetable Jambalaya (page 182) a couple of years ago. We wanted to create a broth that was incredibly rich and full of flavor from the chunks of vegetables so that when we cooked the rice in the broth, the dish was done, just like that. Not only did we make a delicious jambalaya, we realized that the broth alone was a recipe in and of itself. We have since used it to make several other recipes, like the Grits with Creole-Style Mushrooms (page 207) and Creole Pumpkin & Collard Greens Soup (page 104).

YIELDS 6 CUPS (1.5 L)

½ cup (120 ml) olive oil

1 medium onion, diced

½ green bell pepper, diced

1 rib celery, diced

2 cloves garlic, minced

2 tablespoons tomato paste

4 sprigs thyme

1 bay leaf

1 tablespoon salt + more as needed

1 teaspoon paprika

½ teaspoon cayenne pepper

¼ teaspoon freshly ground white pepper

¼ teaspoon freshly ground black pepper

⅛ teaspoon ground cloves

Pinch of ground allspice

2 teaspoons whole-grain mustard

6 cups (1.4 l) Vegetable Stock (page 39) or water

2 tablespoons chopped fresh parsley

Heat a heavy-bottomed stockpot over medium-high heat. Add the olive oil, onion, bell pepper, and celery to the pot and sauté for 7 to 10 minutes, until the vegetables have softened, and the onion has started to brown lightly around the edges. Add the minced garlic and sauté for another minute, or until fragrant. Add the tomato paste, thyme, bay leaf, and the spices up until the allspice and stir rapidly to combine. Continue stirring constantly until the tomato paste and spices deepen in color and are very fragrant, 2 to 3 minutes.

Once the tomato paste has cooked, add the mustard and vegetable stock. Stir to combine, scraping the bottom of the pot to lift off any caramelized tomato paste. Bring the pot to a boil, then reduce the heat to low and simmer until the vegetables are just tender, 45 minutes to 1 hour. Remove from the heat and fish out the bay leaf and thyme sprigs. Add the chopped parsley and adjust the salt to taste. Store in the refrigerator for 3 to 4 days or freeze up to 3 months.

SPREADS & SAUCES

You know what they say: the sauce is the boss. In this chapter, you'll find recipes for sauces that are used throughout this book to create and enhance your culinary delights, alongside standalone dips and spreads that are delicious on their own. One of the recent changes that we made at Greens within the last 10 years is with our hummus. The classic hummus used to be the only hummus, but now we've injected some seasonality and creativity into this classic menu item. Enjoy some of our favorite new spreads, like carrot hummus with sun-dried tomato harissa, or our Green Goddess Hummus, which is a love letter to springtime in San Francisco.

SPRING | SUMMER

Green Goddess Hummus

V | GF | DF | NF | SF

This fun spring take on hummus was inspired by our farm, Green Gulch. As soon as the farm reopens for the spring season, we are just too excited to bring in as much produce as we can, as quickly as we can, so we often over-order for the first few weeks (can you blame us?). With this mountain of new spring herbs, plus some green garlic and avocados from Brokaw, the Green Goddess Hummus was born, and it is still our most popular hummus to date! Lightly sweet, super creamy, and full of those bright herbaceous flavors—you'll be craving this hummus all through the spring.

....

YIELDS 3 CUPS (690 G)

1 medium avocado

2 cups (340 g) chickpeas, cooked and cooled (page 22)

¼ cup (10 g) packed fresh parsley leaves

¼ cup (10 g) packed fresh mint leaves

2 tablespoons fresh dill, stems removed

2 tablespoons fresh Italian Basil leaves, packed

2 tablespoons thinly sliced green garlic coins

1 clove garlic

¼ cup (60 ml) good-quality extra-virgin olive oil (such as Sciabica)

¼ cup (65 g) tahini

¼ cup (60 ml) fresh lemon juice

2 teaspoons salt

Cut the avocado in half and remove the pit. Using a spoon, cut the avocado into chunks and then scoop out from the skin into the bowl of a food processor. Add the remaining ingredients and process for 2 to 3 minutes, until the hummus comes together, and a little texture remains. The herbs will have broken down into small flecks, and the mixture should have the consistency of a thick paste.

We prefer hummus with a bit of texture. But, if you prefer a completely smooth hummus, start by mixing the herbs, olive oil, tahini, and lemon juice in the pitcher of a blender and blend until smooth. Then add the remaining ingredients and blend again until the hummus comes together. Store in the refrigerator for up to 3 days.

NOTE

Green garlic is an essential ingredient in the spring! This immature garlic plant adds a nice bit of springy funky-fresh flavor without too much of a garlic bite. Look for green garlic with small bulbs and bright green tips. Just like scallions, you can use the entire plant—just trim the very tips of the grassy leaves as well as the root. Green garlic is widely available at farmers' markets throughout the spring, but if you can't find any, just substitute a couple extra cloves of garlic and it will be just as delicious.

AVOCADOS

When it comes to avocados, I didn't know what I was missing until I moved to California. Avocados come in so many shapes and sizes, beyond the brown, bumpy-skinned, pear-shaped Hass. Every year, we look forward to Brokaw Ranch's Gwen avocados, which are rounder in shape, impossibly creamy, and are resistant to browning.

44 | SPREADS & SAUCES

ALLIUMS

The spring is full of fresh, funky aromas and flavors. One that we're all familiar with is alliums. Alliums are the family of vegetable that encompasses garlic, onions, leeks, chives, and ramps. During the spring season, the newly grown stalks of garlic are sold in the markets as "green garlic" or "spring garlic." The stalks of the garlic plant are funkier and less garlicky than if you were to use the full bulb. Spring onions pave the way for sweet onions that appear later in the season, and leeks are famously savored all spring long with other light and fresh seasonal vegetables.

SPRING | SUMMER | FALL | WINTER

Chimichurri

V | GF | DF | NF | SF

Chimichurri, an outrageously bright and herbaceous sauce originally from Argentina, is one of those sauces that seems to make just about anything better. It's very versatile and especially lovely on grilled vegetables, like Grilled Zucchini with Mint Pesto (page 158) or used as a marinade, like in the Tofu & Vegetable Brochettes with Chimichurri (page 203).

YIELDS 1½ CUPS (360 G)

1 large bunch curly parsley

1 bunch oregano

1 bunch chives

1 cup (240 ml) extra-virgin olive oil

¼ cup (60 ml) red wine vinegar

1 tablespoon minced garlic

¾ teaspoon salt

¼ teaspoon chile flakes

¼ teaspoon freshly ground black pepper

Start by preparing the herbs, beginning with the parsley. Pick the leaves from the stems and place them on a cutting board, being careful to pick out any yellowed leaves. Save the stems for another recipe, like Vegetable Stock (page 39) or discard. Chop the parsley with a sharp knife until the parsley is incredibly fine, then add to a small bowl. Next, remove the oregano leaves from the stems and chop finely. Add to the bowl with the parsley. Discard the oregano stems. Slice the chives as thinly as possible and add to the bowl of herbs.

Add the remaining ingredients to the bowl and mix until the herbs have been fully incorporated into the oil and vinegar mixture. Adjust the seasonings to taste. Store for up to 1 week in the refrigerator or up to 2 months in the freezer.

NOTE

Alice Waters once told me that a chimichurri is only as good as the time you put into it, and there's no quick and easy way around making it. Even in a restaurant setting, where we're chopping dozens of bunches of herbs at a time, we still chop bunch by bunch to make sure the herbs are prepared correctly. Take your time here. Trying to save time by using a blender or food processor will only bruise the herbs, and they'll turn brown quicker. Use a sharp knife and cut as finely as you can on the first pass so that they stay nice and green.

SPREADS & SAUCES

SPRING | FALL | WINTER

Roasted Carrot Hummus

V | GF | DF | NF | SF

Carrot hummus was the first real recipe that I ever wrote for Greens. It's had multiple iterations over the years, but it's still one of my favorite things to make. We save this recipe for the fall, when the carrots that have spent months in the ground are larger and sweeter, though tender spring carrots would work just as well. Slowly roasting the carrots until they are crinkle-skinned and smell like candy are what makes this autumn spread simply irresistible. Top with Sun-dried Tomato Harissa (page 53) for a truly magical combination.

YIELDS 3 CUPS (400 G)

1 pound (450 g) carrots, skin on, tops removed, and sliced into thin coins

½ cup (120 ml) olive oil

Salt

2 cups (340 g) cooked chickpeas (page 22)

¼ cup (65 g) tahini

¼ cup (60 ml) fresh lemon juice

2 cloves garlic, smashed

1 teaspoon ground coriander

½ teaspoon ground cumin

Pinch of aleppo pepper (or cayenne)

Water or bean cooking liquid, as needed

Preheat the oven to 350°F (180°C). Spread the carrot slices on a baking sheet and drizzle with the olive oil and a generous pinch of salt. Toss to combine. Bake until the carrots are very tender, 40 minutes to 1 hour. Give them a toss about halfway through to allow for even cooking. Use the back of a spoon to smash a carrot. If it smashes easily, they're done. Remove from the oven and allow to cool.

Add all of the ingredients, including the roasted carrots and the olive oil from roasting, to a food processor. Use a spatula to make sure you get all of the oil off the roasting pan. Purée the hummus together until relatively smooth. I prefer a bit of texture to my hummus, but if you like yours smooth, transfer your hummus to a high-speed blender and blend until smooth. In a blender, you may need to add a few tablespoons of water or the chickpea cooking liquid to achieve a smooth consistency. Place in a serving bowl and top with Sun-dried Tomato Harissa (page 53). Keeps for 3 to 4 days in the refrigerator.

A NOTE ON TENDERNESS

In my first semester of culinary school, I had a chef who would always ask the class the same question. "'How do you test if something is fork-tender?' With a fork! Because," he would say, "everything is knife tender, even you!" But for this recipe, fork-tender is still not quite soft enough. We want our carrots to be "pot roast tender"—so testing for doneness with the dull backside of a spoon is best.

CARROTS

Like many root vegetables, carrots have two major seasons. Springtime is the time for baby carrots. They're smaller and sweeter and have a more delicate texture. The fall is the season for giant carrots that spent the better part of the year growing. These carrots have a bolder flavor and hold up well to roasting or puréeing, since the roots are stronger and tougher from the longer growing time.

SUMMER | FALL

Eggplant Caponata

V | GF | DF | NF | SF

Our version of the classic Italian relish caponata features California touches like freshly chopped herbs from our farm, figs in place of raisins, and a smidge of orange zest for brightness. Roasting the eggplant helps deepen the flavor and remove moisture from the vegetable, which will allow it to soak up flavor.

....

YIELDS 2 CUPS (500 G)

1 globe eggplant (about 1 pound/450 g)

¼ cup (60 ml) olive oil + more for roasting

Salt

1 shallot, minced

1 clove garlic, minced

2 tablespoons roasted red peppers, chopped (see page 26)

2 figs, finely chopped or 2 teaspoons chopped dried currants or raisins

1 tablespoon chopped Castelvetrano olives

1 teaspoon capers, drained and chopped

½ teaspoon Calabrian chile paste or ¼ teaspoon crushed red chiles

One 14-ounce (400 g) can diced tomatoes, drained

½ teaspoon chopped fresh rosemary

1 tablespoon sherry or balsamic vinegar

½ teaspoon orange zest

Whipped Garlic Ricotta (page 52) or Macadamia Nut "Ricotta" (page 37), for serving

Crostini, for serving

Preheat the oven to 350°F (180°C). Remove the tough leaves and cut off the stem of the eggplant. Dice the eggplant into ½-inch cubes. It is not necessary to peel the eggplant, but you may if the skin is thick or if that is your preference. Toss with enough olive oil to lightly coat the eggplant and season with a generous pinch of salt. Spread the seasoned eggplant onto a baking sheet in a single layer, then roast the eggplant until it is softened, about 20 to 25 minutes.

While the eggplant bakes, heat a small saucepan over medium heat. Add ¼ cup (60 ml) olive oil, the shallot, garlic, roasted peppers, figs, olives, capers, and chiles together, and cook until the shallot softens, about 5 to 7 minutes.

Add the remaining ingredients along with the roasted eggplant to the pot. Reduce the heat to low and cook at a low simmer for another 20 to 25 minutes to allow the flavors to meld together. Season with salt to taste. Serve warm or cooled with Whipped Garlic Ricotta (page 52) or Macadamia Nut "Ricotta" (page 37). Store in the refrigerator for 3 to 4 days.

SUMMER

Peperonata

V | GF | DF | NF | SF

Peperonata is a great way to feature the many colors and flavors of summer peppers and tomatoes. It's also a wonderful way to use up any older produce you may have, even if their skins are a bit wrinkly or soft. Serve with toasted crostini for a lovely appetizer or toss with some al dente pasta, like in the Pappardelle with Peronata and Shell Beans (page 135) for an elegant, yet easy, dinner.

SERVES 6 TO 8

1½ pounds (680 g) sweet peppers, such as lipstick pimentos, Jimmy Nardello, shishito, cubanelle, Gypsy, etc.

1 to 2 hot Italian peppers or jalapeños, optional

2 cloves garlic, sliced thinly lengthwise

½ red onion, sliced thinly

¼ cup (60 ml) good-quality olive oil

½ pound (225 g) Early Girl tomatoes or other good sauce variety

½ pound (225 g) Sungold tomatoes or other cherry variety

1 sprig oregano or basil

¼ teaspoon freshly ground black pepper

½ teaspoon balsamic vinegar

½ teaspoon red wine vinegar

Salt

Start by cleaning the peppers. Cut the peppers lengthwise and remove the stem and seeds. Slice the peppers lengthwise into strips of various sizes. I like to cut thin-skinned peppers into large chunks, and thicker, meatier peppers into thinner strips. If you are using hot peppers, slice those into coins, and remove the seeds from the slices when you start to cut through the seed core. Set aside.

In a heavy-bottomed saucepan, add the sliced garlic, sliced red onion, and olive oil. Heat the pot from cold over medium-high heat and cook until the onions are translucent and starting to brown on the edges, 5 to 7 minutes. Stir frequently to ensure that the onions and garlic are cooking evenly and not burning on the bottom. Then, add the peppers and cook for about 3 to 5 minutes, until slightly softened.

Reduce the heat to medium-low and then add the Early Girls. Cook, stirring frequently, until the tomatoes get very soft, and the pulp turns into a thick, jammy sauce, about 30 minutes. Once the sauce starts to thicken, add the cherry tomatoes, oregano, black pepper, balsamic, red wine vinegar, and season with salt to taste. Cook the peperonata for another 5 to 10 minutes, until the cherry tomatoes burst. Remove from the heat. Store in the refrigerator for 4 to 5 days.

PEPPERS

You may have noticed that your peppers get hotter as the summer draws on. All of a sudden, your shishito peppers that were once occasionally spicy (about one in a dozen generally) are almost all hot! A lot of this has to do with sunlight. There are dozens of myths out there about growing hot peppers and how to achieve peak spiciness. But really, besides pepper variety, the most major factor is your climate. Peppers tend to get spicier with long hours of hot sun. In the Bay Area, September and October are our hottest months, so our peppers tend to get fiery hot as the weather warms and the days remain long. Make sure to always taste your peppers before using them. If they're very spicy, you might want to start with less in a recipe and add more to taste.

SPREADS & SAUCES

SPRING | SUMMER | FALL | WINTER

Whipped Garlic Ricotta

GF | NF | SF

Whipped ricotta is possibly the easiest and most delicious recipe in this book. Growing up in an Italian-American family, a plain tub of ricotta on the dinner table was a regular thing. At Greens, we use ricotta in many creative ways, from pasta and filo fillings to pizza toppings and dips. This garlic whipped ricotta is the perfect accompaniment to Eggplant Caponata (page 49) and would also be delicious simply spooned onto some sourdough toast. Try it with a drizzle of honey and black pepper, trust me!

YIELDS 1 CUP (230 G)

1 cup (230 g) ricotta cheese

¼ cup (40 g) Garlic Confit (page 33), drained of the oil

½ teaspoon salt

Combine the ricotta, Garlic Confit, and salt in the bowl of a food processor and blend until smooth.

SPRING | SUMMER | FALL | WINTER

Sun-dried Tomato Harissa

V | GF | DF | NF | SF

This harissa is a perfect complement to the Roasted Carrot Hummus (page 48), or when served as a deeply flavored accompaniment with other dishes with a Middle Eastern or Mediterranean influence. It's a touch smoky, boldly spiced, and has the perfect bright pop of fresh lemon.

....

YIELDS 1⅓ CUPS (320 G)

½ cup (60 g) sun-dried tomatoes, (see note, page 16)

½ cup (120 ml) extra-virgin olive oil

¼ cup (60 ml) water + more as needed

¼ cup fresh lemon juice

1 tablespoon chili powder

1 tablespoon paprika

1½ teaspoons ground coriander

1 teaspoon caraway seeds, ground (optional)

½ teaspoon ground cumin

⅛ teaspoon freshly ground black pepper

Salt

Combine all of the ingredients together, except the salt, in a blender pitcher or food processor and process until smooth. Adjust the consistency with more water as necessary by adding a tablespoon at a time. The texture should be thick but spreadable. Season with salt to taste, as different brands of sun-dried tomatoes have varying levels of salt. Once the tomatoes are puréed into the rest of the ingredients, taste the mixture to determine if salt is necessary. Store in the refrigerator for up to a week, or up to 3 months in the freezer.

NOTE

If using Frantoi Cutrera brand tomatoes, you will need approximately ½ cup (120 ml) of water and ¼ teaspoon of salt.

SPRING | SUMMER | FALL | WINTER

Mint Pesto

VP | GF | DFP | SF

This pesto is a wonderfully bright twist on the classic Genovese Pesto (basil pesto) that is particularly beloved in the spring and summer months at Greens. A dollop of this pesto in a soup or added to a vinaigrette is simply wonderful, and it is a handy sauce to have on hand for pastas and veggies off the grill. This pesto also freezes well! I often freeze it in ice cube trays so that I can pull out a tablespoon or so at a time for when I want that extra burst of flavor.

YIELDS 1 CUP (240 G)

1 well-packed cup (20 g) spinach leaves
(about 2 ounces/60 g)

½ well-packed cup mint leaves
(about 1 ounce)

2 cloves garlic, minced

¼ cup (35 g) pine nuts, toasted
(see note, page 25)

⅓ cup (35 g) Grana Padano or similar
hard grating cheese (optional)

2 tablespoons fresh lemon juice

⅓ cup (80 ml) extra-virgin olive oil

¾ teaspoon salt + more as needed

In a food processor, pulse the spinach and mint leaves until they are finely chopped. Add the garlic, pine nuts, Grana Padano, and lemon juice and pulse together until combined. Then, slowly drizzle in the olive oil while the food processor is on until it is fully combined into the pesto. Season with salt and adjust the seasonings as needed to taste. Keeps for 3 to 4 days in the refrigerator or up to 2 months in the freezer.

NOTE

To make this recipe vegan, omit the cheese.

SPRING

Rhubarb Muhammara

V | GF | DF | SF

Muhammara is one of the great sauces of the Middle East. It usually features roasted red peppers, making the original version the perfect sauce for the end of summer, when pomegranates and peppers are both available at the market. But one spring, we decided that muhammara would be perfect for the grilled carrots we were serving, so we developed this recipe with rhubarb instead. It was a clever switch—replacing the sweet-tart roasted peppers with sweet-tart rhubarb. Both share a silky texture when blended, and the rhubarb adds a lovely natural tartness that other spring vegetables lack.

....

YIELDS 2 CUPS (480 G)

¾ cup (100 g) sliced rhubarb, freshly cut or frozen

¾ cup (100 g) walnuts, toasted (see note, page 25)

1½ teaspoons minced garlic

1¼ cups (300 ml) extra-virgin olive oil

¼ cup (60 ml) water

3 tablespoons pomegranate molasses

2 tablespoons agave nectar or maple syrup

¼ cup (35 g) sesame seeds, toasted, or substitute 2 tablespoons tahini

1 tablespoon aleppo pepper or paprika

1 tablespoon salt

1½ teaspoons ground cumin

½ teaspoon smoked paprika

Preheat the oven to 400˚F (200˚C). Lay the rhubarb out on a baking sheet lined with parchment and roast for 10 minutes, or until softened.

Combine the roasted rhubarb with the remaining ingredients in a blender pitcher or food processor and blend until smooth. The sauce should be thick and spreadable. Keeps for 3 to 4 days in the refrigerator or up to 2 months in the freezer.

SPRING | SUMMER | FALL | WINTER

Peanut Hoisin Sauce

V | GF | DF

This sweet and tangy hoisin sauce is the perfect accompaniment to the Sweet Potato Summer Rolls with Peanut Hoisin Sauce (page 76). You can also serve it alongside grilled tofu or use it in stir fries.

YIELDS 2 CUPS (270 G)

½ cup (120 ml) water

2 tablespoons dark soy sauce or tamari

2 tablespoons rice vinegar

1 tablespoon molasses

1 teaspoon Chili Crisp (page 35) or
1 teaspoon neutral oil

¼ cup (30 g) roasted peanuts, chopped
(optional)

2 tablespoons peanut butter

1½ tablespoons brown sugar

1½ teaspoons cornstarch

½ teaspoon Chinese five-spice powder

Combine all the ingredients together in a small saucepan. Heat over medium-low heat, whisking occasionally, until the sauce thickens and starts to boil. Remove from the heat and allow the sauce to cool completely before serving. Store the sauce in an airtight container in the refrigerator for up to a week or up to 2 months in the freezer.

SPREADS & SAUCES

SUMMER | FALL

Grilled Romesco Sauce

V | GF | DF | NF | SFP

Romesco is not a new sauce for Greens, but it is one that we weave into the menu often, pairing it with new, exciting dishes like the Fried Baby Artichokes (page 62) or the Corn & Asiago Arancini (page 75). It's also wonderful on eggs or, of course, with fried potatoes like it was originally intended. In this version, we grill the peppers, tomatoes, and garlic instead of roasting to get a deeper, smokier flavor that enhances anything you put it on.

YIELDS 2 CUPS (240 G)

½ cup (120 ml) extra-virgin olive oil + more for grilling

1 medium red bell pepper

½ fresh hot red pepper, such as Fresno or cayenne

2 Roma tomatoes

1 garlic clove

Salt

¼ cup almonds, toasted

1½ teaspoons sherry vinegar

1½ teaspoons fresh lemon juice

½ teaspoon paprika

⅛ teaspoon freshly ground black pepper

Preheat the grill over high heat. Start by rubbing a small amount of olive oil on the peppers, tomatoes, and garlic cloves so that they shine but aren't dripping with oil. Sprinkle salt over the vegetables.

Grill the vegetables over direct heat, turning occasionally, until they are evenly charred on all sides, about 10 to 15 minutes. To grill the garlic, use a grill mat or lay a bit of aluminum foil directly on the grill grates, then grill the garlic directly on mat or the foil. Cook the garlic until it is well-charred; it does not need to be fully cooked through. You can also skip this step and use raw garlic or Garlic Confit (page 32) instead.

Once the vegetables have cooked, remove from the grill and let sit until cool enough to handle. Remove the skins, cores, and seeds from the peppers and remove the skin and cores from the tomatoes.

Add the tomatoes, peppers, and garlic to a blender pitcher or food processor. Add ½ cup (120 ml) olive oil along with the remaining ingredients and blend until smooth. Adjust the acidity with more lemon juice and add salt to taste. Store in the fridge for 3 to 4 days or up to 1 month in the freezer.

NOTE

Alternatively, the peppers and tomatoes can be broiled in an oven. Broil on high for about 25 minutes, turning the vegetables as they blacken for even coloring. Remove the vegetables from the broiler as they finish blackening, then follow the remaining steps.

SUMMER | FALL

Roasted Cherry Tomato Sauce

V | GF | DF | NF | SF

The most lovely tomato sauce, in my opinion, is one that is made with fresh summer tomatoes. A sauce made exclusively with cherry tomatoes is sweeter and lighter than the average sauce, making it perfect to balance with richer flavors like the Corn & Asiago Arancini (page 75). Our favorite tomatoes to use for this recipe are Juliet tomatoes that we buy from our friend Bill at Everything Under the Sun. The arrabiata variation, a spicy cousin of this sauce, is simply wonderful for braising vegetables, like the Stewed Romano Beans in Arrabiata (page 161).

....

YIELDS 4 CUPS (800 G)

8 cups (1.2 kg) cherry or grape tomatoes

½ cup (120 ml) extra-virgin olive oil + more for roasting

1 tablespoon salt + more for seasoning the tomatoes

1 medium yellow onion, diced small

3 cloves garlic, sliced very thin

¼ cup (60 ml) dry white wine

¼ teaspoon freshly ground black pepper

2 sprigs basil

1 sprig oregano (optional)

Preheat the oven to 300°F (150°C). Start by cleaning the cherry tomatoes by rinsing them with cool water and removing their tops. Halve the cherry tomatoes and spread evenly on a baking sheet. Drizzle with olive oil and a generous pinch of salt. Roast for about 45 minutes, or until the tomatoes are very tender and jammy, not dry.

Next, in a heavy bottomed saucepan, heat ½ cup (120 ml) olive oil over medium-high heat. Add the yellow onion and cook, stirring occasionally, until the onions have softened and have started to brown at the edges, about 10 minutes.

Add the garlic and cook for another 2 to 3 minutes, until fragrant and slightly softened. Carefully add the white wine and deglaze the pan by stirring vigorously. Reduce the wine to nearly dry, then add the cooked tomatoes, taking care to scrape all of the juices from the pan into the pot. Lower the heat to medium-low and allow the sauce to cook and thicken for about 10 minutes. Purée about half of the sauce with an immersion blender and then add the pepper, herbs, and the remaining salt to taste. Continue cooking until the juice thickens into a rich, glossy sauce. Remove from the heat and fish out the whole herbs. Adjust the seasoning to taste with more salt if needed.

Serve immediately or store in an airtight container in the refrigerator for up to 1 week. If a smooth consistency is desired, add the sauce to a blender or food processor and blend until smooth.

ARRABIATA VARIATION

Follow the instructions above and add 1 tablespoon of Calabrian chile paste with the garlic and cook until fragrant and starting to stick to the bottom of the pan. Then, deglaze and follow the remaining steps. Alternatively, add ¼ teaspoon of chile flakes or 1 minced fresh cayenne chile to the sauce when adding the halved tomatoes. The sauce can be left chunky or puréed for braising.

SNACKS & THINGS TO SHARE

In early 2024, the menu at Greens saw a major update, which included the addition of a small bites section. This section of the menu (and of this book) includes one-bite wonders that pack in the flavors of the seasons in small, neat packages—the perfect way to start your meal. I think of the small bites section as the modern-day alternative to bread baskets. Instead of starting your meal with dense, heavy bread, why not start with something seasonal and exciting? These recipes make for excellent hors d'oeuvres for entertaining or can even be enjoyed as side dishes. They also make for wonderful weekend nosh, when you want to experience the joy of snacking all afternoon long without too much of a fuss.

SPRING | FALL

Fried Baby Artichokes

V | GF | DF | NF | SF

Baby artichokes are a springtime marvel, and if you're lucky enough, you might be able to find some in the fall as well. Fresh baby artichokes are much easier to clean than fully grown artichokes because their leaves are still quite tender, and they have not developed the fuzzy inner choke yet. That means with a little patience, you could prepare these baby artichokes even on a weeknight. Serve with your favorite sauce, although I highly recommend Lemon Chive Aioli (page 36), Grilled Romesco Sauce (page 58), or Mint Pesto (page 55).

....

SERVES 2

1 quart (1 l) water

1 bay leaf

1 tablespoon salt

¼ teaspoon whole peppercorns

1 lemon

About 1 dozen baby artichokes, no more than 2 inches (5 cm) tall

1 quart (1 l) of neutral oil for frying, such as canola or grapeseed

Maldon sea salt, for sprinkling

Lemon Chive Aioli (page 36), Grilled Romesco Sauce (page 58), or Vegan Lemon Chive Aioli (page 36)

Start by cleaning and cooking the artichokes according to the instructions on page 64.

Next, heat the oil to about 350°F (180°C) in a high-walled saucepan. If not using a thermometer, test the oil by dropping one artichoke into the oil. It should sink to the bottom of the pot, then quickly rise to the surface and bubble. Once the oil is ready, fry the artichokes in batches and allow to cook until golden brown and crispy. The outer leaves will splay out and darken before the center. Make sure the center of the artichoke is also golden brown. As the artichokes finish frying, remove them from the oil onto a tray lined with a paper towel. Sprinkle with some Maldon salt and serve with Lemon Chive Aioli (page 36) or your favorite romesco sauce.

A Word on Artichokes

A jar of oil packed and seasoned artichoke hearts is a time-saving wonder product. I very much prefer these to the canned stuff, which is often tasteless, and sometimes not cleaned very well (no one likes a tough outer leaf). Artichokes that have been packed in seasoned oil tend to be brighter in color and take less time to make taste good. But, if you can't find the oil-packed variety, a good jar of chokes packed in a seasoned brine would do just fine.

But, of course, at Greens, we are all about using the fresh stuff. The texture, flavor, and appreciation of the vegetable are all heightened when you prepare them from their raw form. To us, it's an honor to spend the time cleaning the artichokes that our farmers so carefully grew for us. If working with artichokes have seemed like a daunting task to you in the past, or if you've simply never cooked them yourself, never fear! Trimming and cleaning baby artichokes, while somewhat time-consuming, is actually quite easy. Once they're prepped, cooking them is also relatively quick and easy, too.

To clean baby artichokes, start by preparing a medium-sized bowl of cold water with the juice of 1 lemon. Add the spent lemon halves to the bowl to add extra acid. This step is essential, as it will prevent the artichokes from oxidizing. Then, working one artichoke at a time, remove the outermost layers of leaves near the stem until you see the pale green flesh underneath. Then, use a paring knife or vegetable peeler to trim the very base of the stem and remove any brown spots.

Next, working with the other side, cut off the top one-third of the tip of the artichoke to remove the tips of the remaining leaves. Halve each artichoke lengthwise and check that the fuzzy choke has not started to develop. If there is no choke to remove, immediately place the cleaned artichoke into the prepared lemon water. If there is some choke, use a spoon or a paring knife to completely remove it all before placing in the lemon water. Repeat this process until all of the artichokes have been cleaned.

Then, to cook, add the artichokes along with the lemon water to a wide, shallow saucepan (rondeau). Add a bay leaf or two along with a pinch of whole black peppercorns, a sprig of thyme, and a generous pinch of salt. Cut a round of parchment so that it sits snug on the surface of the pot. Cut a small hole in the center of the parchment to allow steam to escape.

Heat the pot over high heat until the artichokes come to a boil. Then, lower the heat to a slow simmer. Use a fork to test for doneness. The artichokes are cooked when a fork that's pressed into the core of the artichoke comes out easily. Drain the artichokes and allow them to cool on a cooling rack or baking sheet. Discard the bay leaf, lemon halves, and peppercorns.

SPRING | SUMMER | FALL | WINTER

Slow Roasted Chile-Orange Pecans

V | GF | DF | SF

For the longest time, Greens would make these pecans for our neighbors at The Interval. They ended up becoming one of our favorite snacks, and we recently added them to our main menu in our new "First Bites" section. Don't be afraid of how much chile is in the recipe. The powdered sugar and orange zest round out the spice and earthiness, and you end up with a refreshingly nutty, slightly sweet, and warm, not-too-hot snack.

....

YIELDS 2 CUPS (200 G)

8 ounces (230 g) pecan halves

Zest and juice of ½ medium orange

3 tablespoons refined olive oil or other neutral oil

2 tablespoons powdered sugar

2 teaspoons paprika

1 teaspoon salt

Pinch of cayenne pepper

Preheat the oven to 325°F (160°C). Add the pecan halves to a bowl and add the orange zest and juice and the olive oil. Stir to coat the nuts. In a separate bowl, combine the powdered sugar, paprika, salt, and cayenne together until evenly distributed. Add the sugar mixture to the pecans and toss well to coat. The pecans will be heavily coated.

Lay the nuts out on a baking sheet in a single layer, taking care not to overcrowd the nuts. Be sure to add any remaining oil and spices left on the sides of the bowl to the baking sheet.

Bake the nuts for about 20 minutes total, stirring halfway through to redistribute the nuts so they toast evenly. To test that the nuts are done, remove one nut from the oven and cut it in half. The inner flesh should be a pale golden brown.

Once toasted, remove from the oven and allow to cool completely to room temperature before serving. Store in an airtight container for up to 3 weeks.

SPRING

Grilled Baby Fava Beans

V | GF | DF | NF | SFP

Baby fava beans are a delicacy in the springtime. The favas are harvested when the beans are still very small, and the outer pods are still tender enough to eat. These are only available for a few weeks out of the year, and oftentimes you'll need to ask your farmer to set aside the small ones for you. But, if you can get your hands on these little green gems, you'll have a marvelous snack or side dish worth savoring. These are best served with either Miso Aioli (page 36) or a drizzle of Chili Crisp (page 35).

SERVES 4

1 pound (450 g) baby fava beans in their pods, free of blemishes

2 tablespoons soy sauce, tamari, or soy sauce alternative

2 tablespoons grapeseed oil or other neutral oil

Miso Aioli or Vegan Miso Aioli (page 36) or lemon wedges, for serving

Preheat the grill over high heat until it reaches about 450°F (230°C). In a medium bowl, combine the fava beans, soy sauce, and grapeseed oil together until the fava beans are evenly coated.

Grill the fava beans in a single layer until the pods have nicely charred, 1 to 2 minutes. Then flip the beans over and char the other side. These beans should be cooked quickly to avoid discoloration.

Remove from the heat and serve with Miso Aioli (page 36) or with simply a squeeze of fresh lemon juice.

FAVA BEANS

Unless you are lucky enough to find baby fava beans, favas are the bean so nice you shuck them twice. Once mature, fava pods grow thick and fuzzy, and the beans inside are encased in a "second skin" that needs to be removed before eating. A quick and easy way to remove these skins is by blanching. Cook the fava beans for 15 to 30 seconds in boiling water, then drop into ice water to stop the cooking process. Then, that second skin will be much easier to grab and peel off. Some chefs think it's better to remove this skin before cooking, but I disagree. Blanching with the skin doesn't change the flavor by any discernible means, but it certainly will save you a ton of prep time.

SNACKS & THINGS TO SHARE

SUMMER

Goat Cheese–Stuffed Cherry Bomb Chiles

GF | NF | SF

Cheese-stuffed peppers are the perfect snack on their own, or they make a vibrant addition to any cheese plate. Cherry Bomb chiles are excellent for stuffing, as they are rounded on the bottoms and will stand up straight when placed on a cheese plate. If you can't find Cherry Bomb chiles, you can substitute with mini bell peppers or another kind of fresh, sweet chile pepper.

....

YIELDS 12 STUFFED PEPPERS

12 small Cherry Bomb chiles (12 ounces/ 350 g) or other small, sweet chile pepper

1 cup (240 ml) apple cider vinegar or other mild-flavored vinegar

2 bay leaves

1 tablespoon + ½ teaspoon salt, divided

1 cup soft goat cheese

½ bunch chives, sliced very thin

1 clove garlic, minced

¼ teaspoon dried oregano

1½ cups (360 ml) extra-virgin olive oil

Begin by preparing the peppers. Using a paring knife, cut around the stem of each chile to remove it. Be careful not to cut too deep so that the flesh of the chile remains intact. Remove the seeds and pick out the thin white membranes. Add the prepared chiles to a saucepan along with the apple cider vinegar, bay leaves, and 1 tablespoon salt.

Bring the vinegar to a boil with the chiles, stirring often to ensure that the chiles cook evenly in the vinegar. As soon as the vinegar comes to a boil, remove from the heat and strain the vinegar from the chiles and allow the chiles to come to room temperature in the vinegar mixture. Set aside to cool.

Meanwhile, prepare the filling. Combine the goat cheese, chives, garlic, oregano, and the remaining salt together in a bowl. Mix well to combine and adjust the seasonings as needed.

Use a spoon or a piping bag to stuff each chile with the cheese mixture. The chiles should be stuffed very full. Be sure to pack the cheese into the bottom and sides of the pepper, and level off the top once full.

Next, add the stuffed peppers to a clean glass jar. Pour the olive oil over the peppers to cover with oil. Marinate the chiles for at least 4 to 6 hours before serving.

To serve, remove the chiles from the oil and allow to drain for a minute or two before placing on a serving plate. The chiles will keep for up to a week in the refrigerator.

SPRING

Burrata Toasts with Balsamic Cherries

VP | DFP | SF

Burrata toast is a delightful way to showcase the season's best fruits. In the springtime, when cherries take over the markets, we like to serve a big slice of burrata toast at brunch. This recipe trades the large slice for smaller slices cut from a thin baguette, making it ideal for entertaining, or even just an afternoon snack.

······································

YIELDS 12 BITE-SIZE TOASTS

1 small, thin baguette

Olive oil, for drizzling

½ teaspoon salt

2 cups (300 g) pitted dark-fleshed cherries, such as Bing

2 tablespoons brown sugar

1 teaspoon apple cider vinegar or fresh lemon juice

2 tablespoons balsamic vinegar

4 sprigs thyme

⅛ teaspoon freshly ground black pepper

One 8-ounce (225 g) ball burrata or Macadamia Nut "Ricotta" (page 37)

¼ cup (30 g) toasted almonds, roughly chopped (see note, page 25)

Preheat the oven to 350°F (180°C). Using a sharp serrated knife, slice the baguette on a sharp angle into ¼-inch (.6-cm) thick slices. Lay the slices out on a baking sheet and drizzle with olive oil. Flip the toasts over and drizzle the other side with olive oil as well. Evenly sprinkle the toasts with ¼ teaspoon of salt. Bake for 8 to 10 minutes, until the toasts are golden brown. Remove from the oven and set aside to cool.

Meanwhile, combine the cherries, brown sugar, apple cider vinegar, balsamic vinegar, 2 of the thyme sprigs, the black pepper, and the remaining ¼ teaspoon salt in a small saucepan. Cook over medium heat for 15 to 20 minutes until the cherries have softened and the cooking liquid has thickened to a syrup consistency. Remove from the heat, remove the thyme sprigs, and set aside.

To assemble the toasts, drain the burrata from the whey and cut into 12 equal pieces. Be sure to get some of the filling and outer mozzarella casing in each segment. Spread the burrata on each toast, followed by a small spoonful of the cherries. Remove the leaves from the remaining 2 thyme sprigs and garnish the toasts with the picked leaves. Top each toast with a few chopped almonds and serve immediately.

NOTES

The cherries are wonderful when served warm over the toast, though this recipe can also be made ahead. To do so, toast the baguettes 1 to 2 days before and store in an airtight container at room temperature. The cherries can be made up to a week in advance and stored in the refrigerator. The cherries can be served cold, or they can be reheated in the microwave or on the stove top.

SNACKS & THINGS TO SHARE | 69

SPRING | SUMMER | FALL | WINTER

Smashed Cannellini Bean Toasts

V | DF | NF | SF

Move aside, avocado toast. These beans mean business! Sometimes the most special things come in the simplest packages, and these toasts are no different. The charred bread is the perfect vessel for these flavor-packed toasts, providing a bit of charred bitterness to balance the creamy topping. I love making these in the late summer, when the weather starts to turn, and fresh cannellini beans become available from Iacopi Farms. These are great as a quick snack or for entertaining, too!

SERVES 6 TO 8

FOR THE SMASHED BUTTERBEANS

⅓ cup (80 ml) extra-virgin olive oil

1½ tablespoons minced garlic

1 teaspoon chopped fresh sage leaves

½ teaspoon minced fresh rosemary

4 cups (720 g) cooked cannellini beans (see note, page 22)

Salt

Freshly ground black pepper

FOR THE TOASTS

½ loaf sourdough bread, cut into 1-inch (2.5-cm) slices

½ cup (120 ml) extra-virgin olive oil

Salt

To make the beans, in a 12-inch (30-cm) nonstick skillet, heat the olive oil over medium heat. Add the garlic and swirl in the pan to gently toast, until fragrant and the edges of the garlic start to turn golden brown, 2 to 3 minutes. Add the sage and rosemary and continue to cook until the herbs are fragrant, about 15 to 30 seconds. Add the beans and sauté together until the beans are heated through, then smash the beans gently with the back of a wooden spoon to create a coarse, chunky texture. Remove from the heat and season with salt and pepper. Set aside while you prepare the toasts.

To make the toasts, heat a dry, heavy-bottomed skillet over high heat. While the skillet is heating, generously coat the sliced sourdough with olive oil, until nearly saturated on both sides. Sprinkle each slice with salt.

When the skillet is nearly smoking, working in batches, add the oiled bread and press down with the back of a spatula. Cook until the bread is slightly charred on the edges and golden brown in the centers, about 3 minutes. Flip the bread over and char the other side.

Slice the bread slices in half or in thirds, top with the still-warm smashed beans, and serve immediately.

SUMMER

Savory Johnny Cakes with Marinated Tomatoes

V | GF | DFP | NF | SF

At Greens, we always have a "griddle cake" of some sort on the menu, which, of course, varies seasonally. A few summers ago, I took a particular interest in the American South since the summer just begs for okra and corn. We discovered that the original recipe for "hoe cakes," or johnny cakes, was less of a pancake and more of a cornmeal mush, almost like polenta, that was then griddled on the back of a hoe, hence the name. Our version of johnny cakes takes this more traditional approach, making it delightful when served with bright summer tomatoes. And, while the okra is optional, I encourage you to try it. Cooking it into the cakes imparts a wonderful flavor without any off textures.

....

YIELDS ABOUT 16 CAKES

FOR THE TOMATOES

2 cups (300 g) cherry tomatoes, cut into quarters

¼ small red onion, diced small

1 tablespoon red wine vinegar

1 tablespoon fresh lime juice + more to taste

¼ cup (60 ml) extra-virgin olive oil

2 tablespoons chopped fresh cilantro or parsley

½ teaspoon salt + more to taste

Pinch of freshly ground black pepper

Start by marinating the tomatoes. Tomatoes love salt, and they absorb flavor over time, so it's best to do this first to allow them to absorb flavor. Mix all of the ingredients together in a bowl and season with more salt or lime juice to taste if needed. Set aside.

To make the johnny cakes, mix the cornmeal, sugar, and salt together in a small bowl, and set aside. Then, heat the water in a small saucepan over high heat until boiling. Once boiling, reduce the heat to medium.

While whisking constantly, slowly add the cornmeal mixture to the boiling water in a slow and steady stream, making sure to break up any lumps as you go. Once the mixture has been incorporated, continue whisking until the mixture thickens considerably, 2 to 3 minutes.

Turn off the heat once the cornmeal batter has thickened and immediately add the sliced okra, fresh corn kernels, and the butter. Stir well to combine, then turn the batter out onto a baking sheet and spread evenly to cool. Cover the hot mixture with plastic wrap to prevent a skin from forming.

Once the johnny cake mixture has cooled, heat a nonstick skillet over medium heat with enough canola oil to barely cover the bottom of the pan. Using a cookie scoop or tablespoon, measure the johnny cake mixture into 2 heaping tablespoons per cake. Form each cake into a round ball into round balls.

CONTINUES

SAVORY JOHNNY CAKES WITH MARINATED TOMATOES

FOR THE JOHNNY CAKES

1 cup (140 g) cornmeal

3 tablespoons sugar

1½ tablespoons salt

2½ (540 ml) cups water

4 medium okra, trimmed and sliced into thin rings (optional)

½ cup (80 g) fresh corn kernels

2 tablespoons butter or olive oil

Canola oil, for frying

Crème fraîche, for serving (optional)

Once the oil is heated, it is time to fry the johnny cakes. To test that the oil is ready, toss a small pinch of the johnny cake mixture into the oil. If it sizzles immediately, the oil is ready. Take each ball of johnny cake mixture and gently flatten it between your fingers until it is about ½-inch (12-mm) thick. Gently lay each flattened cake into the oil and fry until golden, 3 to 4 minutes per side. Work in batches to fry all of the cakes—do not crowd the pan! As the cakes finish frying, remove them from the oil and allow them to drain on paper towels.

Serve the johnny cakes immediately with crème fraîche, if desired, and the marinated tomatoes. Before serving, make sure that the marinated tomatoes still taste the way you'd like them to— tomatoes will absorb salt and flavor over time, so you may need to readjust the seasoning.

CORN

Of all the vegetables out there, I think most of us have a pleasant memory with corn. To me, it's a reminder of warm summer evenings on the patio with mourning doves singing and mosquitoes bouncing in the lamplight. It's a Fourth of July barbecue and an autumn run through a corn maze. Whatever your memory, corn is one of the most delicious signs of summer and fall.

SUMMER | FALL

Corn & Asiago Arancini

NF | SF

One of the most magical and impressive qualities of fresh corn is its ability to thicken itself. In this recipe, corn is blended with vegetable stock to create a liquid that has so much natural starch that it will become something of a pudding on its own. And by cooking a risotto in this liquid, you'll end up with the creamiest, "corniest" risotto imaginable. This recipe is meant to make a rather thick risotto so that it can be rolled into balls and fried, but if you'd like to just eat this risotto plain, add a bit more liquid and enjoy it just as it is.

....

YIELDS 12 ARANCINI

2 fresh corn ears

2 cups (480 ml) Vegetable Stock, corn variation (page 39)

1 tablespoon light olive oil

¾ cup (165 g) Carnaroli or Arborio rice

1 small shallot, minced

2 cloves garlic, minced

Salt

¾ cup (180 ml) heavy cream

¼ cup (25 g) Asiago cheese

2 tablespoons Parmesan cheese or similar hard grating cheese

2 tablespoons finely chopped fresh basil

3 scallions, sliced very thin

⅓ cup all-purpose flour

2 large eggs

1 cup (50 g) panko bread crumbs

Canola oil, for frying

Roasted Cherry Tomato Sauce, Arrabiata Variation (page 59), Lemon-Chive Aioli (page 36) or Grilled Romesco Sauce (page 58), for serving

Start by preparing the cooking liquid. Cut the corn kernels off the ears. Blend half of the kernels with the vegetable stock. Set the remaining kernels aside and save the cobs for stock.

Next, heat a skillet over medium heat. Add the olive oil, rice, and shallot. Cook, stirring frequently, until the rice has lightly parched and some of the grains have turned opaque. Add the garlic and stir for another minute, until fragrant. Season the rice mixture with a very generous pinch of salt.

Reduce the heat to low and add the vegetable stock all at once. Cook the rice slowly and stir often. Steam should be visible in the pan, but there should not be any bubbling, or the rice will cook too quickly. Cook until the rice is al dente, 25 to 30 minutes. If you run out of cooking liquid, add some water a little at a time until the rice is the desired consistency.

Then, add the heavy cream, reserved corn, scallions, and basil together, and cook until the risotto is thick and glossy. Do not turn up the heat; allow the cream to slowly cook into the rice. It should take 7 to 10 minutes. At this point, turn off the heat and stir in the cheeses and the herbs. Adjust the salt to taste. Spread the finished risotto on a baking sheet in a thin layer, cover in plastic wrap, and refrigerate for several hours or overnight.

In 3 shallow dishes, prepare the breading station. Place the flour, eggs, and panko each in their own dish. Scramble the eggs using a fork and add a pinch of salt.

When the risotto has cooled and set, scoop it into balls about 1½ inches (3.75 cm) in diameter—about golf ball size. Working in batches, roll a couple of the balls in the flour to coat, then shake to remove excess flour. Then, coat in the egg, letting the excess drip back into the bowl, followed by the bread crumbs, and roll to completely coat the arancini.

Heat a small, tall-walled saucepan with 2 inches (5 cm) of canola oil over medium heat. Allow to heat to 350˚F (180˚C). Fry the arancini a few at a time until golden brown on all sides, 3 to 5 minutes. Once golden, remove from the oil and place on a wired rack lined with paper towels. Sprinkle with a little salt.

Serve immediately with Roasted Cherry Tomato Sauce, Arrabiata Variation (page 59), Lemon Chive Aioli (page 36), or Grilled Romesco Sauce (page 58).

SNACKS & THINGS TO SHARE

SPRING | SUMMER | FALL | WINTER

Fresh Spring Rolls with Sweet Potato

V | GF | DF | SF

Spring rolls have been a mainstay on the Greens menu for what seems like forever. They were the first thing I learned to make when I started at Greens. They take a bit of practice, and you might need to scrap the first couple of rice papers, but once you get that first perfect roll, it'll be worth it. So fresh and delicious, spring rolls can be enjoyed year-round. This sweet potato version can work any time of the year, but I particularly love them in the spring or fall, when the weather is just cool enough to want a sweet potato with its rich, sweet sauce yet still warm enough to enjoy the freshness of the spring rolls.

....

YIELDS 6 ROLLS

1 medium sweet potato

1 tablespoon canola oil

Juice of ½ lime

½ teaspoon salt

Six 8-inch (20-cm) rice paper wrappers, such as Three Ladies brand

2 red Fresno chiles or jalapeños chiles, sliced thinly

3 sprigs Thai basil, leaves picked

¼ red onion, sliced thin

1½ cups (255 g) rice vermicelli noodles, cooked according to package directions

12 little gem leaves or 6 romaine leaves

Peanut Hoisin Sauce (page 57)

Preheat the oven to 400°F (200°C). Peel the sweet potato and cut lengthwise into ½-inch (12-mm) slices. Cut the sweet potato slices lengthwise again to create long, ½-inch (12-mm) strips. Toss the sweet potato strips with the oil, lime juice, and salt. Spread the strips evenly on a baking sheet, leaving space between each strip so they can cook and brown evenly. Bake for 25 to 30 minutes, or until the sweet potatoes are cooked through. Remove from the oven and allow to cool.

To assemble the spring rolls, fill a medium bowl with warm water. Place a clean cutting board next to the bowl of warm water, then neatly place each spring roll ingredient in a row in front of the cutting board in a way that you can quickly and easily grab them as you assemble the rolls. Once your rolling station is ready and your ingredients are easily accessible, you may start rolling.

Dip a rice paper wrapper halfway into the bowl of warm water. When the wrapper starts to soften slightly, but still holds its shape, pull it straight out of the water with one hand, grab the softened side with the other, and turn the wrapper 180 degrees. Dip the other half of the wrapper in the warm water until it is slightly softened like the other side.

Lay the softened wrapper on your clean cutting board. Working quickly, start by adding a few slices of Fresno chile to the bottom third of the rice paper, making sure to leave about ½ inch (12 mm) on each side of the wrapper so you can tuck the ends in later. Then, add 3 to 5 Thai basil leaves and a few slices of red onion directly on top of the chile. Next, add two strips of sweet potato on top of the onion, staggering them a bit, to take up the whole length of the wrapper. Grab a 3-fingered pinch of rice noodles with your hands and pull the noodles up and lay them lengthwise across the sweet potatoes. Finally, top with 2 little gem leaves or one full romaine leaf.

CONTINUES

FRESH SPRING ROLLS
WITH SWEET POTATO

The tricky part is this: Peel up the bottom part of the spring roll wrapper, which is the side where you've laid your vegetables down, with your forefingers and thumbs. Holding your vegetable stack in place with your remaining fingers, pull the rice paper up and over the vegetables to touch the center of the rice paper and roll forward, so the vegetables sit on this seam. Once your vegetables are contained, fold the edges of your spring roll inward to close the ends. Then, roll your spring roll forward until the end of the rice paper seals to itself. Repeat this process with the remaining ingredients until you have made 6 spring rolls. Serve with the Peanut Hoisin Sauce (page 57).

SUMMER | FALL

Chanterelle Shumai with Mirin Sauce

V | DF | NF

Shumai is one our favorite dumplings to make at Greens because they are delightfully easy to prepare and don't involve complicated folding methods. And, since shumai filling is exposed on the top, you don't have to worry so much about overfilling your dumplings. We also, of course, like to tinker with this filling seasonally, so if instead you'd like to make these in the spring with morel mushrooms, or with hen-of-the-woods in the fall, have at it!

....

YIELDS 25 SHUMAI

FOR THE SHUMAI

1 pound (450 g) chanterelle mushrooms, cleaned of debris and dirt with a stiff brush or tea towel

2 tablespoons grapeseed or vegetable oil

2 small shallots, minced

2 cloves garlic, minced

1 teaspoon salt + more as needed

¼ teaspoon freshly ground white pepper

2 scallions, green parts only, minced

½ block (5 ounces/140 g) firm tofu, such as Hodo

1 package 3-inch (7.5 cm) round or 25 wonton wrappers

Start by chopping the chanterelles, so that the largest pieces are about pea sized. Set aside.

In a medium nonstick skillet, heat the grapeseed oil over medium-high heat. Add the shallots and garlic and sauté for 2 to 3 minutes, until fragrant. Add the chopped chanterelles and cook for another 5 to 7 minutes, until the chanterelles have browned slightly and wilted through. Add the salt and white pepper after the chanterelles have cooked down. Remove from the heat and place in a medium bowl to cool. Set aside.

Once the chanterelle mixture has cooled slightly, add the minced scallion. Mix to combine. Then, using a food processor, purée about one-third of the mushroom mixture with the tofu until a somewhat smooth, pasty consistency is achieved. Add this mixture back to the bowl with the mushroom mixture and mix thoroughly to combine and make a thick, sticky filling. Season with salt to taste.

Next, make the shumai. Wet a paper towel and wring it out. Open the wonton wrappers and place the damp paper towel over the wrappers to keep them moist. Then, fill a shallow dish with some water and place a pastry brush in the water, or you can use your finger if you don't have a pastry brush.

Working in batches, 3 to 5 shumai at a time, scoop about 1 tablespoon of filling in the center of each wrapper. It will look quite full. Lightly dampen the rim of the wrapper with the water, either with the pastry brush or simply your finger.

Lift the edges of the wrapper on either side at 3 o'clock and 9 o'clock with your pointer finger and thumb. Press your fingers together to pinch the wrapper from its edge to just touch the filling and create the first folds. Then repeat at 1 o'clock and 7 o'clock to create the second two folds. Finally, pinch the remaining wrapper together at 4 o'clock and 11 o'clock to create the final folds. Your shumai should look like a little star at this point. Then, dampen the pinched points with the water again and fold each point inward clockwise so that they are sticking against the filling.

CONTINUES

SNACKS & THINGS TO SHARE | 79

CHANTERELLE SHUMAI
WITH MIRIN SAUCE

FOR THE MIRIN SAUCE

¼ cup (60 ml) mirin

2 tablespoons white shoyu or soy sauce

½ teaspoon freshly grated ginger

2 scallions, white parts only, minced, green parts reserved for garnish (optional)

Pinch of red chile flakes (optional)

Repeat this process until all of the shumai are made. Once ready, set up a steamer basket over 1 inch (2.5 cm) of boiling water. Add a piece of parchment paper to the bottom of the steamer basket and line with the shumai, leaving about 1 inch (2.5 cm) of space between each dumpling. Steam for 8 to 11 minutes, until the wrappers have become softened and translucent. While the dumplings are steaming, make the mirin sauce.

For the mirin sauce, combine all of the ingredients together in a small dish and mix well to combine. Allow to sit for 10 to 15 minutes before serving to allow the ginger and chile flavors to marinate.

Once the dumplings are cooked, serve immediately with the mirin sauce. For serving a crowd, the dumplings can be garnished with very thin diagonals of scallion.

SPRING

Nettle & Goat Cheese Filo Rolls

NF | SF

Stinging nettles might sound intimidating at first blush. They do sting after all. But this can easily be overcome by wearing a pair of gloves and blanching the nettles for 20 seconds. The barbs that sting you will soften and become limp, making them harmless to handle once cooked. I find most of my nettles at farmers' markets, my backyard, or in the fields at Green Gulch Farm, though if you have a difficult time finding this pesky plant, you can easily substitute spinach or kale instead.

YIELDS 6 FILO ROLLS

Salt

5 ounces (140 g) nettles

1 bunch chives, sliced thin

2 tablespoons chopped fresh dill

2 tablespoons chopped fresh parsley

1 clove garlic, minced

1 cup (230 g) soft goat cheese

2 large egg yolks

1 lemon, zested and juiced

Pinch of freshly grated nutmeg

Pinch of freshly ground black pepper

9 sheets of frozen filo, thawed according to package directions

4 ounces (115 g) (¼ recipe) Lemon Butter (page 33), melted, or plain butter

Fill a large saucepan two-thirds full of water and bring to a boil. Add a generous amount of salt to the water. Using gloves, clean the nettles by removing any thick, tough stems and discarding. Once the nettles are cleaned, dunk the leaves and thin stems into the boiling water and allow to cook for 20 seconds. Drain from the water immediately and allow them to cool completely.

Once cool, ring the nettles out using cheesecloth or a tea towel until they are completely dry. Chop the nettles into ½-inch (12-mm) pieces and add to a bowl along with the herbs, garlic, goat cheese, egg yolks, lemon zest and juice, spices, and 1½ teaspoons salt. Mix together until combined.

When ready to assemble, preheat the oven to 375°F (190°C). Lightly spray or oil a baking sheet and set aside. Lay one filo sheet on a clean surface and brush lightly with the melted butter. Carefully lay a second filo sheet directly on top of the first sheet. Brush this filo sheet with more butter and add a third sheet on top. Then, use a knife or pizza cutter to slice the filo in half lengthwise, then into thirds crosswise to make 6 even stacks.

Take one of the 6 stacks and align it so that the long edge is facing you. Place about ¼ cup of filling at the very bottom of the filo stack. Tuck up the edge of the filo by folding each side inward about 1 centimeter for the entire length of the filo roll. Then, roll the filo loosely away from you until you have a chubby cigar. Place the filo on the prepared baking sheet and brush the top with melted butter. Repeat this process until all of the filo rolls are rolled. Bake the filo rolls for about 35 to 45 minutes, until the filo is uniformly golden brown and crisp. Serve immediately.

A Word on Nettles

I particularly love nettles not only because of their mild, somewhat briny flavor, but also because they are most often thought of as a weed. I've spent enough time helping out the farmers at Green Gulch to know this! Pesky nettles will grow all around the crops and sting you as you walk through to harvest. The farmers don't use gloves when harvesting, despite the nettles, as though it's something you just get used to. I have never particularly desired to be stung by a nettle, but I definitely never desired to be teased either, so I've braved the rows of crops barehanded, getting stung all along the way. Despite this, once I really stopped to think about the somewhat exhausting number of wild nettles that grow on the farm, I realized that it's a free (and delicious) crop that's stubborn enough to grow where it wants to, so we might as well use it. I've been reluctantly enamored ever since, and I always make a point to showcase this plant along with the other green icons of spring.

SOUPS & SALADS

What I love most about soups and salads is their versatility. They can be bright and light or rich and deeply filling, eaten as a starter or as an entire meal, and, my favorite, they always match the seasons. (I don't know about you, but I'm not eating Heirloom Tomato & Stone Fruit Gazpacho (page 121) in the middle of winter.) Like everything on the menu at Greens, we focus on the seasons first, then build the menu off of what we have available to us. Because of this, we change the menu so often that I probably could have written an entire book with only soup and salad recipes, given that there are always at least six choices on any menu. Luckily, I've managed to pare that long list down to my favorite few. The salad recipes in this chapter are all salads that have been featured on the menu at Greens over the last couple of years. The soups, on the other hand, may or may not have graced our menus. The soup of the day at Greens is always vegan, so while I have adjusted some of our classic recipes to include dairy, they are still tributes to the many soups we have served over the years. Enjoy as starters before an entrée or double the portion and enjoy as the main event.

SUMMER

Summer's Bounty Salad

VP | GF | DFP | NF | SF

It's all in the name for this salad. The epic combination of summer beans, corn, tomatoes, and freshly roasted red peppers pairs delightfully with goat cheese and Honey-Dijon Vinaigrette for one of the most refreshing salads of the summer. Once I start to see corn popping up in the farmers' markets, I can't help but count down the days until the rest of the ingredients follow so I can make this salad. This salad is an excellent addition to a barbecue spread, or it can be enjoyed as an entrée.

SERVES 4 TO 6

2 corn ears

Light olive oil, for greasing

8 ounces (230 g) slim and tender pole beans, such as haricot verts, yellow wax beans, or blue lake beans

Salt

3 packed cups (85 g) arugula

4 packed cups (156 g) baby lettuces

¾ cup (115 g) cherry tomatoes, halved

2 roasted red bell peppers, sliced (page 26)

Honey-Dijon Vinaigrette (recipe follows)

2 to 3 ounces (60 to 85 g) fresh goat cheese, crumbled (optional)

HONEY-DIJON VINAIGRETTE— MAKES 1 CUP

2 tablespoons Dijon mustard

3 tablespoons honey or agave

1 tablespoon minced shallot

¼ cup (60 ml) Champagne vinegar

¾ teaspoon salt

½ cup (120 ml) olive oil

Start by roasting or grilling the corn. Remove the husk and any stray hairs from the corn ears. Brush with a small amount of oil and either grill over high heat or broil in the oven on high, turning as needed, until the kernels are charred on all sides. Remove from the heat and allow to cool.

Then, prepare the beans. Fill a medium saucepan two-thirds full of water and bring to a boil. Meanwhile, cut off the tough tips of the beans. For a beautiful presentation, leave the beans whole, though some very long beans can be sliced in half on a pretty bias. Once the water is boiling, salt it generously and add the beans. Cook for 1 to 2 minutes, until the beans are just barely tender, but still have a snap to them. Drain from the water and either add to an ice bath or rinse with cool water to prevent the beans from browning.

For the vinaigrette, combine all of the ingredients in a blender or use an immersion blender in a bowl, and blend until smooth. If making by hand, combine everything together except for the oil and whisk to combine. Then, whisking constantly, slowly drizzle in the oil until emulsified.

Next, assemble the salad. Cut the cooled corn kernels from the cobs and add to a large bowl. Add the arugula, lettuces, tomatoes, bell peppers, and cooked beans. Dress with the Honey-Dijon Vinaigrette to taste (you'll likely have some leftover dressing), and then garnish with the goat cheese.

FRESH BEANS

My mom always had beans in her garden when I was growing up. It's one of the fastest crops to grow, with the first harvest arriving less than two months after planting. Even cleaning beans is rewarding. I quite love stringing snap peas in the spring, trimming pole beans in the summer, and shelling runner beans as fall begins. It's a labor of love worth doing for this incredibly nutrient-dense family of vegetables.

TOMATOES

I never truly loved a tomato until I moved to California (sorry, Mom). It was a Sungold tomato, perfectly ripe and popped when bitten into. I didn't try it willingly; Sue, the woman who trained me to be a line cook at Greens, gasped when I told her I didn't really like tomatoes, and I was not allowed to continue working until I agreed to eat one. After that one tomato, I made it my life's mission to try as many varieties as I could: Black Prince, Green Zebra, Sweet 100, Early Girls, and every other heirloom you could imagine. But what makes these tomatoes so good is when and how they're grown. A fresh, summer tomato simply can't be beat. It puts the mealy, tart, out-of-season hothouse tomatoes to shame. A dry-farmed tomato is even better—boasting a concentration of flavor that you'd never think possible. So, approach tomato recipes with an open mind and palate.

SUMMER | FALL

Roasted Pepper Panzanella

VP | DFP | NF | SF

Summer is the season where the flavors are bold, the ingredients are vibrant, and the flavors are as rich as the sun's rays. One of my favorite ways to use summer produce is in a panzanella, which, unlike the name suggests, is really a salad that's all about the vegetables. This recipe was written on the general side on purpose; use the products that speak to you the most, whether that's a neon green–yellow Gypsy pepper, a slender deep red Jimmy Nardello, small poppable padrons, or a mixture of them all.

SERVES 4 TO 6

½ loaf (8 ounces/227 g) focaccia bread

⅓ cup (80 ml) extra-virgin olive oil + more for roasting

Salt

2 pounds summer peppers, such as Jimmy Nardello, lipstick pimentos, shishitos, etc.

1 pound (450 g) tomatoes, preferably a mix of larger heirloom and cherry varieties, such as Green Zebras, Sweet 100, Sungolds, brandywine, etc.

½ cup (23 g) purslane (optional)

½ cup (80 g) green Castelvetrano olives

2 tablespoons torn fresh basil leaves

1 tablespoon fresh oregano leaves

2 to 3 tablespoons Champagne or white wine vinegar

1 teaspoon Calabrian chile paste or ¼ teaspoon red chile flakes (optional)

½ teaspoon freshly cracked black peppercorns

1 ball burrata cheese or Macadamia Nut "Ricotta" (page 37)

Maldon salt, for serving (optional)

Aged balsamic vinegar, for serving (optional)

Preheat the oven to 375°F (190°C). Tear the focaccia roughly with your hands into 1- to 2-inch (2.5- to 5-cm) pieces. Toss with a generous amount of olive oil to coat the bread nearly completely. Add a pinch of salt and toss to evenly coat. Spread the bread out evenly on a baking sheet and bake for about 10 to 15 minutes, or until the bread is mostly toasted through, but still has a slight chew in the centers.

When the bread is done, remove from the oven and raise the temperature up to 450°F (230°C). Clean the peppers and remove the stems and seeds by slicing each pepper lengthwise and pulling the seed clusters and stems out by hand. Toss the peppers with a very light coating of olive oil and a pinch of salt. Lay on a clean baking sheet and roast for about 5 minutes, until the peppers start to brown but are not completely wilted. Remove from the oven and add to a large bowl.

Cut the various tomatoes into wedges, perhaps leaving some cherry tomatoes whole for variety. Add the cut tomatoes, the toasted bread, and the remaining ingredients except for the burrata to the bowl. Toss together and check the seasoning for salt. Split the burrata into several pieces, place on top of the salad, and serve immediately. For an extra delight, sprinkle the burrata with some Maldon salt and aged balsamic vinegar.

NOTES

Sometimes your tomatoes will be more tart and acidic, so you might need to add sugar. Other times, your tomatoes will be impossibly sweet, and you might need a bit more acidity to bring out all of the flavors. And, no matter what, tomatoes love salt! Don't be afraid to add another sprinkle.

SPRING

Fava Bean & Green Garlic Fattoush

VP | DF | NF | SF

A fattoush is a fried bread salad with origins in the Middle East. It is believed to have originated in Lebanon, when farmers would fry crumbs ("fatteh") of leftover pita in olive oil for extra flavor. This springtime interpretation trades the typical cucumbers and tomatoes for fava beans and romanesco, the fractilic cruciferous vegetable that pops up in the late spring alongside other flowering broccoli varietals.

SERVES 2 TO 4

1 head romanesco

Olive oil, for roasting

Salt

1 package (12 ounces/340 g) fresh pita bread or 6 ounces (170 g) store-bought pita chips

Pinch of sumac

12 ounces fresh fava beans in their pods

1 medium watermelon radish, quartered and sliced into thin triangles

1 stalk green garlic, sliced thin and pickled according to instructions for Standard Pickles (page 32)

1 head radicchio, chopped into 1-inch (2.5-cm) segments

4 ounces (115 g) little gem lettuces, halved lengthwise and cut into 1-inch (2.5-cm) segments crosswise

2 ounces fresh fava greens, chopped into 1-inch (2.5-cm) segments, or more baby lettuces

½ bunch curly parsley, stems removed

5 ounces (140 g) feta cheese, crumbled (optional)

Preheat the oven to 400˚F (200˚C). Cut the romanesco into medium-small florets by removing the thick core and slicing into the top segments, following along the stems of the romanesco. Toss with a small amount of olive oil and a pinch of salt and place on a baking sheet. Bake for about 25 minutes, or until the romanesco is fork-tender and nicely browned. Remove from the oven and allow to cool.

Next, slice the pita into ½-inch (12-mm) strips, then turn and slice into 2-inch (5-cm) tiles. Toss with enough olive oil to generously coat the pita and add salt and a pinch of sumac to taste. Place on a baking sheet. Bake for 10 to 15 minutes, stirring halfway through until the pita is golden brown and crisp. Remove from the oven and allow to cool. If using pita chips, you can skip this step.

While the romanesco and pita are baking, prepare the fava beans. Bring a medium saucepan of water to a rolling boil. Remove the fava beans from their outer pods and add to the boiling water with a generous handful of salt. Boil for about 30 seconds, then remove from the heat and rinse under cool water to stop the cooking process. Working one bean at a time, use your thumbnail or a paring knife to cut open the outer skin of the bean, and with your other hand, squeeze the bottom of the bean to pop out of the skin. Discard the skins and place the beans in a large bowl.

Add the roasted romanesco, sliced watermelon radish, pickled green garlic, all of the greens, curly parsley, and feta cheese (if using) to the bowl. Just before serving, add the pita chips and dress with the Green Garlic Vinaigrette to taste and adjust the seasonings as needed.

To make the vinaigrette, blend all the ingredients with an immersion blender until smooth. If mixing by hand, finely chop the herbs and whisk with the remaining ingredients, though the dressing will be less creamy than when fully blended.

FOR THE GREEN GARLIC VINAIGRETTE

½ cup mint leaves

2 tablespoons minced green garlic

2 tablespoons curly parsley, chopped

¼ cup fresh lemon juice

1 teaspoon sumac

2 teaspoons pomegranate molasses or agave vinegar

¾ teaspoon

¾ cup light olive oil

FALL | WINTER

Roasted Cabbage & Farro Salad

NF | SF

Cabbage is one of those vegetables that, for whatever reason, doesn't get the credit it deserves. Cabbage is used around the world in so many ways, but it's seldom seen as the star of the show. Enter: this salad. Cabbage takes on a wonderfully nutty character when roasted in a hot oven, and it really shines alongside a chewy whole grain like farro. A mildly funky cheese like Taleggio provides richness and balance. Don't skip the pickled mustard seeds! They really provide that "je ne sais quoi" that ties everything all together.

SERVES 4

1 large (3 pounds/1.4 kg) napa cabbage

2 tablespoons light olive oil

½ teaspoon salt + more as needed

1 head (8 ounces) Treviso radicchio

1 cup (100 g) cooked farro (page 25)

½ bunch curly parsley, stems removed and roughly chopped

4 ounces (115 g) Taleggio cheese, cut into ½-inch (12-mm) cubes

¼ cup (55 g) Pickled Mustard Seeds (page 29)

2 tablespoons fresh lemon juice

1 tablespoon extra-virgin olive oil

Preheat the oven to 425°F (220°C). Halve the cabbage lengthwise, then cut each half into thirds lengthwise to create 6 wedges. Place the cabbage wedges cut-side up on a baking sheet. Drizzle the cabbage with the light olive oil, sprinkle with salt, and roast for 25 to 30 minutes, until the cabbage is tender and well-browned on the surface. Remove from the oven and let cool just enough to handle.

While the cabbage is cooling, prepare the remaining ingredients. Quarter the radicchio lengthwise, then cut the core out of each quarter. Thinly slice across the radicchio wedges to form long ribbons. Add to a large bowl along with the farro, parsley, and Taleggio cheese.

When the cabbage is still warm, but cool enough to handle, slice out the cores of each wedge. Then, slice the cabbage wedges crosswise as thin as possible. Add to the bowl with the radicchio. Add the Pickled Mustard Seeds, lemon juice, and olive oil and toss the salad to dress. Adjust the seasonings to taste.

SOUPS & SALADS

SPRING | SUMMER | FALL

Celery & Peanut Noodle Salad

V | GFP | DF | SF

My dream is to live in a world where people rejoice over the crisp, vegetal, and refreshing glory that is celery. While often overlooked as merely an ingredient in vegetable stock, celery is an incredible vegetable to use in salads, especially when served with something creamy and nutty like peanut butter. (The creator of ants-on-a-log was really onto something!) I particularly love this salad with the addition of fresh edamame, a delicacy that is only available for a few weeks every October.

....

SERVES 2 TO 3

One 5-ounce (142 g) package soba noodles, ramen noodles, or rice noodles, cooked according to package directions and cooled

4 ribs celery, sliced thinly on a bias

¼ head purple cabbage, shredded finely

4 ounces (115 g) snap peas, trimmed and halved on a bias

4 to 6 red Flambeau radishes, sliced very thinly

2 scallions, sliced thinly on a bias

1 red Fresno chile, sliced into thin coins

¼ bunch cilantro, stems removed

Peanut Vinaigrette (recipe follows)

1 cup (140 g) toasted peanuts (see page 25)

PEANUT VINAIGRETTE

½ cup (70 g) well toasted peanuts (see page 25)

¼ cup (68 ml) peanut oil or canola oil

3 tablespoons brown sugar

2 tablespoons rice vinegar

1½ teaspoons salt

2 teaspoons sambal oelek

Combine the soba noodles, celery, cabbage, snap peas, radishes, scallions and Fresno chile together in a bowl. Add half of the cilantro leaves and peanut vinaigrette to taste. Garnish with the toasted peanuts and remaining cilantro leaves.

To make the vinaigrette, in a food processor or mortar and pestle, grind the peanuts together until they form a thick, shiny, and somewhat chunky paste. Add to a small bowl with the remaining ingredients and stir well to combine.

CELERY

Celery is yet another incredibly underrated vegetable. While it firmly has its place in things like mirepoix, it's seldom used as the main ingredient in a dish. When paired with the right components, celery offers a marvelously juicy crunch, making it ideal for cold, bright salads.

SPRING | SUMMER

Strawberry Tatsoi Salad

V | GF | DF | NF | SF

One year, our beloved friend and farmer Sidney Weinstein from Star Canyon Ranch asked us if we'd be interested in serving tatsoi on our spring menu. Sidney grows the most darling baby greens, and when I tasted her tatsoi, I couldn't resist them. Tatsoi is often called a supergreen for its many health benefits, but it's truly special for its buttery, light flavor. It is closely related to bok choy, but is wonderfully mild and perfect in salads, especially when paired with spring strawberries and nutty sesame seeds.

....

SERVES 4 TO 6

6 packed cups (8 ounces/230 g) baby tatsoi or spinach

8 to 10 medium strawberries, quartered

4 scallions, sliced thinly on a bias

2 medium carrots, shredded into a thin julienne with a mandoline or food processor

¼ jicama, peeled and shredded into a thin julienne with a mandoline or food processor

½ cup (10 g) Thai basil leaves

2 tablespoons toasted sesame seeds (see note, page 25)

Creamy Sesame Vinaigrette (recipe follows)

Combine the prepared salad ingredients together in a large bowl and dress with the Creamy Sesame Vinaigrette to taste.

To make the Creamy Sesame Vinaigrette, combine the ingredients together and whisk until combined.

CREAMY SESAME VINAIGRETTE

½ cup Aioli (page 35) or prepared mayonnaise

¼ cup (60 ml) yuzu juice or fresh lime juice

¼ cup (60 ml) agave nectar or maple syrup

¼ cup (60 g) toasted sesame paste, black sesame paste, or tahini

2 tablespoons mirin

¾ teaspoon salt

FALL

Kale & Apple Salad

V | DF | SF

At Greens, the end of the summer is marked by the Green Gulch apple harvest. The groundsmaster Carolyn tends to the many varieties (34!) of heirloom apples each year, and through her efforts, these apple trees, despite their great age, are producing dozens and dozens of apples every year. She pulls a cart with several planter buckets along the rows of trees that are all entangled and leaning on one another for support. Each bucket has a little handwritten sign to denote which apples are which. Some are sweet and tart and have great textures for baking, others are light and crisp and perfect for salads like this one. Green Gulch also happens to have some of the best kale in the Bay Area (or world!), so this salad was a natural fit on our menu for the early fall. At Greens, we prefer a slightly heavier dressing for hearty kale salads.

SERVES 4 TO 6

2 bunches kale, such as blue curled, lacinato, Russian, etc.

2 medium apples, sliced thin

1 large shallot, sliced into thin rings and pickled according to the instructions for Standard Pickles (page 32)

1 cup (150 g) small, sweet seedless grapes, such as Bronx or Flame

2 cups (430 g) cooked and cooled purple barley (see page 25)

Pecan Vinaigrette (recipe follows)

⅓ cup (40 g) toasted chopped pecans

Start by cleaning the kale. Cut out the thick stems of the leaves and stack 4 to 5 leaves neatly on top of one another. Roll the kale up into a tight cigar and slice into 1-inch (2.5-cm) segments crosswise. Then, cut across each segment 1 to 2 times to make smaller bite-sized pieces of kale. Repeat until all of the kale is cut. Add the prepared kale to a large bowl and squeeze the leaves firmly with your hands to massage the leaves and slightly wilt them. This will soften the kale and bring out its natural sweetness.

Next, add the apples, pickled shallots, grapes, and barley together in a bowl. Toss with the Pecan Vinaigrette to taste. Garnish with the toasted chopped pecans.

To make the vinaigrette, combine all of the ingredients together in a blender or use an immersion blender in a bowl, and blend until smooth.

PECAN VINAIGRETTE

⅔ cup (160ml) light olive oil

¼ cup (60 ml) apple cider vinegar

1 tablespoon agave nectar

½ cup (60 g) toasted pecans (see note, page 25)

2 tablespoons crumbled tofu

1½ teaspoons whole-grain mustard

1½ teaspoons salt

SPRING

Baby Lettuces with Snap Peas & Extra-Herby Ranch

GF | NF | SF

Spring is the season of regrowth and new life, so the flavors tend to be GREEN— vegetal, grassy, funky, and sweet. The way spring smells on a bright, sunny April morning is the way it tastes, too. This salad features our Extra-Herby Ranch that highlights the absolute best parts of the spring. Paired with lovely, sweet snap peas, earthy radishes, aromatic spring carrots, and nutty toasted seeds, this will become your favorite salad of the spring.

SERVES 4 TO 6

8 ounces (230 g) snap peas

Salt

6 packed cups (about 9 ounces/255 g) baby lettuces

3 medium spring carrots, shredded finely on a mandoline or food processor

8 to 10 small red Flambeau radishes, sliced very finely on a mandoline

½ cup (60 g) toasted pumpkin seeds

½ cup (70 g) toasted sunflower seeds

Extra-Herby Ranch (recipe follows)

Start by destringing the snap peas. Fill a medium saucepan three-quarters full of water and bring to a boil. Meanwhile, using your index finger and thumb, or a paring knife, pinch off the top of the snap pea, pulling inward to remove the string along the inside edge of the pea. Repeat this process along the outside edge of the pea to remove the outer strings.

When all of the peas have been destringed, add them to the boiling water along with a generous amount of salt and cook for 30 seconds, until the peas have slightly softened, but still have a snap to them. Drain from the water and either dunk in an ice bath or place under cool running water to stop the peas from cooking and discoloring.

Next, add the peas, lettuces, carrots, and radishes to a bowl. Just before serving, add the toasted seeds and dress the salad to taste (you will likely have extra dressing).

To make the Extra-Herby Ranch, combine the garlic, shallot, Aioli, buttermilk, and sour cream together in a blender or use an immersion blender in a bowl, and blend until smooth. Season with the salt and pepper. Fold in the chopped herbs and allow to sit in the refrigerator for at least 10 minutes to thicken up a bit before using.

EXTRA-HERBY RANCH

1 clove garlic

1½ tablespoons minced shallot

½ cup (115 g) Aioli (page 35) or mayonnaise

½ cup (120 ml) buttermilk

¼ cup (60 g) sour cream

½ teaspoon salt

⅛ teaspoon freshly ground black pepper

½ cup (50 g) finely fresh chopped chives (about 1 bunch)

⅓ cup (30 g) finely chopped fresh dill (about ¼ bunch)

SPRING | WINTER

Avocado & Citrus Salad with Chimichurri

V | GF | DF | NF | SF

While this salad might make you think of summer sunshine, it's actually in season in the early winter and through the spring. Avocados are local in California until early winter, well into the start of citrus season, and they return around early March, before citrus leaves us for another year. This is a lovely salad to enjoy when you'd like a pop of brightness among the rather rich flavors of the winter.

....

SERVES 4

1 large red beet

1 tablespoon sugar

½ teaspoon salt

¼ cup (60 ml) light olive oil

2 tablespoons golden balsamic vinegar

2 medium blood oranges

1 cara cara orange

1 navel orange

1 oro blanco grapefruit or pomelo

3 to 4 small satsuma mandarins

Chimichurri (page 47)

1 to 2 avocados

Flaky sea salt, for garnish

1 Belgian endive, leaves separated and core removed

Start by cooking the beet. Place the beet in a small saucepan that is deep enough to cover the entire vegetable. Cover the beet with water and place on the stove top. Bring to a boil over high heat, then reduce to a strong simmer and cook until the beet is fork-tender, about 1 hour. Meanwhile, prepare the beet marinade by combining the sugar, salt, olive oil, and golden balsamic vinegar together in a bowl.

While the beet cooks, begin preparing the oranges and grapefruit. On a clean cutting surface, using a sharp knife, slice across the top and bottom of each piece of citrus so that the flesh is exposed. Then, place the citrus on the cutting surface on one of the flat sides to hold it in place. Cut away the skin and pith carefully, so that the bright flesh is exposed. Be careful not to cut away too much of the flesh with the pith.

Next, prepare a mixture of orange slices and "supremes." You can use whichever citrus for either cut, but each citrus can only be cut into one or the other. I prefer to slice the citrus that have smaller, tighter segments and cut supremes of the citrus that have larger, more defined segments.

CONTINUES

BEETS

Beets are one of the healthiest vegetables you can eat besides leafy greens. These powerhouse roots boast plenty of antioxidants for heart health and better blood flow. If you're afraid of the earthy taste, start with roasting the beets and tossing with some orange juice and olive oil. The citrus sweetens the beets and tones down those earthy flavors.

AVOCADO & CITRUS SALAD
WITH CHIMICHURRI

To cut slices, simply slice the citrus crosswise to create little wheels. To cut supremes, take the skinless citrus and hold it in your nondominant hand. Place the bowl with the beet marinade underneath you as you work to catch the excess juices. Using a paring knife, cut away each segment from the inner membranes by slicing as close to the membrane on either side of the segment as possible, then push the segment out with the side of the knife. Repeat this process until all of the segments have been removed from the core. Squeeze the core well over the bowl to collect any remaining juices.

Next, prepare the mandarins. Peel the mandarins with your hands as you normally would to eat them. Dip the peeled mandarins in water for a few seconds, then use a paring knife to remove the stringy pith. Once the mandarins are cleaned, separate them into individual segments.

When the beet is cooked to fork-tender, remove it from the cooking water and let it cool for a few minutes on a clean cutting surface. Once cool enough to handle, use a tea towel or gloves to rub away the skin of the beet. Then, slice the beet into 1-inch (2.5-cm) chunks and place in the prepared marinade. Stir to combine and let sit for at least 10 minutes.

To assemble the salad, place the citrus wheels flat on a large serving plate. Leave space in between the wheels and vary the color and sizes of the citrus as you lay them out. Top these citrus segments with the mandarins and "supremes." Next, top the citrus with the beets, then drizzle the entire salad with dollops of Chimichurri. Slice the avocado into thin strips and neatly fan over the citrus. Salt the avocados lightly with the flaky salt and garnish with endive leaves. Serve immediately.

SPRING | SUMMER | FALL | WINTER

Escarole & Potato Salad

VP | GF | DVP | NF | SF

Baby potatoes are the star of this salad, and it's important to use the smallest ones you can find. These tiny potatoes, because of the skin-to-surface-area ratio, will keep their shape after boiling and won't break up as easily as larger potatoes. This salad can be enjoyed warm or cold, so it's imperative that the potatoes are adequately cooked, or else they will become chalky upon cooling. If you can't find escarole or simply find it to be too bitter, finely chopped kale makes an excellent substitution. Or you can omit the leafy greens altogether and enjoy simply as a delicious potato salad.

....

SERVES 4 TO 6

2 pounds (900 g) small new potatoes or baby creamer potatoes

1 teaspoon salt + more for cooking the potatoes

1 pound (450 g) cremini mushrooms, sliced thin

1 tablespoon light olive oil

1 large head escarole

½ cup (115 g) Aioli (page 35), Vegan Aioli (page 36), or mayonnaise

¼ cup (60 g) sour cream or cashew cream

1½ tablespoons whole-grain mustard

1 medium shallot, minced

1 clove garlic, minced

¼ cup (10 g) capers, chopped

½ bunch chives, finely sliced

2 tablespoons finely chopped fresh parsley

2 tablespoons finely chopped fresh dill

½ teaspoon freshly ground black pepper

Start by cooking the potatoes. Halve the smallest potatoes and cut any potato larger than 1 inch (2.5 cm) in diameter into quarters. Place in a pot and cover completely with cold water. Add a generous handful of salt and bring to a boil on high heat. Once boiling, reduce the heat to medium-low and continue cooking until the potatoes are very well cooked, but not yet falling apart, about 20 minutes. A fork should easily pierce through the flesh. Drain the potatoes well, and then spread on a baking sheet to cool slightly. Set aside.

Next, sauté the mushrooms. Add the mushrooms and olive oil to a nonstick skillet and cook over medium-high heat, stirring often, until the mushrooms release their liquid and then reabsorb it. The mushrooms should brown and become somewhat crisp. Salt the mushrooms after they've cooked to avoid overseasoning. Remove from the heat and set aside.

Next, clean the escarole, then halve down the center lengthwise. Cut out the core, then chop the escarole into 1½-inch (3.75-cm) pieces by cutting the leaves down the center lengthwise and then across into chunks. Set aside.

In a large bowl, prepare the dressing by whisking together the remaining ingredients with the 1 teaspoon salt. Add the still-warm potatoes, pan-roasted mushrooms, and prepared escarole. Toss together to coat and adjust the seasonings to taste.

POTATOES

"New" potatoes are a delicacy in the Bay Area in June and July. These potatoes are eaten right after harvesting, before undergoing the typical "curing" process to preserve them at room temperature. New potatoes should be refrigerated and eaten quickly, but not to worry—it's hard to keep such perfect spuds around for long! New potatoes have sweet, juicy flesh and thin, papery skins that can easily be rubbed off even with your bare hands. They feel lighter and are wonderfully refreshing. I love them in potato salads, particularly because they don't get as chalky when cooled.

SPRING | FALL

Couscous & Baby Artichoke Salad

V | GFP | DF | SF

This couscous salad is inspired by the flavors of Northern Africa, while also celebrating the marvel that is the California artichoke. Most of the artichokes grown in the United States come from California, and if you are lucky enough to visit a springtime farmers' market, you'll see stands flooded with artichokes of all shapes, sizes, and colors. At Greens, we love to use baby artichokes because they're quick and easy to clean, and you don't have to worry about the fuzzy choke like you do with fully grown artichokes.

SERVES 4 TO 6

8 cups (160g) arugula

2 cups chopped cooked baby artichokes or artichoke hearts

1½ cups (240 g) cooked couscous or quinoa (page 25)

⅔ cup (115 g) cooked chickpeas (page 22)

¼ cup (30 g) toasted almonds (see note, page 25), roughly chopped

2 scallions, sliced thin

1 roasted red pepper, sliced into thin strips crosswise

FOR THE DRESSING

1 cup (240ml) extra-virgin olive oil

⅓ cup (80 ml) fresh lemon juice

1¼ teaspoons salt

½ teaspoon coriander, ground

Pinch of freshly ground black pepper

Pinch of saffron threads

Mix the salad ingredients together in a large bowl and toss to combine. To make the dressing, blend the olive oil, lemon juice, and spices together with an immersion blender until smooth. Season with the salt.

Just before serving, add about half of the vinaigrette into the bowl and toss to combine. Taste the salad and adjust the seasoning as necessary. The couscous will absorb dressing after a few minutes, so it should be dressed a bit on the heavy side.

FALL | WINTER

Creole Pumpkin & Collard Greens Soup

V | GF | DF | NF | SF

This soup is just about as hearty as it gets, and it's one of my favorite recipes to make when the season turns colder. It's almost a ritual of mine to make this on the first rain of the year in the Bay Area, as though this soup itself has the power to kick off soup season and make the house cozy for the holidays. Most of the work for this soup is in making the Creole Broth (page 40). While it takes some time and prep work, the deep flavor you get from this rich broth is worth every second. I suggest making the broth ahead of time and freezing it, so that this soup can be a quick weeknight venture whenever you need it. Serve with crusty bread or over a chewy whole grain such as brown rice, barley, or wheat berries.

....

SERVES 4

1 large sweet potato (about 2 pounds/900 g)

1 tablespoon olive oil

Salt

1 bunch collard greens or curly kale

1 recipe Creole Broth (page 40)

¾ cup (165 g) uncooked black-eyed peas, soaked (page 22)

Preheat the oven to 400°F (200°C). Prepare the sweet potato. Peel the sweet potato and cut into 1-inch (2.5-cm) cubes.

Toss the sweet potato cubes with the olive oil and a pinch of salt. Spread evenly on a baking sheet and bake for about 35 minutes, until the sweet potato is tender and browning on the edges.

Meanwhile, clean the collard greens well and cut out the large stems; discard. Then, working with 3 to 4 leaves at a time, roll up the collard greens into a tight roll and cut crosswise into ¼-inch (6-mm) slices to make thin ribbons. Slice down the center of the cut collards lengthwise to cut each of these ribbons in half.

In a medium saucepan, heat the Creole Broth over medium-high heat. Drain the soaking black-eyed peas and add to the Creole Broth along with the sliced collard greens. Bring to a strong simmer, then reduce the heat to low, cover with a lid, and allow the beans and greens to simmer in the broth until the beans are tender and the greens have softened and discolored, about 40 to 45 minutes.

Once the sweet potato is cooked, remove from the pan and add to the soup. Simmer for another 10 minutes to allow the flavors to meld together.

COLLARD GREENS

If I had to choose between collard greens and kale, I'd almost always go with collards. Both are hearty, dark bitter greens that are great for sautéing and braising, but collards tend to be a bit less bitter than kale and are arguably healthier, too. When braised, the leaves become velvety and satisfyingly sweet. If you can't find collards at your local grocery store, kale is still an excellent substitute.

SPRING | SUMMER | FALL | WINTER

Turmeric Chickpea Soup

V | GF | DF | NF | SF

This is one of the simpler soups in this book, but that doesn't mean it lacks in flavor. I first made this soup back when I was a sous chef. I remember that it was a particularly busy day, and before I knew it, I only had about 30 minutes to make soup before we opened for dinner, and the only two things in our refrigerator that I had extras of were chickpeas and kale. With those, plus some other staples, I ended up creating one of our most requested recipes to date!

SERVES 4

2 tablespoons light olive oil or grapeseed oil

1 medium onion, diced

2 cloves garlic, minced

One 1-inch (2.5-cm) knob ginger, minced

1 serrano chile, stem and seeds removed and minced

1 tablespoon ground turmeric

¼ teaspoon freshly ground black pepper

2 cups (480 ml) Vegetable Stock (page 39)

Two 14.5 ounce (410 g) cans coconut milk

2 cups (340 g) cooked chickpeas (see note, page 22)

1 bunch kale (curly or lacinato preferred)

2 teaspoons salt + more as needed

1½ tablespoons sugar + more as needed

Juice of ½ lime + more as needed

In a large saucepan, heat the oil over medium-high heat. Add the onion and sauté until translucent, stirring frequently, 5 to 7 minutes. Then, add the garlic, ginger, and serrano and sauté for another 2 to 3 minutes, or until fragrant and sizzling. Add the turmeric and black pepper and toast for 30 seconds, stirring constantly so the spices don't burn.

Add the Vegetable Stock, coconut milk, and chickpeas. Scrape the bottom of the pan to lift off any aromatics that may be sticking. Bring to a boil, then reduce the heat to medium-low and simmer slowly.

While the soup is simmering, prepare the kale. Strip the kale of its large stems; discard. Then, working with 3 to 4 leaves at a time, roll the leaves up crosswise to create a long log. Slice across the rolled leaves to create ¼-inch (6.35-mm) ribbons of kale. Then, roughly chop across the sliced leaves to create small pieces.

Add the kale to the soup and continue to simmer for about 15 to 20 more minutes, until the kale is softened and turned a deep green color. Season with salt, sugar, and lime juice, adding more to taste as necessary.

SUMMER | FALL

Roasted Eggplant & Pepper Soup

VP | GFP | NF | SF

Eggplant is one of the most controversial of vegetables, but this soup is the one to convert even the eggplant-suspicious to eggplant-enthusiast. Roasting the eggplant whole softens the flesh to a velvety texture that, when mashed and added to the soup, creates a richness and lightness that is nothing short of extraordinary.

....

SERVES 6 TO 8

1 globe eggplant (a little over 1 pound/450 g)

⅓ cup (80 ml) extra-virgin olive oil

2 large shallots (about 5 ounces/140 g), diced

6 cloves garlic, sliced thin

2 teaspoons Calabrian chile paste (optional)

¼ cup (60 ml) dry white wine

2 roasted red bell peppers, diced (see note, page 26)

One 14-ounce (400-g) can crushed tomatoes

4 cups (1 l) Vegetable Stock (page 39)

4 sprigs thyme

1 bay leaf

2 teaspoons salt

¼ teaspoon freshly ground black pepper

2 tablespoons chopped fresh basil

2 tablespoons chopped fresh parsley

4 cups baby spinach (optional)

Cooked orzo pasta or fideos, for serving

Grated Pecorino cheese, for garnish (optional)

Preheat the oven to 450°F (230°C). Place the whole eggplant on a baking sheet. Roast the eggplant until the skin is blackened and the eggplant is very tender in the center, about 25 to 30 minutes.

Once the eggplant has blackened, remove from the oven, and allow to cool until it is cool enough to handle. Then, carefully remove the blackened skin, leaves, and stem; discard. Remove any large seed clusters. Place the remaining eggplant flesh in a bowl and roughly mash with a fork or chop with a knife. Set aside.

Next, heat the olive oil in a large saucepan over medium-high heat. Add the shallots and garlic and sauté, stirring often, for about 4 to 5 minutes, until fragrant and starting to brown lightly. Add the chile paste, if using, and sauté another 30 seconds to toast. Add the white wine and deglaze the pan by stirring vigorously to lift off any stuck bits to the bottom. Reduce the wine to nearly dry.

Once the wine has reduced, add the mashed eggplant, roasted red bell peppers, crushed tomatoes, Vegetable Stock, thyme, and bay leaf. Bring to a boil, then reduce to a slow simmer. Cook for about 25 minutes to allow the flavors to marry and to break up the eggplant a bit more. Season with the salt and pepper and adjust accordingly to taste. After 25 minutes, remove the bay leaf and thyme sprigs.

Finish the soup with the herbs and spinach, if using. Stir to gently wilt. Add ½ cup of cooked orzo to the bottom of each serving bowl before adding the soup on top, and garnish with pecorino cheese, if desired.

SPRING

Spring Minestrone

VP | GFP | DFP | NF | SF

The kitchen team at Greens gets so excited when the first signs of spring start to show. It's the true season of the color green—peas, fava beans, asparagus, ramps, green garlic, baby spinach, pea greens, and herbs, all re-emerging after what feels like an eternity. Spring produce brings grassy and funky flavors to our dishes, which pair so deliciously with creamy beans and hearty pasta. Featuring almost every spring vegetable you can imagine, this soup is a celebration of this new growth and also the end of winter.

SERVES 6 TO 8

1 leek

¼ cup (60 ml) extra-virgin olive oil

1 rib celery, sliced thin

2 cloves garlic, sliced or grated

1 pound (450 g) Yukon gold or fingerling potatoes, diced

6 cups (1.5 l) Vegetable Stock (page 39)

Salt

Freshly ground black pepper

1 cup (140 g) snap peas

1 cup (145 g) shelled fresh or frozen English peas

½ bunch asparagus

1½ cups (270 g) cooked cannellini beans (page 22) or one 14.5-ounce (410-g) can, drained and rinsed

4 cups (340 g) spring greens, such as baby spinach, nettles, fava greens, or pea tendrils

Juice of ½ lemon

2 tablespoons chopped fresh dill

2 tablespoons chopped fresh basil

1 cup (60 g) small pasta, such as orzo, ditalini, or small shells, cooked according to package directions

2 ounces (60 g) pecorino cheese, grated (optional)

Start by cleaning the leek. Remove the dark green tops of the leek, leaving only the light green and white bottom. Halve the leek lengthwise and clean well under running water, being careful to remove any dirt that is caught between the layers. Then, slice the leek crosswise into thin strips.

Heat a large sauce pot over medium heat. Add the olive oil, leek, celery, and garlic, and sauté for 5 to 7 minutes, or until the leek has wilted and the garlic is fragrant. Add the potatoes, Vegetable Stock, and a generous pinch of salt. Bring to a boil and then reduce the heat so the liquid just simmers.

While the potatoes are cooking, thinly slice the snap peas on a bias. Snap off the ends of the asparagus and cut them on a diagonal into thin ½-inch (12-mm) chunks.

When the potatoes are fork-tender, add the snap peas, English peas, cannellini beans, spring greens, and lemon juice. Allow to simmer for 7 to 10 minutes, or until the asparagus and snap peas are tender.

Just before serving, add the dill and basil. Season with salt and black pepper to taste. To serve, add about ¼ cup (50 g) of cooked pasta to the bottom of each serving bowl, then ladle soup over the top. Garnish with pecorino cheese, if desired.

SOUPS & SALADS | 109

SUMMER | FALL

Creamy Corn Chowder

VP | GF | DFP | NF | SF

Ah, the famous corn chowder. There are so many wonderful versions, but this one is particularly beloved because it relies less on heavy cream and more on the natural starches inside puréed corn to thicken it to a luscious, velvety consistency. It's easily made vegan, and the touch of bell pepper gives this sweet corn soup a little more balance.

SERVES 6 TO 8

3 ears fresh corn

6 cups (1.5 l) Vegetable Stock (page 39, corn variation)

¼ cup (60 ml) light olive oil

1 medium onion, diced

½ green bell pepper, diced

3 cloves garlic, minced

¼ cup (60 ml) dry white wine

1 large Yukon gold potato (about 8 ounces), peeled and cut into ½-inch (12-mm) cubes

1 tablespoon salt

1 cup (240 ml) heavy cream or vegan alternative, such as coconut milk

¼ teaspoon freshly ground black pepper

½ bunch cilantro, stems removed and roughly chopped

Start by preparing the corn. Strip the husk from the corn ears and remove as many of the corn silks as possible. Cut each corn cob in half crosswise, then stand the cob halves upright and cut the kernels off the cobs. Cutting the cobs in half first helps keep the corn from flying all over the place when cut, since the kernels won't fall as far. Reserve 1 cup of corn kernels for later. Place the remaining corn kernels in a blender pitcher with the Vegetable Stock. Then, scrape each corn cob of any remaining juice and corn bits by sliding the edge of your knife across the cobs on a 45-degree angle. Add this juice and pulp to the blender. Blend until smooth; set aside.

Next, heat the oil in a large saucepan over medium-high heat. Add the onion and bell pepper and sauté together, stirring often, until the onion is translucent, but not yet browning, 5 to 7 minutes. Add the garlic and cook for another 3 minutes, until the garlic is fragrant and starting to stick to the bottom of the pot. Add the white wine and deglaze the pot by scraping the bottom with a wooden spoon. Allow the wine to almost evaporate before adding the potatoes, vegetable stock purée, and the salt.

Bring the mixture to a boil, then reduce the heat to a slow simmer and allow the potatoes to completely cook though, about 15 to 20 minutes. Once the potatoes are cooked, add the heavy cream and black pepper. Allow to simmer for another 10 minutes to fully heat the cream. Add the chopped cilantro right before serving.

FALL | WINTER

Black Lentil Mulligatawny

V | GF | DF | NF | SF

Mulligatawny as we know it today is a British soup that was inspired by a Southern Indian dish called "rasam" several hundred years ago during the British colonization of India. Since its popularization in the eighteenth century, mulligatawny has seen countless iterations, though many share some key components. The most surprising of which is the addition of apples, which lends a touch of sweetness to an otherwise bold and savory soup. At Greens, we make this soup in celebration of our farm's apple harvest. It is important to cook the rice separately from the soup, or it will become too soft and begin to break as it sits in the soup.

SERVES 6 TO 8

2 tablespoons grapeseed oil

1 medium onion, diced

1 large carrot, diced

1 small rib celery, diced

1 tablespoon curry powder, such as vadouvan

½ teaspoon ground coriander

Pinch of cayenne pepper (optional)

¾ cup (130 g) cooked chickpeas (see note, page 22)

⅓ cup (70 g) beluga lentils, cleaned and sorted (page 22)

One 14-ounce (400-g) can diced tomatoes

6 cups (1.5 l) Vegetable Stock (page 39)

1 large tart apple (about 8 ounces), such as Honeycrisp

One 14-ounce (400-g) can coconut milk

1½ tablespoons salt + more as needed

Cooked rice, for serving (see note, page 25)

Heat the oil in a large saucepan over medium-high heat. Add the onion, carrot, and celery and cook, stirring occasionally, until the onions are translucent, about 10 minutes. Add the curry powder, coriander, and cayenne and cook for another 30 seconds to toast the spices.

Next, add the chickpeas, lentils, tomatoes, and Vegetable Stock. Bring the soup to a boil, then reduce the heat to medium-low and simmer slowly until the lentils are cooked through.

Once the lentils have softened, peel and core the apple. Grate the apple coarsely using a box grater or food processor. Add to the soup along with the coconut milk and salt and cook for another 5 to 10 minutes to infuse the flavor. Adjust the seasoning to taste.

To serve, add about ¼ cup (60 g) of cooked rice to the bottom of each individual soup bowl. Spoon the hot soup over the rice.

SOUPS & SALADS | 111

SPRING | SUMMER | FALL | WINTER

Coral Lentil Dal

V | GF | DF | NF | SF

This dal is a mainstay on all of our menus, from brunch to lunch to dinner. There are no tricks to this soup, but because it's so simple, it's important to use the best ingredients you can find. The curry powder that we like to use is a French variety called vadouvan, which is a touch sweeter than your average curry powder thanks to the addition of fried shallots.

....

SERVES 6 TO 8

¼ cup (60 ml) grapeseed oil

1 medium onion, diced

1-inch (2.5-cm) knob ginger, minced

1 small serrano, stem and seeds removed, minced

1½ tablespoons vadouvan curry powder

2 cups (420 g) pink or red lentils, cleaned and sorted (page 22)

6 cups (1.5 l) Vegetable Stock (page 39)

1 tablespoon salt + more as needed

Chopped fresh cilantro, for serving

In a large saucepan, heat the grapeseed oil over medium-high heat. Add the onion and cook, stirring often, until translucent and starting to brown at the edges, 8 to 10 minutes. Add the ginger and serrano and cook for another minute, until fragrant. Then, add the curry powder and toast for about 30 seconds.

Add the lentils, Vegetable Stock, and salt to the pot. Bring to a boil and then reduce the heat to a slow simmer. Cook, stirring occasionally, until the lentils have completely broken down and the soup has thickened to a homogeneous consistency, adding more water as necessary so that the lentils don't dry out. Adjust the seasoning to taste. Sprinkle with chopped fresh cilantro before serving.

SUMMER | FALL

Portobello Tamarind Soup

V | GF | DF | NF

This soup is quite different from the others in this book. The tamarind, mushrooms, and tomatoes combine to make a broth that is both tangy and bright, sweet, and savory. And, because of the punchy ingredients, this soup develops a surprising amount of flavor in a short amount of time, making this a great option for weeknights. This soup is best in the early fall, when cherry tomatoes are plump and sweet, and mushroom season is on the horizon. Using "seedless" tamarind pulp that comes in blocks is best, as it is less sour and has a better flavor than the liquid concentrate, but you'll still need to wrap this in cheesecloth.

....

SERVES 4

2 tablespoons grapeseed oil

1 medium yellow onion, diced small

2 cloves garlic, minced

8 ounces (230 g) portobello mushrooms, cut in half and then sliced thin

¼ cup (30 g) tamarind pulp or 3 tablespoons liquid tamarind concentrate

1 cup (150 g) cherry tomatoes, halved

6 cups (1.5 l) Vegetable Stock, Asian variation (page 39)

½ block (5 ounces/140 g) firm tofu, cut into ½-inch (12-mm) cubes

¼ cup (60 ml) tamari

2 tablespoons sugar + more as needed

2 tablespoons chopped fresh cilantro

4 scallions, green parts only, sliced thin

Salt

Heat a large saucepot over medium-high heat. Add the grapeseed oil and onions and cook until translucent, 5 to 7 minutes. Add the garlic and portobellos and cook until the mushrooms have softened and released their liquid, another 7 to 10 minutes.

If using tamarind pulp, wrap it in cheesecloth and tie tightly so that the seeds do not escape. Add the tamarind, cherry tomatoes, Vegetable Stock, tofu, tamari, and sugar. Bring to a boil, then reduce the heat to low and simmer slowly for about 20 minutes. Remove the cheesecloth from the soup and press it against the side of the pot with the back of a spoon to release the tamarind into the broth.

Garnish with the cilantro and scallions just before serving. Adjust the seasoning to taste with salt and sugar as needed.

FALL | WINTER

Butternut Squash Soup

VP | GF | DFP | NF | SF

Cream cheese may seem like an unorthodox addition to this soup, but its tartness and creamy texture is the easiest way to achieve a perfectly balanced soup. Butternut squash is my favorite squash to use for this soup, since it's naturally more moist than other varieties and lends itself well to soups. However, any winter squash would be delicious here, from kabocha to red kuri. Choose your favorite and enjoy.

SERVES 6 TO 8

1 large butternut squash
(about 3 pounds/3.4 kg)

1 tablespoon light olive oil

2 tablespoons butter

1 teaspoon salt + more as needed

½ teaspoon freshly ground black pepper + more as needed

1 medium onion, diced

2 tablespoons fresh marjoram or 1 teaspoon dried oregano

3 to 4 cups (720 to 960 ml) Vegetable Stock (page 39)

1 teaspoon fresh thyme leaves

One 8-ounce (225 g) block cream cheese, cut into 8 cubes (or a vegan alternative, such as Oatly)

1 teaspoon apple cider vinegar

Preheat the oven to 400°F (200°C). Cut the squash in half lengthwise, being careful to avoid the stem, to expose the seeds. Use a spoon to scrape out the stringy flesh and seeds; discard. Place the squash face up on a baking sheet and evenly coat with the olive oil. Make sure to coat the entire surface with oil by spreading with your hand or a pastry brush. Place ½ tablespoon of the butter in each cavity of the squash. Then, evenly sprinkle the squash halves with the salt and pepper. Roast until very tender, about 60 to 90 minutes, depending on the density of your squash.

In a large saucepan, heat the remaining 1 tablespoon butter over medium heat. Add the onions and cook until the onions are very soft and are starting to brown at the edges. Add the marjoram leaves and 3 cups (720 ml) of the Vegetable Stock and heat to a boil, then reduce the heat to low. Use a spoon to scrape the cooked butternut squash flesh away from the skin and add to the soup. Make sure to add any melted butter and juice from the squash cavity to the soup as well. Allow the soup to simmer for about 15 minutes, then add the cream cheese. Simmer for 5 minutes more, then purée until smooth using a high-powered blender or immersion blender. If the soup is too thick, add the remaining 1 cup stock to achieve the desired consistency and return to a boil before serving. Add the apple cider vinegar at the very end and adjust the seasoning to taste.

WINTER SQUASH

While Annie taught me a long time ago that it's best to hold on to summer produce for as long as possible, I can't help but look forward to the arrival of winter squashes. As a born and raised New Yorker, I always looked forward to the weather cooling down, cozy scarves, warm tea, and of course, pumpkins. Pumpkins come in all shapes and sizes, and their qualities vary from squash to squash. The dryer squashes, like honeynut, kabocha, and acorn, are ideal for recipes like gnocchi (page 128), roasting, and baked goods. Other squashes like butternut are wonderful in soups, as their light, creamy texture is ideal for puréeing. With so many things to do with winter squashes, how could you not look forward to their arrival every year?

SOUPS & SALADS | 115

SPRING | SUMMER | FALL | WINTER

Kimchi Noodle Soup

VP | GFP | DF | NF

Our veganized kimchi jjigae is a touch lighter and less fiery than the traditional version, but that doesn't mean that it lacks in flavor. We also trade the traditional rice accompaniment for ramen noodles, which are wonderfully chewy and stand up to the funky kimchi flavors with ease. This soup is best in the dead of winter, when you need a little fire to warm you up. Enjoy through the early spring—it's great with ramps!

SERVES 6 TO 8

2 cups (16 ounces/473 ml) just-boiled water

½ cup dried shiitake mushrooms

½ bunch mustard greens

2 tablespoons grapeseed oil

2 cups (4½ ounces) shimeji (beech) mushrooms, bottoms trimmed

1 bunch scallions or ramps, sliced thin, green and white parts separated

2 tablespoons minced fresh ginger

4 cloves garlic, minced

1½ cups (225 g) Quick Kimchi (page 29) or store-bought kimchi, chopped finely

6 cups (1.5 l) Vegetable Stock, Asian variation (page 39)

1 tablespoon sugar

2 teaspoons salt

2 tablespoons toasted sesame oil

2 packages (3 ounces each) ramen noodles or other noodle as desired, such as rice or udon

1 block silken tofu, sliced into 2-inch (5-cm) by ½-inch (12-mm) strips

4 large eggs, soft- or hard-boiled, peeled and rinsed

Black sesame seeds, for garnish

Start by preparing the dried shiitake mushrooms. Soak the mushrooms in the boiling water for 20 minutes, or until cool enough to handle. Once the mushrooms have rehydrated, drain the soaking water, and cut into quarters. Set aside.

Next, clean the mustard greens. Cut out the tough stems from each leaf. Then, working 3 to 4 leaves at a time, roll the mustard greens up crosswise to create a tight log. Cut across the leaves in ¼-inch (6-mm) segments to make thin strips. Cut lengthwise down the center of the cut leaves to shorten the length of each strip. Set aside.

Heat a large saucepan over high heat. Add the beech and shiitake mushrooms and sauté until the beech mushrooms are softened and starting to brown. Reduce the heat to medium, then add the whites of the scallions, ginger, and garlic to the pot and sauté until fragrant, 2 to 3 minutes.

Add the kimchi, mustard greens, Vegetable Stock, sugar, salt, and sesame oil. Bring to a boil, then reduce to a simmer and cook for 15 minutes. Add the ramen noodles and half of the scallion greens and cook for another 2 to 3 minutes, until the noodles are fully cooked.

To serve, place a few slices of silken tofu to the bottom of each bowl. Use tongs or chopsticks to place some noodles to the side of the tofu, then ladle some broth into the dish. Garnish with soft- or hard-boiled eggs, sliced in half, the remaining scallion greens, and sesame seeds.

NOTE

To make this recipe vegan, omit the eggs.

SUMMER

Pozole Verde

V | GF | DF | NF | SF

Whenever we make this soup, we make double our normal daily amount to account for the staff requesting it for their family meal. Everyone loves the tartness from the tomatillos paired with the sweet summer corn and filling hominy. Roasting the zucchini gives the soup a bit more richness and depth of flavor, but if you're short on time, you can simply throw it in the pot and the resulting soup will be just as delicious.

SERVES 6 TO 8

4 large zucchini, sliced into 1/8-inch rounds

Light olive oil or grapeseed oil

3/4 teaspoon salt + more as needed

1 large onion, diced

2 cloves garlic, minced

1 poblano chile, diced small

1 green jalapeño, seeds and stem removed, minced

6 tomatillos, husks removed and diced

6 cups (1.5 l) Vegetable Stock (page 39), divided

1 teaspoon dried oregano

1/2 teaspoon ground cloves

2 to 3 bay leaves

1 1/2 cups (250 g) cooked hominy (see page 22) or one 14-ounce (400-g) can

3 ears fresh corn, kernels removed

2 bunches cilantro

Juice of 1/2 lime

Preheat the oven to 425°F (220°C). Toss the zucchini slices with just enough olive oil to coat and season with 3/4 teaspoon salt. Spread the zucchini in a single layer on 1 or 2 baking sheets and roast until the zucchini is cooked through and browning on the edges, about 15 to 20 minutes.

While the zucchini is roasting, heat 2 tablespoons olive oil in a large saucepan over medium-high heat. Add the onion and cook, stirring occasionally, until softened and starting to brown at the edges, about 10 minutes. Add the garlic, poblano chile, and jalapeño and continue to cook for another 5 to 8 minutes. Next, add the tomatillos, 5 cups (1.2 l) of the Vegetable Stock, the oregano, cloves, and bay leaves. Reduce the heat to medium-low, place a lid on the pot, and cook until the tomatillos are discolored and starting to fall apart. Stir occasionally to prevent them from sticking to the bottom of the pan.

Add the cooked hominy, corn, and the roasted zucchini and bring to a boil, then turn off the heat.

In a blender pitcher, combine the cilantro with the remaining 1 cup (240 ml) stock and blend until smooth. Pour into the hot soup, add the lime juice, and adjust the seasoning to taste. Serve immediately.

SUMMER SQUASH

Unlike winter squash, summer squash is a relatively neutral tasting, juicy addition to your summer meals. It's one of those vegetables that can take on the flavor of most anything, and its texture depends on how it's cooked. For a luscious, melt-in-your-mouth texture, grill, roast, or sauté halved zucchini until it is pliable and softened. For a crisper texture, a quick pan-fry of thinly sliced wedges or shaving raw into salads are options, too.

SUMMER

Heirloom Tomato & Stone Fruit Gazpacho

V | GF | DF | NF | SF

A great way to use up excess summer produce is with this gazpacho. In my eyes, this recipe only gets better with somewhat dry, wrinkled tomatoes and bruised, sugary stone fruit. It's perfect for a hot summer day and is wonderful served in shot glasses for a party. It might be cold and foggy for most of the year in San Francisco, but there are always a couple of days in September and October when a heat wave inevitably passes through. These are Greens' gazpacho days, and they are the very best. Don't be afraid of the amount of olive oil in this recipe—this is what makes the gazpacho thick and helps bring out the flavor.

SERVES 4

3 pounds heirloom tomatoes, preferably red or yellow

1 very ripe plum (8 ounces)

½ cup (80 ml) diced red onion

1 small clove garlic

1 persian cucumber

2 sprigs basil, stems removed

2 tablespoons sherry vinegar + more as needed

½ teaspoon black pepper

½ cup (120 ml) extra virgin olive oil

2 tablespoons salt + more as needed

Start by preparing the vegetables. Cut the cores out of the tomatoes and dice them into large chunks. Remove the pit from the plum and dice into chunks as well. Crush the garlic with the side of a knife and slice the Persian cucumber into thick chunks.

Place all the ingredients into a blender pitcher and blend until smooth, adjusting the seasoning with salt and sherry vinegar as needed. Tomatoes will vary in acidity as the season evolves, so you may need more or less vinegar and salt depending on when you make this soup. For a soup with a bit more texture, place the ingredients in a saucepan or bowl and blend with an immersion blender.

To serve, ladle into bowls and garnish with a drizzle of olive oil and some chopped basil. The soup can be stored in the refrigerator for up to 3 days and served cold.

CUCUMBERS

When I think of cucumbers, I think of my mom. They're our favorite snack in the summertime, and we always grew them in the garden. Most of the time, our Burpee cukes would grow into little round balls or into curly monsters, but they were delicious no matter their peculiarities. You don't have to be a bad gardener to enjoy some variety with your cukes. You can choose from so many types of cucumbers, some purposefully round and yellow skinned, like lemon cucumbers, or long twisted varieties like serpentine.

SOUPS & SALADS | 121

DOUGHS & SAVORY PASTRIES

Savory doughs form the foundation for a generous portion of the meals at Greens, and for good reason. Doughs are an incredible vessel—blank canvases on which to create veggie works of art. Pasta is certainly an important player here, as its many shapes lend themselves well to different sauces and components. We always have pasta on the menu at Greens, and we change this offering every two months or so in order to showcase the best of what the seasons have to offer. I'm also particularly fond of the pierogi stuffed with peas and feta. Growing up in a Ukrainian-American family, on my mom's side, I often looked forward to pierogi day with my mom and grandma. Putting pierogi on the menu for the first time at Greens was a moment that I'll never forget; it was the first time I really felt that I put my own stamp on the menu. Other doughs in this section are also quite special because they're more commonly used for our special events, like New Year's Eve or during wine dinners, when we have some extra time to make dough and transform it into something extraordinary. These dishes are best served as entrées and would be wonderful served with a salad on the side to balance the entrées.

SUMMER | FALL

Spinach & Ricotta Dumplings

NF | SF

These dumplings are like pillowy, giant gnocchi. We make these dumplings in the summertime and serve them with our light and sweet Roasted Cherry Tomato Sauce (page 59) along with roasted summer vegetables like zucchini, eggplant, and peppers. These dumplings would be fantastic with Lemon Butter (page 33) and spring vegetables like English peas and sautéed pea tendrils, too. The ricotta that we like to use is Bellwether Farms, but any good quality ricotta will do.

SERVES 4

8 ounces (227 g) fresh spinach

1 pound (450 g) ricotta cheese

2 large eggs

Pinch of freshly ground black pepper

½ cup (45 g) Parmesan cheese, grated + more for serving

½ teaspoon lemon zest

1½ cups (180 g) all-purpose flour + more for dusting

Salt

¼ cup (60 ml) light olive oil + more for greasing

Roasted Cherry Tomato Sauce (page 59)

Start by preparing the spinach. Clean the leaves well and remove any large stems. Heat a saucepan over medium-high heat. Add the spinach and a couple tablespoons of water and immediately cover with a lid. Allow the spinach to steam for about 20 seconds. Remove the lid and stir the spinach, making sure that it has completely wilted. Remove the spinach from the pan and set aside to cool completely.

Once the spinach has cooled, dry it well by squeezing out all of the excess water through a tea towel or cheesecloth. Finely chop the dried spinach and add to a bowl.

Next, add the ricotta, eggs, pepper, Parmesan, and lemon zest together in a bowl until the mixture is fluffy and well combined. Add half of the flour and mix until just combined, then add the remaining flour and mix until a dough forms. The dough should be a bit sticky. Once all of the flour is incorporated, cover with plastic wrap, and refrigerate for at least an hour.

Once rested, remove the dumpling dough from the refrigerator and place on a clean, heavily floured surface. Cut the dough into 4 pieces. Working with one piece at a time, gently roll the dough into 1-inch (2.5-cm) logs, flouring as needed to prevent the dough from sticking. Once rolled, cut the log into dumplings about 1½ inches (3.75 cm) long. Set aside while you roll out and cut the remaining dough.

Once the dumplings have been cut, bring a saucepan filled halfway with heavily salted water to a simmer over medium heat. Do not boil the water or it will break the dumplings. Grease a baking sheet with the olive oil; set aside.

Drop a few dumplings into the simmering water and allow to cook for about 8 to 10 minutes until the dumplings float and have firmed up. Carefully remove from the water with a spider or slotted spoon. Place on the oiled tray, tossing the dumplings in the oil to prevent sticking. Repeat this process until all of the dumplings have been cooked.

Once cooked, heat a nonstick skillet over medium heat with enough olive oil to coat the bottom of the pan, about ¼ cup or more as needed (light olive oil is ideal). Pan-fry the dumplings until they are golden brown on both sides, about 4 minutes per side. Serve with Roasted Cherry Tomato Sauce (page 59) and sprinkle with additional Parmesan cheese.

FALL | WINTER

Caramelized Mushroom & Onion Pasta

VP | DFP | NF | SF

My friends at Shared Cultures are masters of their craft of miso making. This pasta recipe was originally written to honor the fabulous, funky, cheesy qualities of their cashew miso. That, plus Grana Padano, roasted mushrooms, and chili crisp, make for an unusual, but delightful, fusion of flavors that are incredibly umami rich. I'd highly recommend making the Chili Crisp on page 35 for the perfect balance of sweetness and spiciness, but any store-bought chili crisp will do. And while Shared Cultures ships their misos nationwide, if you're in a pinch, any miso would work well here, too.

SERVES 6 TO 8

1 pound (450 g) mushrooms, such as cremini, black trumpet, oyster, or maitake, cut into bite-sized chunks

1½ teaspoons salt + more as needed

¼ cup (60 ml) grapeseed oil

1 recipe Basic Cut Pasta (page 134) or 1 pound (450 g) dried fettuccine or pappardelle

1 large onion, sliced thin

2 tablespoons soy sauce or tamari

1 tablespoon brown sugar

2 cloves garlic, sliced thin

1 bunch lacinato kale, stems removed and torn into 1- to 2-inch (2.5 to 5-cm) pieces

6 tablespoons (90 g) Miso Butter (page 33), made with Shared Cultures cashew miso or mushroom miso

2 ounces (60 g) Grana Padano or similar hard grating cheese (optional)

½ cup (115 g) Chili Crisp (page 35)

1 bunch scallions, sliced thin into ribbons or on the bias

Preheat the oven to 425°F (220°C). Toss the mushrooms with 1 teaspoon of salt and about 3 tablespoons of grapeseed oil. Spread in a single layer on a baking sheet and roast for about 20 to 25 minutes, until the mushrooms have dried out a bit and have caramelized nicely. Remove from the oven and set aside.

If using fresh pasta, prepare that next. Roll the pasta to very thin, nearly translucent sheets (about 1/16-inch/1.6 mm thick). Roll the sheets up into a long, loose cigars and slice crosswise into ¾-inch-thick ribbons for pappardelle, or into ½-inch (12-mm) thick ribbons for tagliatelle. Bunch into nests and set aside.

Heat a large skillet over medium heat. Add a small drizzle of grapeseed oil and the sliced onion and allow it to deeply caramelize, about 20 to 25 minutes. Stir the onions occasionally, so that they have time to sit and caramelize. While the onions cook, bring a large pot of water with a generous handful of salt to a rolling boil.

Once the onions have caramelized, deglaze the pan with the soy sauce, scraping up any stuck bits from the bottom of the pan. Add the brown sugar and salt to the onions and stir to dissolve. Reduce the heat to medium-low and add the cooked mushrooms to the pan along with the garlic and cook for 3 to 5 minutes, until the garlic is softened. Add the kale and cook until wilted, about 3 to 4 minutes.

Next, add the fresh pasta to the pot of boiling water and cook for about 2 minutes, until the pasta is al dente. If using dry pasta, cook according to package directions. Drain the pasta, reserving 1 cup of pasta water, and add to the pan with the mushrooms and kale. Add the miso butter and stir to coat. Add about half of the pasta water and the cheese. Stir to create a thick, rich, glossy sauce. Add more pasta water as needed. Adjust the seasonings to taste.

Portion the pasta into bowls and garnish with Chili Crisp and scallions.

DOUGHS & SAVORY PASTRIES | 127

FALL | WINTER

Honeynut Squash Gnocchi with Brown Butter

VP | DFP | NF | SF

Honeynut squash is a special variety of squash that was bred to look like a tiny butternut and have a drier consistency. We often like to use this squash in its whole form because the shape and size are so magnificent on a plate, but this recipe is an exception. Because honeynut has more of a dry, creamy sweet potato consistency, it's the ideal squash for making something that typically requires dry potatoes, like gnocchi. Serve this with a simple brown butter with sage and a spoonful of Garlic Confit (page 32) for the perfect cold weather meal.

....

SERVES 4

2 medium honeynut squash (about 2 pounds/907 g)

2 cups (240 g) all-purpose flour + more as needed

⅛ teaspoon freshly grated nutmeg

½ teaspoon salt + more for seasoning

¼ cup (½ stick/60 g) butter or vegan butter, such as Miyoko's

2 tablespoons light olive oil

2 tablespoons roughly chopped fresh sage leaves

2 cloves smashed Garlic Confit (page 33)

Freshly ground black pepper

½ ounce pecorino romano cheese (optional)

Preheat the oven to 400°F (200°C). Halve the honeynut squash lengthwise and place face up on a baking sheet. Bake until the squash is very tender and dry, about 90 minutes. Remove from the oven and allow to cool completely.

Then, purée the squash in a food processor until smooth. Combine the squash purée with the flour, nutmeg, and salt in a bowl and mix gently to form a shaggy dough.

Turn the dough out onto a lightly floured surface and gently knead the dough just until it comes together. Do not overmix. Cover the dough with plastic wrap and refrigerate for at least 15 minutes. After the dough has chilled, return it to the floured prep area and divide it into 6 equal pieces.

Working with one piece at a time, roll each piece of dough out into ropes about ¾ inch (2 cm) in diameter and 13 inches long. Cut across the length of each rope in 1 inch (2.5 cm) lengths to form the gnocchi. If desired, use a gnocchi board or a fork to create a design by rolling the gnocchi across the ribbed surface. As you finish the gnocchi, place them on a lightly floured baking sheet.

Next, prepare the brown butter. Melt the butter in a 12-inch (30-cm) nonstick skillet over medium heat. Add a pinch of salt and stir constantly until the butter solids begin to turn golden brown and the butter smells nutty. Pour into a heat-safe dish and set aside. Wipe out the skillet, add the olive oil, and place over medium low heat.

Bring a large pot of water to a rolling boil. Add the gnocchi, shaking off any excess flour before dropping in the water. Cook until the gnocchi float, about 3 to 4 minutes. Drain the gnocchi and pat dry with a paper towel, then add to the skillet with the olive oil.

Allow the gnocchi to cook, without touching, until the edges of the gnocchi are golden brown. Give the pan a toss and continue cooking until most sides of the gnocchi are crisp. Add the reserved brown butter, sage, and garlic confit and cook for another minute to crisp the sage leaves.

Garnish with freshly ground black pepper and the pecorino cheese, if using. Serve immediately.

128 | DOUGHS & SAVORY PASTRIES

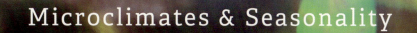

Microclimates & Seasonality

Seasonality is subjective, and what's in season near you might depend on the microclimates around you. In the Bay Area, we are fortunate to have many different microclimates that offer a wide array of seasonal produce at any given time. So, while the summer might make you think of tomatoes, corn, and peppers, you might also find great quality kale and broccoli, too.

Microclimates are just what they sound like—they are tiny climates that exist within bigger environments. One of the most well-known examples of microclimate expressionism is in wine. Wines from hotter climates tend to have bolder flavors and higher alcohol compared with wines from cooler regions. There are coastal wines that taste a bit briny from the sea air and mountaintop wines that are ripe from the sun, but acidic because of the cool high-elevation air, and have notes of the granite or limestone that they're grown in. Wines can even differ depending on where they were grown on the same hillside. This is what we call terroir—the wine's unique expression of the earth.

In the world of vegetables, you don't hear the term *terroir* thrown around much, but I think it works its way into our lives in various ways. If you frequent farmers' markets, you probably already know who you're going to get strawberries from in the springtime. Maybe this vendor changes for you as the seasons progress. Why is that? Maybe some of it is the varietal—I certainly wait for Mara des Bois strawberries later on in the season—but another likely cause is the climate the berries were grown in. Certainly, strawberries get better as the season goes on, but I would bet that the hot-climate farms are likely to get sweeter strawberries first. As the season gets hotter, you might find that the farmer in the hottest climate has fewer berries than one in a more temperate area.

Of course, the climate isn't the only factor when choosing produce. Farm practices, varietal, size, color, and texture all contribute to what fruits and vegetables we buy and when. It's so important to us to know our farmers and create relationships with them. Each farmer, in every microclimate, plays a critical role in helping us understand the seasons so we can make the menu just right.

SUMMER

Fettuccine with Herb-Marinated Tomatoes & Burrata

VP | NF | SF

This incredibly light, bright, and summery pasta takes about 20 minutes from start to finish, making it the perfect weeknight meal. You can make the tomatoes up to two days ahead, which is not only a time-saver, but also helps to build flavor. I often keep a big batch of the tomato mixture in my refrigerator during the summer months so that I can add a bit of brightness to my cooking whenever I need it. This pasta makes my favorite summer staple the star, and when finished with a bit of good balsamic and a ball of burrata, it's sensational. To keep this vegan, replace the compound butter with olive oil and use Macadamia Nut "Ricotta" (page 37) as the creamy topping.

....

SERVES 4

1 to 2 heirloom tomatoes, diced (about 1½ cups diced)

2 tablespoons minced shallot

1½ teaspoons minced garlic

1½ teaspoons chopped fresh chives

1 tablespoon thinly sliced fresh basil

1½ teaspoons chopped fresh oregano

1 tablespoon balsamic vinegar

1 tablespoon olive oil

¾ teaspoon salt + more as needed

⅛ teaspoon freshly ground black pepper

1 recipe Basic Cut Pasta (page 134) or 1 pound (450 g) dry fettuccine pasta, cooked to package directions

4 tablespoons (60 g) Lemon Butter (page 33)

1 ball (6 ounces/170 g) burrata cheese or Macadamia Nut "Ricotta" (page 37)

¼ cup (60 ml) aged balsamic vinegar

Start by making the tomatoes. Combine the tomatoes, shallot, garlic, herbs, balsamic, olive oil, and salt, and pepper together in a bowl. Stir until well mixed, then set aside. If you are making tomatoes fresh for the pasta dish, leave it out so that it's room temperature. If you are making it ahead of time, place it in the refrigerator until ready to use. It is best to temper the tomatoes so that it isn't too cold when it's mixed with the pasta.

Next, bring a large stockpot to a boil. Add a generous handful of salt. Flouring as necessary, roll the Basic Cut Pasta dough out until it is very thin. It should be nearly translucent, about $1/16$-inch (1.6-mm) thick. Roll the pasta sheet into a loose cigar and cut crosswise in ¾-inch (2-cm) by ½-inch (12-mm) segments to create fettucine noodles. Add the pasta to the boiling water and cook al dente for about 2 minutes, until just cooked. Strain out 1 cup of the pasta cooking liquid, then drain the pasta.

Next, with the heat off, add the Lemon Butter to the pot with half of the pasta water. Add the pasta back to the pot and toss to combine. The butter should glaze the pasta to make a nice, thick glossy sauce. If the butter looks shiny or oily, add a bit more pasta water and stir rapidly to emulsify the butter sauce. Add half of the tomatoes and toss to combine.

Add the pasta to a large serving bowl. Top with the remaining tomatoes. Break the ball of burrata over the top and drizzle with the balsamic glaze and add a pinch of salt directly onto the cheese. Serve immediately.

130 | DOUGHS & SAVORY PASTRIES

SPRING | FALL | WINTER

Escarole & Fagioli Pasta

NF | SF

I grew up in an Italian-American family from the Bronx on my dad's side, so I also grew up in the land of "fazool." My favorite of the "fazool" (bean) based soups was the lovely and light escarole and fagioli. This pasta, inspired by the famous soup, is wonderfully brothy, rich with flavors of Parmesan and bright lemon. The best part is that this takes not more than 15 minutes to make if you exclude the time it takes to boil water, making this the perfect cozy winter and chilly spring weeknight dish. If you're making this in the spring, consider swapping out half of the garlic for a stalk or two of green garlic for a funky, springier rendition.

SERVES 4 TO 6

2 large heads escarole, outer leaves removed

10 cloves garlic

½ teaspoon Calabrian chile paste or ¼ teaspoon crushed red chile flakes

1 tablespoon butter

⅛ teaspoon freshly ground white pepper

2 cups (360 g) cooked cannellini beans (page 22)

4 cups (90 ml) bean cooking broth or Vegetable Stock (page 39)

½ teaspoon salt

12 ounces (340 g) small shells, orecchiette, or ditalini, cooked 2 minutes short of al dente

2 tablespoons Lemon Butter (page 33)

2 ounces (60 g) Grana Padano cheese or similar hard grating cheese, grated

Clean the escarole well under running water and dry well. Halve lengthwise and cut out the core. Then, rip the leaves into ragged pieces 2 to 3 inches in length. Set aside.

Next, peel and thinly slice the garlic as finely as possible. A mandoline is helpful here.

Heat a large saucepan over medium-high heat. Melt the butter and add the garlic and chili paste. Fry until the garlic begins to turn golden brown at the edges. Add the escarole and white pepper and cook until just wilted. Add the beans and their cooking broth or vegetable stock along with the salt. Bring to a boil, then reduce the heat to a slow simmer. Add the pasta and allow to cook in the garlicky escarole broth for a couple of minutes, until al dente. Add the Lemon Butter and stir well to create a rich, somewhat glossy broth. Portion the pasta with its broth into bowls and top with the Grana Padano cheese. Serve immediately.

SPRING | SUMMER | FALL | WINTER

Linguine with Cauliflower & Chard

VP | DFP | NF | SF

This pasta was inspired by a classic Sicilian dish but reimagined for the California springtime. Green olives and golden raisins make for one of the most euphoric flavor combinations with sweet, briny, and citrusy notes; and when paired with lemon butter and deeply roasted cauliflower, they create the most perfect pasta of them all. While we love this pasta in the springtime for its lovely lemony flavor, these ingredients are able to be found year-round—something I find most comforting, since I can and do want to eat this pasta all the time.

....

SERVES 6 TO 8

1 recipe Basic Cut Pasta (page 134) or 1 pound (450 g) linguine, bucatini, or spaghetti

1 to 2 heads cauliflower (about 3 pounds/ 1.4 kg), cut into florets

3 tablespoons olive oil

1 tablespoon salt + more as needed

1 large bunch Swiss chard

2 tablespoons butter

1 cup (50 g) panko bread crumbs

1 bunch spring onions or scallions, sliced thin

2 cloves garlic, sliced thin

½ cup (75 g) golden raisins

½ cup (80 g) Castelvetrano olives, pitted and chopped

½ cup (120 ml) dry white wine

6 tablespoons (90 g) Lemon Butter (page 33)

¼ cup (25 g) Grana Padano or similar hard grating cheese (optional)

Flouring as necessary and working in batches, roll the Basic Cut Pasta dough out until it is very thin. It should be nearly translucent, about 1/16-inch (1.6-mm) thick. Roll the pasta sheet into a loose cigar and cut crosswise in ⅛ inch (3 mm) segments to create long, thin linguine noodles. Wrap the linguine into nests and set aside on a floured baking sheet to dry.

Preheat the oven to 425°F (220°C). Toss the cauliflower florets with 2 tablespoons of olive oil and a teaspoon of salt and spread evenly on a baking sheet. Roast for about 20 to 25 minutes, until the cauliflower is softened and browned on the edges. Set aside.

While the cauliflower is cooking, clean the Swiss chard. Remove the thick stems and slice them on a thin bias; set aside. Then, tear the chard leaves into 1- to 2-inch (2.5- to 5-cm) pieces. Set aside.

Next, toast the panko bread crumbs. Melt the butter in a nonstick skillet over medium heat, then add the bread crumbs and ¼ teaspoon of salt. Stir the bread crumbs constantly until they are golden brown; set aside.

Bring a stockpot filled with water to a boil. Add a generous handful of salt. Cook the pasta for 1 to 2 minutes, until al dente. Reserve 1 cup of the pasta water and drain the pasta. Set aside.

Next, heat a large skillet over medium heat. Add the remaining tablespoon of olive oil, the chard stems, spring onions, and garlic. Sauté for 2 to 3 minutes, until the alliums are fragrant and slightly softened. Add the raisins and olives and cook for another 15 seconds, then add the white wine. Reduce the wine until nearly dry, then add the cooked pasta and the pasta water, the Swiss chard leaves, roasted cauliflower, and Lemon Butter. Stir to combine and cook until the sauce has thickened slightly and coats the noodles.

Remove from the heat and stir in the cheese. Top with the bread crumbs and serve immediately.

132 | DOUGHS & SAVORY PASTRIES

CAULIFLOWER

Cauliflower is a great vegetable to have in a vegetarian's back pocket. Its mild, buttery flavor lends well to many different flavors from around the world, and its texture is creamy and soft when cooked correctly. As a member of the brassica family, cauliflower takes well to roasting, where deep caramelization brings out the sweet, nutty flavors that we all love.

SPRING | SUMMER | FALL | WINTER

Basic Cut Pasta

NF | SF

My recipe for homemade pasta is a bit unusual, but it's my absolute favorite recipe for nearly any type of pasta. It's hearty enough to stand up to filled pastas like ravioli and tortellini, yet delicate enough to be cut into thin spaghetti or linguine. Since the dough is so strong, these thin shapes also don't stick together as much as other pasta doughs, so I find it to be quite a useful recipe that's very beginner friendly. You can repurpose them for the Blueberry Lavender Cake with Cream Cheese Frosting (page 230).

YIELDS 1 POUND (450 G)

2 cups (320 g) semolina flour + more as needed for dusting

3 eggs

3 egg yolks

Salt

NOTE

This dough is too stiff to knead in a stand mixer. It's best to do it by hand.

On a clean flat surface, pour the semolina flour out into a small mound. Use your fingers to create a 4-inch (10-cm) well in the middle of the flour mound. Make sure the edges of the well are supported and don't have any thin spots, or the egg may run.

Once the well is formed, add the eggs and egg yolks to the center of the well. Use a fork to slowly begin incorporating the flour into the egg yolk. Once a shaggy dough has formed, switch to using your hands. Knead the dough in a circular motion, turning the kneaded edges toward the center of the dough ball until the dough is smooth and very stiff. Add more flour as necessary if the dough feels sticky. To test that the dough is ready, press into the top portion of the ball with your pointer finger. If the dough quickly bounces back, it's ready. If it appears to bounce back lazily, continue kneading until it bounces back quickly. The entire process should take about 10 to 15 minutes of steady kneading.

Once the dough is ready, wrap it with plastic wrap and allow it to rest for 30 minutes in the refrigerator. Remove the rested dough from the fridge and allow it to sit for about 10 minutes to get the chill out, then begin rolling.

Cut the dough ball into 4 equal pieces. Dust one of the dough portions with semolina and cover the remaining pieces until ready to use. Use a pasta roller to roll the dough to a thin sheet between 1/8-inch and 1/16-inch (1.6-mm) thick, adding more flour as needed to prevent it from sticking. Then, use the desired pasta cutter to cut the dough into its shape. For long pasta like linguine or fettuccine, cut the rolled pasta sheet into 12- to 15-inch (30- to 38-cm) lengths. Roll up the sheet starting from the short edge, then slice crosswise to create the long pasta shapes. Wrap the pasta into nests and place on a baking sheet sprinkled with semolina.

Continue this process with the other three dough balls until all the pasta is made. At this point, the pasta can be frozen and saved for later, or cooked immediately.

To cook, bring a large pot of water to a boil with a generous amount of salt. Add the pasta and cook for 45 to 60 seconds, until al dente. Serve with the desired sauce.

SUMMER | FALL

Pappardelle with Peperonata & Shell Beans

V | DF | NF | SF

When the summer finally peaks and begins to come to a close, one of my favorite ways to celebrate the season over and over again is to make peperonata and use it in EVERYTHING. Because peperonata boasts bold summer flavors from various chiles, heirloom tomatoes, herbs, and a generous amount of olive oil, it is a great one-ingredient wonder when used to build a pasta sauce. Fortunately, peperonata is a cinch to make once the peppers are prepared, and it can easily last over a week in the refrigerator. Freezing is another great way to keep the flavors of summer around, but unfortunately I have never quite been able to keep peperonata on hand long enough to ever freeze any— it's just too delicious!

SERVES 2

1½ cups (210 g) Peperonata (page 50)

¼ pound fresh shelling beans, such as fresh cannellini or cranberry, removed from pods

Kosher salt

2 sprigs fresh basil

4 tablespoons (60 g) Miso Butter (page 33), prepared with Shared Cultures pepper miso

1 recipe Basic Cut Pasta (page 134), cut into pappardelle, or 1 pound dry pappardelle pasta

2 ounces (60 g) freshly grated Grana Padano or other salty aged cheese + more for garnish

2 cups (40 g) arugula

Aged balsamic vinegar, for serving

Maldon sea salt (optional)

Start by preparing the Peperonata on page 50 up until you remove it from the heat. If you have prepared your peperonata ahead of time, let it stand at room temperature for at least 45 minutes to allow the olive oil to melt.

Meanwhile, prepare the fresh shelling beans. Strip the shelling beans from their pods. The weight of the beans without their pods should weigh about 4 ounces (115 g). Place the beans in a sauce pot and fill the pot with water to cover the beans by about 1 inch (2.5 cm). Bring the beans to a boil over high heat, then reduce the heat to a simmer and cook until the beans are tender, about 20 minutes.

Once the beans are cooked, remove from the heat and add a generous pinch of kosher salt and allow the beans to absorb the salt for another 5 minutes. Then, drain the beans. Set aside.

To prepare the pasta, bring a pot of generously salted water to a boil. Meanwhile, heat a large skillet over medium-low heat. Add the Peperonata and allow it to slowly heat through. Once the Peperonata is sizzling in the pan, add the cooked shelling beans, fresh basil, and the Miso Butter. Stir to combine and allow the vegetables to cook in the Miso Butter for a minute or two. At the same time, add the fresh pasta to the pot of boiling water. Cook the pasta until al dente, 1 to 2 minutes. Spoon about ½ cup (120 ml) pasta water into the skillet with the Peperonata. Then, drain the pasta and add to the skillet.

Use tongs or a pasta spoon to toss the pasta to combine with the vegetable mixture. Add the grated cheese and continue to stir until the pasta creates a luscious, creamy sauce.

To serve, place the pasta in a large bowl and top with the fresh arugula. Drizzle the pasta with aged balsamic and finish with some more grated cheese and some Maldon salt, if desired.

NOTES

If using dry pasta, cook ahead of time and reserve the pasta water separately. This will ensure that the sauce comes together at the right moment.

For a smoother consistency for the pasta sauce, pulse the prepared peperonata in a food processor a couple of times to break the peppers up a little more.

DOUGHS & SAVORY PASTRIES | 135

SPRING

Pierogi with Peas & Feta

NF | SF

My mom's side is Rusyn, a small group of people that has been residing in the Carpathian Mountains for millennia. Prior to immigrating to the United States, the town my family inhabited was part of Austria-Hungary, but now it is part of Southern Poland. Regardless of borders, the Rusyn people have lived on in their own way and have wonderful traditions that are much like that of other Eastern European countries. Lucky for me, one of the traditions that made it to the States is the art of pirohi (pierogi). I first introduced pierogi to the menu at Greens in the springtime, so we filled ours with buckwheat groats, feta cheese, and green garlic. This recipe is similar to that very first version, but instead uses sweet, plump English peas as the base. These are delightfully sweet and savory, and they freeze very well, so you can double or triple this recipe and make a weekend out of it like my family does whenever our freezer stock starts to get low.

SERVES 4 TO 6

FOR THE FILLING

2 tablespoons butter

1½ cups (220 g) freshly shelled or frozen English peas

4 spring onions, sliced thin

⅔ cup (80 g) feta cheese

¼ teaspoon freshly ground white pepper

¾ teaspoon salt

Juice of ½ lemon

Start by making the filling so it can cool. Melt the butter in a medium skillet over medium heat. Add the peas and spring onions and cook them together until the peas have cooked through and the onions have softened. Remove from the heat and lightly mash the peas with a fork or potato masher, allowing some to remain whole for a chunky texture. Fold in the feta cheese, pepper, salt, and lemon juice, and stir to combine. Set aside to cool.

Next, make the dough. Add the flour to a bowl. In a separate bowl, mix together the sour cream and egg yolk, then add in the warm water and salt and mix until combined. Add the wet ingredients to the flour and stir until a shaggy dough forms.

Turn the dough out onto a lightly floured surface and knead together just until smooth. The dough should be on the softer side, but not sticky at all. Wrap the dough in plastic wrap and refrigerate for about 30 minutes.

Once the dough has rested, cut it into 4 equal pieces. Work with one piece at a time, and wrap the remaining pieces with plastic to prevent them from drying.

With the working dough, roll out the dough, flouring as necessary, until it is about $1/16$-inch (1.6-mm) thick. Use a 3-inch (7.5-cm) round cutter or a glass to cut as many circles as possible into the dough. Remove the scraps, ball them up, and cover with plastic wrap for later.

Place a small dish of water near your work surface. Place a dough round across the fingers of your nondominant hand. Use your finger or a pastry brush to brush the rim of your dough lightly with water. Add about 1 tablespoon of filling to the center of the dough.

Then, using your dominant hand, lift the side of dough closer to your palm and stretch it over the filling to neatly touch the other half of the dough to form a semicircle. Use your nondominant hand to help pinch the dough closed.

CONTINUES

DOUGHS & SAVORY PASTRIES | 137

PIEROGI WITH PEAS & FETA

FOR THE DOUGH

1½ cups (180 g) all-purpose flour + more as needed

2 tablespoons sour cream

1 large egg yolk

½ cup (120 ml) warm water

½ teaspoon salt + more for cooking pierogi

Butter or oil, for the baking sheet

4 tablespoons (57 grams) butter

Herb Butter or Lemon Butter (page 33)

Hold the dough from the pinched top with your nondominant hand. Using your other hand, neatly pinch the rest of the dough edges together to create a firm seal. Pinch firmly so that both layers of dough merge to become one layer. The rim of dough should be about ¼ inch wide.

Place the finished pierogi on a tea towel sprinkled with flour and allow the pierogi to dry a bit. Repeat with the remaining dough until all of the pierogi are made. You may reroll the scrap dough, but do not roll out the scraps more than once or the dough will become too tough.

While the pierogi are drying on the tea towels, bring a large pot of water to a boil. Add a generous pinch of salt to the water. Then, working in batches, boil the pierogi for a couple of minutes, until they begin to float in the water. Strain from the pot with a spider or slotted spoon and set on a lightly buttered or oiled baking sheet. Repeat until all of the pierogi have been boiled.

At this point, the pierogi can be frozen. If freezing, lay the pierogi on a baking sheet lined with a double layer of parchment paper. Make sure they are not touching one another, or they will stick together when frozen. Freeze on the baking sheet until completely frozen, then transfer to a freezer bag for longer term storage.

If serving immediately, heat a nonstick skillet over medium heat. Melt the butter, Herb Butter, or Lemon Butter (page 33) to the pan. Fry for a minute, then add the cooked pierogi and fry together until the pierogi have a bit of color on some edges, about 3 minutes per side. Pierogi are best when lightly fried, so as to keep them soft and pillowy, rather than golden and crunchy. Serve immediately with some crème fraîche, if desired.

SPRING | SUMMER | FALL | WINTER

Basic Flaky Pastry

V P | D F P | N F | S F

There's puff pastry, then there's "rough puff," and then there's this recipe. If there's anything more bothersome than making homemade pastry that takes hours upon hours of resting and turning and measuring and ratios and, and, and . . . I'd be surprised. This recipe is a somewhat simplified version of a "rough puff," which yields something in between a puff pastry and a super-flaky piecrust. Here, the butter just needs to be cold from the refrigerator and can stay at room temperature throughout the process. The dough's chilling time is much more manageable than many other recipes, and it only takes a few easy folds to make an incredibly flaky dough that would surprise anyone who tries it. Plus, it's an incredibly versatile pastry that can be used in many ways, from galettes (page 145) to empanadas (page 140).

....

YIELDS 1 BLOCK

1 cup (2 sticks/230 g) cold butter

1⅔ cups (245 g) all-purpose flour + more for dusting

1 teaspoon salt

4 tablespoons (60 ml) ice water

NOTE

This recipe works well with vegan butter, but because vegan butter tends to be a bit softer, make sure the butter is kept in the refrigerator until ready to mix.

Remove the butter from the refrigerator and let sit for about 10 minutes. Cut each stick into 8 equal pieces. Add one of the cut sticks to the bowl of a stand mixer fitted with a paddle attachment. Add the flour and salt and mix on medium speed until the mixture resembles coarse fresh bread crumbs with pea-sized bits of butter throughout. Add the ice water, a little at a time, until the dough just barely starts coming together into some larger chunks, while still quite crumbly toward the bottom.

Turn the dough out onto a clean surface and press the dough together into a rough 8-inch by 5-inch (20- by 12-cm) rectangle. The crumbly dough should stick together easily when pressed. If there are some crumbs that won't stick because they're too dry, add a couple of drops of water to hydrate them and press to form the brick of dough.

Lightly flour both sides of the dough and roll out into 8-inch by 5-inch (20- by 12-cm), flouring as needed to prevent the dough from sticking. Add half of the remaining butter cubes to the middle third of the rolled dough. Break up the butter with your fingers to cover the entire third of dough. Fold the left side of the dough inward on top of the buttered dough, like you are folding a letter. Add the last of the butter to the top of the folded dough, breaking it up and covering the entire surface like the first layer. Fold the right side of the dough inward to cover the second buttered layer to finish the letter fold. You should be left with an 8-inch by 5-inch (20- by 12-cm) rectangle again. Wrap the dough with plastic wrap and refrigerate for about 20 to 30 minutes, or until the dough has firmed up a bit.

Once the dough is firm, remove it from the refrigerator and place it on a lightly floured surface. Dust the top of the dough with flour. Roll the dough out from the short end until it is about ¼-inch thick. The dough should be about 8 inches by 18 inches in size or 8 inches by 4½ inches once folded. Create a book fold by folding the two long ends inward so that they touch at the center of the dough. Fold the dough in half so that you are left with an 8-inch by 5-inch rectangle with 4 layers of dough. Repeat this process twice more, roll out again, and repeat the book fold, dusting with flour as needed to prevent the dough from sticking.

Finally, wrap the dough in plastic wrap and rest the dough in the refrigerator until it is quite firm, at least 30 minutes to 1 hour. The dough can also be frozen at this point. Simply transfer to the refrigerator from the freezer one day before using to thaw.

DOUGHS & SAVORY PASTRIES | 139

SUMMER

Corn & Poblano Empanadas

NF | SF

These little empanadas are a mainstay on our special events menus. I remember the first time I tried them, nearly ten years ago, and I still love them to this day. The mixture of sweet corn, cheese, charred poblanos, and smoky grilled onions is so summery and delicious! My favorite way to enjoy these is by deep-frying them, but baking them will still yield lovely, crisp empanadas. These are excellent for entertaining or can be a fun snack to make on the weekends. Even better, these empanadas freeze very well, so you can make them ahead of time and pull them out as needed.

....

YIELDS 24 MINI EMPANADAS

½ medium red onion, sliced into ½-inch (12 mm) rings

1 small poblano chile

Grapeseed oil, for grilling and frying

½ teaspoon salt + more for roasting

½ cup (80 g) corn kernels, cut fresh from the cob

½ cup shredded cheddar cheese

½ chipotle chile in adobo, minced

2 tablespoons chopped fresh cilantro

Juice of ½ lime + more as needed

1 recipe Basic Flaky Pastry (page 139)

1 large egg, if baking

Milk, for egg wash (optional)

Cilantro-Lime Crema (page 37)

Preheat the grill over high heat. Lightly coat the red onion rings and the poblano with the oil and a pinch of salt. Grill the onions until they are nicely browned and softened. Grill the poblano until the skin is charred on all sides. Remove the onions and pepper from the heat and allow to cool. You may also broil the onions and pepper in the oven if you do not have access to a grill.

Once cool, chop the onions to a fine dice and add to a bowl. Remove the skin, stems, and seeds from the chile. Slice into ¼-inch (3-mm) strips, then turn and cut into a small dice and add to the bowl with the onions. Add the remaining ingredients to the bowl except for the pastry and egg and mix to combine. Adjust the seasonings to taste with salt and lime.

Roll the pastry out to ⅛-inch (3-mm) thickness. Using a 3-inch (7.5-cm) round pastry cutter, cut the pastry into circles and remove the trim. The trim may be balled together and rolled out a second time, but should be handled gently. After the second roll, the scraps should be discarded.

Crack the egg into a small dish and add 2 tablespoons of milk or water. Mix well to combine to make the egg wash. Brush some egg wash on one half of each round of dough. Place 1 teaspoon of filling in the center of each dough round. Fold the egg washed half over to touch the dry half and press to seal, making sure the filling doesn't spill out on the seams. Use a fork to gently press the edges of the empanadas together for a decorative and firmly sealed edge. At this point, the empanadas are ready to be cooked or frozen for later.

To freeze, lay on a baking sheet lined with parchment and spread the empanadas evenly so that they are close together but not touching. Freeze completely, then remove from the baking sheet and place in a freezer bag. If cooking from frozen, do not thaw before baking or frying.

CONTINUES

140 | DOUGHS & SAVORY PASTRIES

CORN & POBLANO EMPANADAS

FRYING INSTRUCTIONS

Heat a medium saucepan with 2 inches (5 cm) of oil over medium heat to 375°F (190°C). To test that the oil is ready, place a small scrap of dough into the oil. It should sizzle immediately but not smoke or brown immediately.

Add a couple of empanadas at a time to the oil, being careful not to crowd the pan. Fry for about 2 to 3 minutes until golden brown on all sides. Remove from the oil and place on a tray lined with paper towels. Sprinkle with a little salt and serve immediately with Cilantro-Lime Crema (page 37).

BAKING INSTRUCTIONS

Preheat the oven to 400°F (200°C). Place the empanadas 1 inch (2.5 cm) apart on a baking sheet. Brush the tops of the empanadas with the remaining egg wash. Bake for about 20 minutes, or until golden brown, turning halfway through. Serve immediately with Cilantro-Lime Crema (page 37).

SPRING | SUMMER | FALL | WINTER

Ethiopian Cabbage & Potato Puffs

VP | DFP | NF | SF

These flaky cabbage and potato puffs are inspired by tikil gomen, an Ethiopian dish consisting of cabbage, potatoes, and carrots. The filling is richly spiced while still feeling light, and it is simply incredible when served in a delightful little hand pie. While serving this dish in a flaky pastry instead of on injera bread is certainly unorthodox, the combination of buttery pastry and deeply spiced cabbage and potatoes is a true winner. We served this dish as part of our New Year's Eve prix fixe menu in 2022, along with sautéed kale and Berbere Spiced Lentils (page 172).

SERVES 4

¼ cup (60 ml) olive oil + more for brushing

½ medium yellow onion, sliced

4 cloves garlic, minced

1 tablespoon minced fresh ginger

½ serrano chile, minced (optional)

½ teaspoon ground turmeric

¼ teaspoon ground cumin

1 black cardamom pod (optional)

Pinch of ground cinnamon

Pinch of freshly ground black pepper

1 carrot, sliced into thin coins

1 large (1 pound/450 g) Yukon gold potato, cut into ½-inch (12-mm) cubes

½ small green or napa cabbage, shredded thinly

1 teaspoon salt

1 recipe Basic Flaky Pastry (page 139) or 1 sheet frozen puff pastry, thawed according to package directions

Start by making the filling. In a large skillet over medium-high heat, add the olive oil and onion. Cook until the onion begins to soften, 5 to 7 minutes, then add the garlic, ginger, and serrano (if using). You may add more or less chile depending on your desired heat level. Fry for another minute, until fragrant, then add all of the spices. Fry the spices for just 10 seconds before adding the carrot and potato. Stir together and add ¼ cup (60 ml) water to the skillet to prevent sticking. Reduce the heat to medium low and cook for about 8 to 10 minutes.

After 8 to 10 minutes, the potatoes should be nearly cooked, but not quite, and the water should have evaporated fully. At this point, add the cabbage and allow to cook for another 15 to 20 minutes over medium low heat, until the cabbage is very soft, and the potatoes are fully cooked through. The cabbage will release moisture as it cooks, but if the mixture is sticking and dry, add a few tablespoons of water as needed. Once cooked, the mixture should not have too much residual liquid. Remove from the heat and allow to cool completely.

While the cabbage mixture is cooling, prepare the pastry. Roll out the Basic Flaky Pastry to a 12- by 16-inch (30- by 41-cm) rectangle. Using a pizza cutter or a sharp knife, halve the pastry on the long end. Then, halve each half again to create 4 long strips. Slice each strip in half to create 8 rectangles that measure 4 inches by 6 inches.

Divide the filling into 4 equal portions and place in the centers of 4 of the rectangles. Brush the edges of these rectangles with water, then top with the remaining dough. Use a fork to firmly crimp the edges of the dough so that they stick together to form the hand pies. Then, use a paring knife to cut 2 equal diagonal vents ½ inch (12 mm) in length in the center of the pastry.

Preheat the oven to 400°F (200°C). Brush the 4 hand pies with oil. Bake for about 20 to 25 minutes, until the pastry is golden brown. Serve immediately, while still warm with Berbere Spiced Lentils (page 172).

DOUGHS & SAVORY PASTRIES | 143

BRUSSELS SPROUTS

I've never understood why Brussels sprouts were the hated vegetable of my youth. I remember characters in TV shows turning their nose up at even the thought of them. These tiny cabbages are one of my favorite vegetables, right up there with broccoli. They're excellent roasted, but I also quite like them shaved thin and cooked with butter, just long enough to set the color and soften slightly.

FALL | WINTER

Brussels Sprouts, Caramelized Shallot & Taleggio Galette

NF | SF

This galette hits all the right notes. It's flaky, buttery, and has just the right amount of funky cheese to make the Brussels sprouts sing. Not to mention the winter herbs and caramelized shallots add a wonderfully festive note to make this dish a gorgeous centerpiece at a holiday table. The shallots take a bit of preparation time, but it's worth the effort. In a pinch, you could also substitute an equal amount of sliced yellow onion.

SERVES 6 TO 8

5 to 6 large (1 pound/450 g) shallots, sliced thin

1 tablespoon butter

1 tablespoon mashed Garlic Confit (page 33)

1½ teaspoons fresh thyme leaves

¾ teaspoon finely chopped fresh or dried rosemary

¼ teaspoon crushed red chile flakes

¼ teaspoon freshly ground black pepper

¼ cup (60 ml) Vegetable Stock (page 39) or water

1 pound (450 g) Brussels sprouts, shaved very thin on a mandoline (about 6 cups shredded)

1 teaspoon salt

Zest and juice of 1 lemon

1 recipe Basic Flaky Pastry (page 139)

6 ounces (170 g) Taleggio cheese, cut into small cubes

Heavy cream or olive oil, for brushing the crust (optional)

Start by cleaning the shallots. Peel the shallots and remove any discolored bits. Slice off the papery ends. Then, slice the shallots thinly, between ⅛- to ¼-inch (3- to 6-mm) thick, stopping just before hitting the tough core.

Add the shallots and butter to a 12-inch (30-cm) stainless-steel skillet. Heat from cold over medium-high heat until the butter is melted, and the shallots start to sizzle. Stir well to coat the shallots with the butter, then allow the shallots to cook untouched for about 2 to 3 minutes, until they begin to brown on the bottom of the pan. Stir the shallots and continue this process until they are golden brown, and the bottom of the pan also has a golden brown fond, about 10 to 15 minutes. Add the Garlic Confit, thyme, rosemary, crushed red chile flakes, and black pepper. Cook for 2 minutes more, until fragrant. Deglaze with the Vegetable Stock, scraping up the browned bits on the bottom of the pan.

Cook until the stock is nearly evaporated, then add the shaved Brussels sprouts and the salt. Cook for just a minute or so, until the sprouts brighten in color and have softened slightly. Remove from the heat and add the lemon zest and juice. Set aside to cool.

Next, roll out the Basic Flaky Pastry. Lightly flour a clean work surface and place the prepared pastry block in the center. Lightly dust the top of the pastry with flour. Gently roll the pastry into a circle about 14 inches (36 cm) in diameter, dusting with flour and flipping the dough as necessary to prevent it from sticking to the work surface.

Transfer the rolled dough to a baking sheet lined with parchment paper. Preheat the oven to 425°F (220°C). Add half of the cheese to the pastry, leaving 2 inches (5 cm) of space from the edges of the pastry. Then, add the prepared filling on top of the cheese. Dot with the remaining cheese, making sure to leave some of the Brussels sprouts exposed so they can brown nicely in the oven. Then, working clockwise and with 2-inch (5-cm) segments at a time, fold the edges of the galette dough up and over the edge of the filling to set the crust. Brush with some cream or oil, if desired.

Bake the galette at 425°F (220°C) for about 10 minutes, then reduce the temperature to 375°F (190°C) and continue baking for 25 to 30 minutes or until the pastry is golden brown and fully cooked on the bottom. Remove from the oven, slice into 6 to 8 equal wedges, and serve warm.

DOUGHS & SAVORY PASTRIES | 145

VEGETABLE SIDES, BEANS & GRAINS

In a vegetarian world, it may be a bit confusing to tell what constitutes a side dish vs. an entrée. To me, a dish isn't considered a full entrée unless it satisfies a range of textures, flavors, and components. Side dishes, on the other hand, are much more focused. I say "focused" and not "simpler" because sides are not to be underestimated! Think of a luscious corn and herb mixture topped over roasted summer peppers (page 162) as a perfect accompaniment to Chipotle & Lime Grilled Tofu (page 187). In my eyes, a side dish is a way to celebrate a vegetable in its simplest form. While some sides are building blocks that support a fully composed entrée, others could turn into entrées themselves with the simple addition of a grain. Others still can be eaten just as a snack, like Asparagus with Cannellini Beans, Creamy Tarragon Vinaigrette & Pickled Mustard Seeds (page 171). Have some fun, mix and match, and enjoy these vegetable preparations however you like.

SPRING | SUMMER | FALL | WINTER

Yuca "Fries" with Beet Slaw

V | GF | DF | NF | SF

If you're looking for a French fry, but better, yuca is the vegetable for you. Yuca lends itself well to dry-heat cooking. It's easier to get a crispy crust with yuca than your average potato, while boasting a sweetness akin to a white-fleshed sweet potato. The one caveat to this spud-superior is a thin, fibrous vein that runs through the center of the root that needs to be dealt with. It's simple enough to remove, though; one should not fear the yuca just because of this one extra step. Enjoy this incredible root in the fall, though it could be found year-round in most Latin markets. You can also enjoy the yuca "fries" plain with salt, as you would potato fries.

SERVES 4

2 medium yuca roots

5 cloves garlic, smashed

1 bay leaf

Salt

2 medium red beets, cooked

½ medium yellow onion, sliced thin

2 tablespoons Champagne vinegar

1 tablespoon white distilled vinegar

Grapeseed oil, for frying

Chimichurri (page 47)

Slice the yuca into 3- to 4-inch (7.5- to 10-cm) segments. Then, stand the yuca wedges up on their cut ends and carefully cut away the tough skin so that the bright white flesh is exposed.

Add the yuca to a saucepan with enough water to cover the vegetable by at least 1 inch (2.5 cm). Add the garlic cloves and bay leaf along with a generous pinch of salt. Bring the water to a boil, then reduce to a simmer and cook until the yuca starts to break apart from the center, depending on the thickness of the yuca, about 25 to 30 minutes or longer. Drain, remove the garlic and bay leaf, and set aside to cool.

While the yuca cools, start on the beet slaw. Slice the beet into thin matchsticks. Combine with the sliced yellow onion, the vinegars, and salt to taste. Let the beet slaw sit for at least 20 minutes so the flavors can meld together.

Once the slaw has been mixed, finish the yuca. Take the slightly cooled yuca segments and cut them down the center lengthwise if they haven't already broken open. Cut out the thin, fibrous vein that runs through the centers. Then, slice the yuca into wedges about ¾ inch (2 cm) in diameter and 3 to 4 inches (7.5 to 10 cm) in length.

Heat a nonstick skillet over medium heat. Add about ¼ inch of grapeseed oil and allow to heat for about 5 minutes, or until a piece of yuca bubbles immediately when touched to the oil. Fry the wedges in batches, being careful not to crowd the pan, about 5 minutes per side until golden brown and crispy.

Once cooked, remove the wedges from the oil and toss in a bowl with enough Chimichurri to coat. You can also salt the yuca "fries," pile them on a platter, and serve the Chimichurri and beet slaw on the side. Top with the beet slaw and serve immediately.

YUCA

Not to be confused with yucca, the ornamental shrub, yuca, also known as cassava, is a starchy root vegetable native to South America. This root is incredibly starchy, even more so than potatoes, making it ideal for frying. It crisps up easily and stays crisp for a long while, and its flesh stays sweet and tender beneath the golden crisp exterior.

SPRING | SUMMER | FALL | WINTER

Gigante Beans With Mint Pesto & Barley

VP | DFP | SF

Gigante beans, as the name suggests, are large white beans that are similar in flavor to cannellini. I love beans of all sizes, but using larger varieties is useful when creating salads and sides that revolve around the bean. This salad is a great transition dish—a dish that we put on the menu in between seasons because it works in both. The dried beans and barley from the winter pair so perfectly with the springy mint pesto for a dish that feels like opening the window the first time after winter passes. Iacopi Farms grows our absolute favorite gigantes, and Rancho Gordo grows a lovely Royal Corona bean that works wonderfully as well.

SERVES 4

1 cup (180 g) gigante beans or Italian butterbeans, cooked (page 22)

½ cup (110 g) barley, cooked (page 25)

¼ cup (60 g) Mint Pesto (page 55)

1 cup (20 g) arugula

2 tablespoons Pickled Red Onions (see Standard Pickles, page 32)

2 tablespoons grated pecorino fiore sardo (optional)

Combine the gigante beans, barley, and Mint Pesto together in a bowl. Toss to evenly coat the beans with the pesto, then add to a serving dish. Add the arugula to the same bowl to lightly dress with the mint pesto that remains on the sides of the bowl.

Add the arugula to the serving dish, then garnish with pickled red onions and pecorino cheese, if using.

SPRING | SUMMER | FALL | WINTER

Grilled Cabbage with Makrut Lime Sambal

V | GF | DF | NF | SF

I have an endless appreciation for cabbage and its versatility. This Southeast Asian take on grilled cabbage turns makrut lime leaves into a sambal (chili paste) and mixes it with coconut milk for an incredible marinade that just gets better with some char from the grill. Makrut lime also grows in California, and I have the pleasure of living nearby one of these marvelous trees, so I often pinch off a few leaves for myself and store them in the freezer for when I need its unique touch of flavor. You can find makrut lime leaves at well-stocked specialty grocery stores or in specialty Asian and Indian markets.

SERVES 4

½ cup (7 g) makrut lime leaves

2 to 5 green Thai chiles

2 cloves garlic, minced

1-inch (2.5-cm) knob ginger, peeled and minced

1 small shallot, minced

¼ lemongrass stalk, finely minced, or 1½ teaspoons lemongrass paste

Zest and juice of 2 limes

1 bunch cilantro, stems removed

2 tablespoons sugar

½ teaspoon seaweed powder, such as kelp or dulse (optional)

One 14.5-ounce (429 ml) can coconut milk

½ cup (120 ml) grapeseed oil

2½ teaspoons salt

1 head (2 pounds) cabbage, such as savoy, green, or arrowhead

Grapeseed oil, for grilling

Start by making the marinade. Combine all the ingredients except for the cabbage in a blender pitcher and blend until very smooth.

Next, cut the cabbage into 8 equal wedges, keeping the core intact so that the cabbage doesn't fall apart during grilling. Place the cabbage in a casserole dish and pour the marinade over the top, turning the wedges over a couple of times so that the marinade completely coats the wedges. Cover with plastic wrap and place in the refrigerator for at least 1 hour or up to 24 hours.

When ready to grill, remove the cabbage from the refrigerator and let it temper for a few minutes. Heat the grill over high heat and run an oiled rag over the grill grates to clean and lubricate them. Take the cabbage wedges out of the marinade and allow them to drain for a moment so the grill does not flare up. Place each wedge of cabbage on the grill and cook for 3 to 5 minutes per side, until the cabbage is deeply charred and softened. Remove the cabbage from the heat and brush some of the excess marinade over the top. Serve immediately.

SPRING

Sautéed Pea Tendrils with Calabrian Chile

V | GF | DF | NF | SF

Pea tendrils are one of spring's many delights. Beautiful, crispy, and mild, pea tendrils make a lovely substitute for spinach in the spring months. I quite prefer pea tendrils to spinach anyway, as the little shoots stay crisp for a nice textural element, and I find the little curly q's to be utterly adorable. There's an extra sustainability bonus here, too; pea tendrils are the mature leaves of the snap pea plant, a part of the plant that is generally discarded in favor of the vegetable it bears. These are best found at California farmers' markets from March through May, and while you may find these delectable leaves through June, keep in mind that the tender, crunchy stems tend to become fibrous and woody later in the season. This recipe is also delightful with spinach or steamed broccoli.

SERVES 4

1 pound (450 g) pea tendrils, cleaned and chopped into 2-inch (5-cm) segments

¼ cup (60 ml) light olive oil

2 tablespoons capers, drained and chopped

1 teaspoon Calabrian chile paste or ¼ teaspoon crushed red chile flakes

2 tablespoons Garlic Confit (page 33), lightly mashed with the back of a spoon

Salt

Clean the pea tendrils well, dry them, and check their size. If they have stems longer than 3 inches (7.5 cm), cut them down so that they are 3 inches or shorter.

Heat the olive oil in a large skillet over medium high heat. Add the capers, chile paste, and garlic confit to the pan and cook for 15 seconds, until fragrant. Then, add the prepared pea tendrils. Be careful—the greens may sputter and pop. Allow the pea tendrils to wilt ever so slightly, tossing them frequently to prevent them from overcooking. Once lightly wilted, remove from the pan and serve immediately.

VEGETABLE SIDES, BEANS & GRAINS | 153

Green Gulch Farm

Tucked away in a little valley in the Marin Headlands is our very own farm, Green Gulch. Also known as the Green Dragon Temple (Soryu-ji), Green Gulch Farm Zen Center is a thriving space focused first and foremost around Zen meditation and practice. The farm itself is part of a Zen work program that brings Zen practices like functional speech and mindfulness into the workplace. Through this work, the vegetables are treated with immaculate care and respect, fostering a sense of gratitude for the food that sustains us. To this day, Green Gulch remains a symbol of our commitment to the freshest vegetables, the best farming practices, and our overall celebration and appreciation for the bounty that grows in our very backyards.

The concept that food comes from real people and real farmers is somewhat lost in today's busy society. My first real experience in understanding this was in a little lettuce patch at the farm. Emila Heller, along with Sara Tashker, welcomed some of the Greens team to Green Gulch one dewy Monday morning to teach us how to help with a particularly bountiful harvest. We were excited and chatty, unsure of what to expect, and were quickly hushed by the seasoned farmers. "We practice functional speech here on the farm. We only speak when absolutely necessary. Your attention needs to be on the practice," Emila told us. She is, without a doubt, refreshingly no-nonsense, and incredibly committed to her practice.

With grace and calm, Emila knelt down in one of the beds of lettuce. She unsheathed an odd-looking knife on her hip and gently touched it to the soil. "Cut just below the soil line. We want to keep the roots intact and allow the heads to regrow. Each cut must be precise." She passed the knife to me and handed a backup knife to another line cook. We cut a few heads as instructed, when, with a terse nod of apparent approval, Emila turned away to check the other fields.

In the next hour or so of silence, I couldn't help but feel an immense wave of gratitude for that moment of time. The mist had started to burn off and the sun was kissing our skin as we touched the still cold, crisp lettuce. The birds were chirping, and we heard every moment of our work, the crunch of the knife against the fresh vegetables and the squishing of the earth beneath our feet as we moved along the rows. The air was crisp and clean, and you could just smell the nutrients wafting out of the healthy earth. Despite being peaceful, intentional work, it worked our bodies hard. We had only so much time to gather the lettuces before moving onto Swiss chard, hakurei turnips, and beets.

By the end of the day, we were wiped out. We gathered together in the vegetable washing station and quietly cleaned and bunched beets, working in a conveyor belt fashion. Sara offered us each a turnip for a sweet and earthy reprieve from our long day. She told us that some of the beets were headed to Mill Valley Market the following morning, and the rest would be saved for the farmers' market the day after that. I never really thought about how much work went into preparing this $6 bunch of beets, and from that day forward, I have never taken a farmer's work for granted.

You might be surprised to learn that our menu planning process starts not with a dish, but with a vegetable. We are delighted to see what our farmers have in store for us each season. The menu is a love letter to the vegetables and people that make the dish possible, because we recognize that even a simple head of lettuce or a bunch of beets took time, care, and intention.

SUMMER

Grilled Zucchini with Mint Pesto

VP | GF | DFP | SF

Of all the "all-star" ingredients that appear in the summer months, zucchini is one of the most versatile. Its subtle flavor and unique texture grants zucchini a wide array of cooking methods and flavor profiles. One of my favorite ways to prepare zucchini is to grill it over high heat to char it, while cooking it just enough so that it is tender but not mushy, charred but not burnt. The mint pesto adds a cool, refreshing flavor that is at once surprising and familiar.

SERVES 4 TO 6

2 tablespoons grapeseed oil + more for greasing the grates

6 medium zucchini

Salt

Mint Pesto (page 55)

2 ounces (60 g) feta cheese (optional)

2 tablespoons toasted pine nuts (page 25)

Preheat the grill over high heat. Make sure to clean the grates well with an oiled rag to ensure proper charring.

Halve the zucchini lengthwise. Using a paring knife, score the zucchini diagonally ½-inch (12-mm) apart in one direction, then again in the other direction, making a diamond shape. Be careful not to score too deep—about a quarter to halfway through is plenty. Drizzle with the oil and season with salt.

Grill the zucchini, scored-side down, until the squash has nice char marks and is starting to soften. Flip to grill the other side. The zucchini should be lightly pliable, but not breaking apart, when fully cooked, and there may be some moisture showing on the scored side.

Remove from the grill and brush with the pesto. Crumble the feta cheese over the top and sprinkle with toasted pine. Serve immediately.

VEGETABLE SIDES, BEANS & GRAINS

SPRING | SUMMER | FALL | WINTER

Grilled Sweet Potatoes
with Tahini Garlic Cashew Cream

V | GF | DF | SF

There are only a few vegetables that I truly enjoy all year long, and one of them is sweet potatoes. This delicious root vegetable is great with almost anything because it lends sweetness while balancing more savory flavors. In the summer, I enjoy grilling my sweet potatoes and serving with a sauce. In this case, sweet potatoes with thick, rich Tahini Cashew Cream are excellent alongside Tofu & Vegetable Brochettes with Chimichurri (page 203).

SERVES 4 TO 6

2 medium sweet potatoes

2 tablespoons olive oil

Juice of ½ lemon

¾ teaspoon salt

1 recipe Cashew Cream (page 36)

2 tablespoons chopped fresh cilantro or parsley

Preheat the grill over high heat. Clean the sweet potatoes well and slice on a slight bias into ¾-inch (2-cm) ovals. Toss with the olive oil, lemon juice, and salt until the sweet potatoes are evenly coated.

Grill the sweet potatoes for about 5 to 6 minutes per side, until they are well charred and cooked through. If they are charred before they are cooked through, turn off the heat on one side of the grill and move the sweet potatoes to the side that is turned off and allow them to continue cooking with the grill lid closed until tender.

Once cooked, transfer the sweet potatoes to a platter, drizzle with the Tahini Garlic Cashew Cream, and garnish with the chopped herbs.

SUMMER

Stewed Romano Beans in Arrabiata

VP | GF | DFP | NF | SF

Say what you will about long cooked, discolored green vegetables, but to me, there is nothing better. While there is a time and place for a snappy summer bean, I find that the more gratifying meal takes place after a long, lazy Sunday afternoon. I just love the soft, tantalizing mouthfeel of these braised beans, and the tomato-soaked flavor that comes along with them. Arrabiata is the spicier brethren to marinara, which is simply the perfect sauce for the summer. I find that it becomes even more pleasurable when made with cherry tomatoes because the sweetness of those summer beauties expertly balances the spiciness of the chiles.

SERVES 4 TO 6

2 pounds (900 g) romano beans

1 recipe Roasted Cherry Tomato Sauce Arrabiata Variation (page 59), purée

2 sprigs Italian basil

¼ teaspoon freshly ground black pepper

Salt

2 ounces (60 g) pecorino cheese, grated (optional)

Clean the romano beans by snapping them at their tips and peeling any strings away down the length of the beans. Very long romano beans are visually appealing when served at the table in larger serving dishes but will require a knife to cut. If desired, cut the beans on a pretty bias to a shorter length for easier serving.

Once the beans have been cleaned, add them to a saucepan and top with the tomato sauce. Take one of the sprigs of basil and remove the leaves from the stem. Roughly tear the basil leaves and add them to the pot along with the pepper and a pinch of salt to taste. Turn the heat on to medium and bring the sauce to a boil, then reduce the heat to a slow simmer and allow the beans to cook directly in the sauce for about 45 minutes, or until they are very tender and have turned a to a deep green color. If the sauce begins to thicken too much, add a bit of water to reach the desired consistency.

Once cooked, adjust the seasonings to taste along with freshly grated pecorino cheese (if using). Finely chop the remaining basil leaves and sprinkle on top of the cheese. Serve immediately.

SUMMER

Grilled Peppers with Herby Corn Salsa

VP | GF | DFP | NF | SF

The best months to make this dish are in August and September, when peppers have had time to become sweet and juicy, and corn is still very much at its peak. The seasons, of course, vary year-to-year, so it's possible to make this dish sooner, but there's something about the late summer that makes peppers and corn all the more desirable. This is a dish that makes summer feel almost eternal, even if the days are already starting to get shorter, and the nights crisper.

SERVES 4

2 pounds (900 g) sweet summer peppers, such as Jimmy Nardello, Gypsy, lipstick pimentos, and bell peppers

2 ears fresh corn, husks removed

½ medium red onion, sliced into ¼-inch rings

Grapeseed oil, for coating

Salt

2 scallions, sliced thin

½ bunch cilantro, chopped + cilantro sprigs, for garnish (optional)

2 sprigs oregano, stems removed and chopped

1 sprig sage, stems removed and chopped

½ teaspoon coriander seeds

¼ teaspoon cumin seeds

Pinch of red chile flakes

2 tablespoons Aioli (page 35), Vegan Aioli (page 36), or prepared mayonnaise

¼ cup (30 g) crumbled feta cheese (optional)

Juice of ½ lime

Olive oil, for garnish (optional)

Maldon salt, for garnish (optional)

Preheat the grill over high heat. Lightly coat the peppers, corn, and onion rings with the oil. Season the vegetables with salt and grill, turning as necessary, until charred and cooked through. The peppers should cook the fastest, about 3 to 4 minutes per side, followed by the corn and onions, about 10 to 15 minutes. Remove the vegetables from the grill as they finish cooking. Allow to cool slightly.

While the vegetables are cooling, prepare the corn salsa. Place the scallions, cilantro, oregano, and sage in a bowl.

Add the coriander and cumin seeds to a small sauté pan. Heat over medium-low heat until fragrant, about 3 to 4 minutes. Transfer to a mortar and pestle and crush the seeds so that they are coarsely ground. Add to the bowl with the herbs.

Next, add the chile flakes, Aioli, feta (if using), and lime juice to the bowl and mix until combined. Cut the grilled corn kernels off of the cobs and add to the bowl. Finely chop the grilled onion rings and add to the bowl. Mix until combined and season with salt to taste.

To serve, arrange the grilled peppers on a serving platter or divide them among individual plates, varying the colors and sizes for an ideal presentation. Spoon the corn salsa over the peppers in dollops or next to the peppers, leaving some space in between so the peppers show underneath. If desired, garnish with a drizzle of olive oil, a sprinkle of Maldon salt, and/or cilantro sprigs. This dish is best served at room temperature, but the chiles can also be reheated in a 400°F (200°C) oven until warm.

FALL | WINTER

Masala Roasted Winter Squash

VP | GF | DFP | NF | SF

While it's tough to say goodbye to summer veggies, I'm always excited for the emergence of pumpkin season. There are countless varieties of pumpkin, and all of them are wonderful for different things. For roasting, I personally love kabocha, which has a lovely flavor and a texture closer to that of a sweet potato than the wet, stringier butternut. Other thin-skinned varieties are wonderful here as well, like carnival, red kuri, or delicata. These pumpkins have edible skins, which saves you a step when preparing; but if the skin isn't to your liking, peeling them would be fine, too. To make this vegan, substitute vegan yogurt or use Cilantro-Lime Crema (page 37).

SERVES 4

1 kabocha squash or other thin-skinned winter squash (about 2 pounds)

3 tablespoons brown sugar

1½ teaspoons salt

1½ teaspoons garam masala

1½ teaspoons curry powder, such as vadouvan

3 tablespoons olive oil

1 cup plain yogurt

2 limes

¼ cup (30 g) toasted pumpkin seeds (see page 25)

2 tablespoons chopped fresh cilantro

Preheat the oven to 375°F (190°C). Start by preparing the squash. Cut the hard stem off by slicing across, just underneath where it ends. Halve the squash lengthwise to expose the seeds. Use a spoon to scrape out the stringy flesh and seeds; discard. Slice the squash lengthwise into 1-inch (2.5-cm) strips by laying the squash cavity-side up and rocking it to one side so that it lays relatively flat. Then, make your slices across the squash, adjusting your grip as you go so that you cut through the squash evenly. Slice the squash wedges into 1-inch (2.5-cm) chunks.

In a medium bowl, add the brown sugar, salt, garam masala, curry powder, and olive oil. Add the squash to the bowl and toss to coat. Pour the squash into a casserole dish, being sure to include all of the spices by scraping down the sides of the bowl.

Bake the squash for 35 to 40 minutes, flipping the squash cubes halfway through to allow for even cooking until the squash is fork-tender. While the squash is cooking, prepare the yogurt and pumpkin seeds. Add the yogurt to a small bowl. Zest the limes and add to the yogurt. Add the juice of 1½ limes and season with salt. Set aside. Coarsely chop the roasted pumpkin seeds. Add the cilantro and juice of ½ lime. Taste the yogurt and pumpkin seed salsa, and season with salt as needed.

When the squash is cooked, remove it from the oven and place on a serving dish. Top with the pumpkin seed mixture. Serve with the lime yogurt on the side for dipping.

VEGETABLE SIDES, BEANS & GRAINS | 165

SUMMER | FALL

Blistered Shishito Peppers

V | GF | DF | NF | SF

Shishito peppers, nicknamed "Russian roulette" peppers, are a wonderfully thin-skinned, and usually mild pepper, though like the name suggests, one out of every dozen or so will be fiery hot. Despite this spicy challenge, shishitos are one of the best peppers to snack on because of their thin skin. They blister beautifully and are juicy, a little sweet, and vegetal. I love serving these with a dipping sauce, one as simple as plain Aioli (page 35) or something fun, like Turmeric Ginger Cashew Cream (page 36), if you're looking for something a touch lighter and faster, a squeeze of fresh lemon juice and a pinch of flaky sea salt would do the trick, too.

SERVES 4

8 ounces (225 g) shishito peppers

2 tablespoons grapeseed oil

Maldon sea salt

1 recipe Aioli or a variation (page 35)

Lemon wedges, for serving

Prepare the shishitos by removing any leaves and debris from the peppers. Clean and dry them well.

Heat a large skillet over high heat. Add the oil and heat until it is nearly smoking, then add the whole peppers. Allow the peppers to cook for 2 to 3 minutes untouched, then toss. Continue this process until the peppers are well blistered and have blackened spots on the skin, about 4 to 6 minutes more.

Remove the peppers from the heat and sprinkle with sea salt to tastes. Serve with Aioli or a squeeze of fresh lemon.

SPRING | SUMMER | FALL | WINTER

Mayocoba Beans with Urfa Biber

V | GF | DF | NF | SF

There's nothing like a big, warm pot of beans to warm you from the inside out. This recipe utilizes urfa biber, an incredibly complex, dark purple Turkish chile powder. Serve with grilled or toasted crusty bread.

SERVES 4

2 cups (350 g) mayocoba beans, soaked overnight, or another bean, such as pinto, vaquero, or cannellini

⅓ cup (80 ml) olive oil

1 medium yellow onion, diced

2 bay leaves

2 tablespoons tomato paste

2 teaspoons garlic, minced

2 teaspoons urfa biber chile + more for garnish (optional)

1 teaspoon cumin, ground

1 teaspoon coriander, ground

¼ teaspoon freshly ground black pepper

1½ teaspoons salt

Vegetable Stock (page 39), as needed

2 tablespoons fresh lemon juice

Cook the beans according to instructions on page 22.

In a second saucepan, heat the olive oil over medium-low heat and add the onion and bay leaves. Cook until the onion is very tender and golden brown at the tips, about 15 minutes. Add the tomato paste, garlic, urfa biber, cumin, coriander, and black pepper and cook for another 2 to 3 minutes until the spices have toasted and the tomato paste has deepened in color.

Add the cooked beans and their cooking liquid to the saucepan with the onions and stir to combine. Add the salt and simmer the beans for 15 to 20 minutes to fully infuse the flavors together. If the beans start to look dry, add some stock or water to the pot to keep the beans saucy. The beans should have a chili-like consistency—not too dry nor too watery.

Just before serving, stir in the lemon juice. Divide the beans among serving bowls. Garnish with more urfa biber, if desired.

VEGETABLE SIDES, BEANS & GRAINS | 167

FALL | WINTER

Steamed Brussels Sprouts with "Cali" Kosho

V | GF | DF | NF | SF

While brassicas, the family of vegetables that encompasses Brussels sprouts, love being roasted, they're also delightful when steamed. The flesh softens nicely and becomes sweet, making it the perfect vessel for sharper flavors like citrus and spice. The sauce that accompanies these steamed sprouts is based off of yuzu kosho, a Japanese fermented condiment that combines the zest of the yuzu citrus and hot chile peppers with salt to create a bright and spicy paste. Our Cali kosho is not only delicious, but it allows us to save these peels from the compost bin. This is a great dish to make if you have extra peels from the Avocado & Citrus Salad with Chimichurri (page 98). Or you can save your peels over time in a freezer bag until ready to use.

....

SERVES 4

FOR THE CALI KOSHO
(MAKES ONE CUP)

1½ cups (100 g) citrus peels from oranges, lemons, limes, or grapefruits

⅓ cup (50 g) red Fresno chiles, stems and seeds removed

1 tablespoon salt

⅓ cup (80 ml) water

FOR THE BRUSSELS SPROUTS

1½ pounds (680 g) Brussels sprouts

3 tablespoons Cali Kosho or store-bought yuzu kosho

⅓ cup (80 ml) rice vinegar

2 tablespoons agave nectar

Salt

To make the Cali Kosho, add the citrus peels, Fresno chiles, salt, and water to a blender pitcher. Blend into a thick, fine paste, adding more water as needed to blend. Store in an airtight container in the refrigerator for at least 3 days (ideally 1 week) before using. Yuzu kosho can last for several months when refrigerated in an airtight container.

To prepare the Brussels sprouts, set up a pot with a steamer basket and a lid. Fill the pot with 1 inch (2.5 cm) of water and heat over medium-high heat until the steam is visible. Trim the ends of the Brussels sprouts and halve each one lengthwise. Add the Brussels sprouts to the steamer basket and steam until cooked through, about 7 minutes.

While the sprouts are steaming, prepare the Cali Kosho glaze. Combine the Cali Kosho, rice vinegar, agave, and salt together in a medium saucepan off of the heat. When the Brussels sprouts are cooked through, remove them from the steamer basket and place in the pot with the glaze. Heat the saucepan over high heat until the glaze thickens and sticks to the Brussels sprouts. Adjust the seasoning to taste, remembering that the kosho is quite salty. Serve immediately.

168 | VEGETABLE SIDES, BEANS & GRAINS

ASPARAGUS

The Sacramento River Delta is where
Bay Area asparagus is king. Here, asparagus
can grow to be over an inch thick in peak season,
and it blesses the Bay usually from mid-March to late May.
It's one of the harbingers of spring. Its grassy, vegetal flavor pairs
wonderfully with butter, cream, lemon, and herbs like dill and basil.

SPRING

Asparagus with Cannellini Beans, Creamy Tarragon Vinaigrette & Pickled Mustard Seeds

VP | GF | DFP | NF | SF

After many long months of limited varieties of fruits and veggies, chefs everywhere rejoice when asparagus finally graces their order lists. It is arguably the first harbinger of spring, aside from maybe green garlic, which can pop up as early as December in California. Asparagus is quite versatile; it can be consumed raw, roasted, grilled, pickled, and blanched. One of my favorite preparations of asparagus is lightly pan-steaming them in their own juices. To make this a meal, serve with Creamy Garlic & Herb Polenta (page 173).

SERVES 4

1 bunch asparagus

½ cup (4 ounces/118 ml) water

½ teaspoon salt + more as needed

2 tablespoons chopped fresh tarragon

1 tablespoon Dijon mustard

1½ teaspoons whole-grain mustard

1 tablespoon Champagne vinegar or white wine vinegar

3 tablespoons extra-virgin olive oil

2 tablespoons sour cream or ⅓ cup Vegan Aioli (page 36)

¼ cup (60 g) Aioli (page 35) or prepared mayonnaise

1½ cups (270 g) cooked cannellini beans, gigante beans, or corona beans (see note, page 22)

Pickled Mustard Seeds (page 29)

Trim the bottom 2 to 3 inches (5 to 7.5 cm) of the asparagus and place the trimmed bottoms in a blender pitcher. Add the water and a pinch of salt and blend on high until completely smooth. Strain the liquid through a fine-mesh sieve into another container. Set aside.

Next, make the vinaigrette by combining the tarragon, mustards, vinegar, olive oil, sour cream, Aioli, and salt together in a bowl. Stir to combine and adjust the salt to taste.

When you're ready to cook the asparagus, heat a large skillet over high heat. Allow the skillet to preheat for at least 5 minutes, until very hot. Add the asparagus stalks and then quickly add the reserved asparagus juice to create steam. Cook the asparagus until it is just tender, or until the asparagus liquid has nearly evaporated, about 4 minutes.

Remove the asparagus from the heat and place on a serving platter. Top with the cannellini beans, then drizzle generously with the vinaigrette and Pickled Mustard Seeds around the plate. You can also toss the beans with the vinaigrette and mustard seeds and spoon everything over the asparagus. Serve immediately.

NOTE

To make vegan, substitute sour cream or prepared mayonnaise for more Vegan Aioli (page 36).

VEGETABLE SIDES, BEANS & GRAINS | 171

SPRING | SUMMER | FALL | WINTER

Berbere Spiced Lentils

V | GF | DF | NF | SF

Also known as misir wat, these Ethiopian spiced red lentils are easy to make and pack in a ton of flavor in a simple-looking package. We made misir wat when Adiam Tsegaye joined us for a collaboration dinner in 2022. The flavor in this dish comes from berbere, a complex spice blend consisting of various chiles, warm spices like allspice and cinnamon, and punchy, earthy spices like cumin and cardamom. While we were lucky enough to use Adiam's mother's homemade berbere, any store-bought kind will do. Pair these lentils with the Ethiopian Cabbage & Potato Puffs (page 143) for a delightful main course.

SERVES 4

½ cup (120 ml) grapeseed oil

1 yellow onion, diced

4 cloves garlic, minced

1 tablespoon minced fresh ginger

2 to 3 tablespoons berbere, depending on your desired heat

3 Roma tomatoes, diced

1 cup (200 g) red lentils, washed and sorted (see note, page 22)

3 cups (720 ml) Vegetable Stock (page 39) or water

Heat the oil in a medium saucepan over medium-high heat. Add the onion and cook for 5 to 7 minutes, until it begins to turn translucent. Add the garlic, ginger, and berbere and cook, stirring constantly, until the berbere is toasted and starting to stick to the bottom of the pan, 2 to 3 minutes longer. Add the Roma tomatoes and stir vigorously to deglaze the stuck bits on the bottom of the pan. Reduce the heat to medium and cook until the tomatoes have thickened and turned into a somewhat thick paste.

Add the lentils and the Vegetable Stock and bring back to a boil. Reduce the heat to a simmer and allow the lentils to cook, stirring occasionally, until they are plump and fully cooked. Adjust the seasoning to taste and serve.

VEGETABLE SIDES, BEANS & GRAINS

SPRING | SUMMER | FALL | WINTER

Creamy Garlic & Herb Polenta

V | GF | NF | SF

This polenta makes an outstanding accompaniment to savory entrées, like Wild Mushrooms "Au Poivre" (page 181), and can elevate simple side dishes to full meals, like with the Stewed Romano Beans in Arrabiatta (page 161). This polenta is meant to be served soft, but you can also cut the water by 1 cup (8 ounces/237 ml) and let it firm up on a baking sheet overnight for grilling or pan searing.

....

SERVES 4

5 cups (40 fluid ounces/1.18 liters) water

1 cup (160 g) polenta

2 tablespoons Garlic Confit (page 33), mashed to a paste

4 tablespoons Herb Butter (page 33) or olive oil

½ cup (120 ml) heavy cream or Cashew Cream (page 36)

2 teaspoons salt

¼ cup (30 g) grated Asiago cheese (optional)

2 tablespoons grated Grana Padano cheese (optional)

Heat the water in a medium saucepan over high heat until boiling. Slowly add the polenta in a steady stream while whisking constantly until it is all combined. Lower the heat to medium-low and allow to cook, stirring constantly, until the polenta fully combines with the water and starts to become thick. Add the Garlic Confit paste and allow the polenta to slowly bubble for about 30 minutes, stirring occasionally to prevent it from sticking to the bottom of the pot.

Once the polenta has cooked, add the Herb Butter, heavy cream, and salt. Cook for another 5 minutes to allow the flavors to infuse. After 5 minutes, remove the polenta from the heat and whisk in the cheeses, if using. Serve immediately.

NOTE

For a vegan version, use olive oil instead of the butter and use cashew cream instead of heavy cream.

SPRING | SUMMER | FALL | WINTER

Roasted Potatoes with Dill & Garlic

VP | GF | DFP | NF | SF

I can hardly wait until the new, freshly dug potatoes end up on the Green Gulch order list. When they do arrive, I buy them all, no matter what. We end up buried in potatoes for a couple of weeks, but who can resist? These potatoes haven't been cured (a several-week process that helps to preserve them), so their skins are still paper thin, and their flesh still sweet from the earth. You can also enjoy this recipe with regular cured fingerling potatoes. Add some of the incredible dill from the farm along with some lemon butter and garlic, and you're in for some of the best potatoes around.

SERVES 4 TO 6

2 pounds (900 g) small new potatoes or fingerling potatoes

Salt

3 tablespoons light olive oil

2 tablespoons Lemon Butter (page 33) or more olive oil

2 tablespoons chopped fresh dill

2 tablespoons chopped fresh parsley

1 tablespoon minced garlic

Halve the smaller creamer potatoes and quarter the larger ones. If using fingerlings, halve them lengthwise and then again crosswise if the potatoes seem too long. Place in a pot with enough cold water to cover the potatoes by 1 inch (2.5 cm). Give the water a handful of salt, and then bring to a boil on the stove.

Once boiling, reduce the heat to a simmer and cook the potatoes until they are very tender, but not quite falling apart. Drain the potatoes well and spread on a tray lined with paper towels to cool and finish draining.

Once the potatoes have cooled slightly, their flesh will have firmed up a bit so that they can be handled. Preheat the oven to 425°F (220°C). Toss the potatoes with the light olive oil and spread on a baking sheet, leaving enough space between them so they can become crisp.

Bake the potatoes for about 10 minutes, until the bottoms have started to crisp. Stir the potatoes, lifting them off the baking sheet with a spatula to ensure that you lift the crisped bottoms from the pan. Return the potatoes to the oven and bake for another 10 minutes or until the potatoes are fully cooked "fork tender."

Finally, add the Lemon Butter in small knobs across the pan to evenly distribute it, along with the chopped herbs and garlic. Toss well and return to the oven once more for just a few minutes, until the butter has completely melted and the garlic is fragrant. Adjust the seasoning with salt as needed and serve immediately.

MAIN COURSES

Unlike sides, main courses often have more complexity, textures, and flavors. They're the fully composed meals that incorporate a "star" component, plus "supporting characters" like grains, sauces, and sides. This section boasts some of the most beloved entrées from recent years—recipes that guests often ask me to share, staff favorites, and a couple of recipes that haven't yet made it to the menu but are still incredible enough to share. You'll also notice that I've included a couple of recipes that don't have more than a couple of steps but are best served with other dishes throughout this book, like the Chipotle & Lime Grilled Tofu (page 187). Other dishes are a bit more self-contained, like the ultra-famous Root Vegetable Biryani (page 200), one of my favorite recipes that I have ever developed. Whatever recipe you choose, you'll find delicious vegetables worthy of being the main event.

SPRING

Spring Vegetable Piccata

GF | NF | SF

Romanesco, one of the most mathematically pleasing vegetables— the spiral pattern on romanesco broccoli exhibits the golden ratio—is also one of the most delicious. It has a flavor somewhere between a cauliflower and broccoli, meaning that it will pair well with creamy, luscious sauces. In this case, romanesco, along with other fabulous spring vegetables, are steamed and then smothered in piccata sauce— a sauce consisting of white wine, capers, and just the right amount of butter. Serve this with Roasted Potatoes with Dill and Garlic (page 174) or Creamy Garlic & Herb Polenta (page 173) to make this the perfect spring dinner.

SERVES 4

½ teaspoon salt + more for blanching

1 medium head romanesco

1 cup (160 g) snow peas

1 cup (185 g) pearl onions

1 bunch baby carrots

½ cup (75 g) shelled fresh English peas
(discard the pods or save them for stock)

½ cup (1 stick/115 g) butter

3 cloves garlic, sliced thin

2 shallots, finely minced

2 tablespoons capers, roughly chopped

⅓ cup (80 ml) dry white wine

½ cup (120 ml) Vegetable Stock (page 39)

Juice of 1 lemon

½ bunch parsley, chopped

½ bunch chives, sliced thin

Pinch of freshly ground black pepper

Bring a large saucepan two-thirds full of water and a handful of salt to a boil. While waiting for the water, prepare the vegetables. Cut the romanesco into 4 large wedges and remove any tough stems. Remove the strings from the snow peas by slicing into the tough tops and pulling away from the direction of the cut. Cut off the tops and bottoms of the pearl onions, but do not peel them. Remove the tops of the carrots.

Once the water is boiling, blanch the vegetables one at a time to properly cook them. Cook until the vegetables are just al dente—6 minutes for the romanesco, onions, and carrots, and just 30 seconds for the snow peas and English peas. As they finish cooking, remove the vegetables and place them on a clean plate.

Next prepare the sauce. Heat 2 tablespoons of the butter in a large skillet over medium heat. Add the garlic and shallot and cook for 2 to 3 minutes, until fragrant and starting to soften. Add the capers and cook for another minute, then add the white wine. Reduce the wine by half, then add the stock and the lemon juice. Add the blanched vegetables to the skillet and cook for a couple of minutes to reheat as necessary. Then, remove from the heat and add the herbs, remaining 6 tablespoons (85 g) butter, ½ teaspoon of salt, and a pinch of pepper. Stir the contents of the skillet rapidly to emulsify the butter so that it creates a thick, glossy sauce that coats the vegetables. Serve immediately.

MUSHROOMS

When the weather starts to turn cold and everyone's thoughts turns to cozy scarves, warm lattes, and pumpkins, I start thinking about mushrooms instead. Wild mushrooms are my favorite flavor of cozy in the winter months, pairing with winter favorites like sage, rosemary, and caramelized onions. The best part is that these fabulous fungi will cycle through their seasons through the beginning of spring, so you can enjoy them until spring melts the last frost.

SPRING | FALL | WINTER

Wild Mushrooms "Au Poivre"

VP | GF | DFP | NF | SF

This is the holiday dish of my dreams! The deep, rich, glossy cream sauce and the savory roasted mushrooms are the perfect indulgence for a special day. I like to serve this dish around Easter with buttered peas or asparagus and Roasted Potatoes with Dill & Garlic (page 174). It's a bit of a labor of love, but once you have the sauce prepared, it's a cinch to put together. It's crucial to make the sauce and mushroom sauce from scratch so you have a thick, rich, mushroom-forward flavor that will hold up to the stronger flavors of Dijon mustard and peppercorns. I like to make the mushroom sauce ahead of time in double- or triple-sized batches so I can freeze some for future dinners (even weeknight ones!), and also so that I can split up some of the work.

SERVES 2

1½ teaspoons coarsely cracked five-peppercorn blend

¼ cup (60 ml) dry white wine

1 cup (240 ml) Porcini Jus (page 39)

1 cup (240 ml) heavy cream (or Cashew Cream page 36)

1 tablespoon Dijon mustard

1 sprig tarragon

1 pound (450 g) wild mushrooms, such as maitake, royal trumpet, oyster, black trumpet, etc.

¼ cup (60 ml) light olive oil

Salt

2 tablespoons butter or Miso Butter (page 33)

Start by making the peppercorn sauce. In a small saucepan over medium heat, toast the cracked peppercorns until fragrant, about 30 seconds to 1 minute. Add the white wine. Reduce the wine to nearly dry, then add the Porcini Jus, heavy cream, mustard, and tarragon. Bring the sauce to a simmer, then reduce the heat to low and simmer until the sauce thickens enough to coat the back of a spoon, about 20 minutes.

While the sauce is simmering, prepare the mushrooms. Preheat the oven to 425°F (220°C). Cut the mushrooms into large chunks about 1½ to 2 inches (3.75 to 5 cm) in length. Some mushrooms will cook faster than others, so if you are using a mix of mushrooms, keep them separate from one another. Toss the mushrooms with the olive oil and enough salt to lightly coat the mushrooms. Lay on a baking sheet in a single layer, leaving plenty of space between the mushrooms. Roast the mushrooms until they have cooked through and are browned on the edges, about 25 minutes.

Remove the mushrooms from the oven and add them to the peppercorn sauce. Add the butter and stir until it incorporates to make a rich, glossy sauce. Adjust the salt to taste and serve.

FALL | WINTER

Autumn Vegetable Jambalaya

V | GF | DF | NF | SF

As long as you have Creole Broth (page 40) on hand, this recipe comes together in a cinch. While preparing the stock is admittedly time-consuming, by making it in advance and freezing it in portions, recipes like this jambalaya can be made even on a weeknight. By far, our favorite rice to use for this dish is Carolina Gold from Anson Mills. This rice was once a major cash crop in the United States in the late eighteenth century, but by the end of the Civil War, the variety grew close to extinction. The rice has been revived over the last couple of decades as part of a "cultural revival," and is our preferred variety when making dishes from the South. If you can't find Carolina Gold, a medium grain rice or sturdy long-grain rice such as jasmine would work fine.

SERVES 6 TO 8

2 cups (400 g) Carolina Gold rice or other sturdy medium- to long-grain rice

¼ cup (60 ml) olive oil

1 cup medium diced sweet potato

2 cups cauliflower florets

1 block Hodo tofu (10 ounces/287 g), cut into ½-inch (12-mm) cubes

½ bunch lacinato kale or collard greens

6 cups (1.42 l) Creole Broth (page 40)

1½ cups cooked pinto beans, red kidney beans, or an heirloom bean, such as Rio Zape (270 g) (see bean cookery instructions, page 22)

2 cups water or Vegetable Stock (page 39) + more as needed

1 tablespoon salt

2 scallions, sliced thin

Preheat the oven to 400°F (200°C). Place the rice in a bowl and wash it several times with cold water to remove the starch. The water should turn cloudy with starch for the first couple of times. Continue washing the rice until the water runs clear.

Next, heat the olive oil in a large oven-safe skillet or Dutch oven over medium-high heat. Add the sweet potato, cauliflower, and tofu and cook, stirring occasionally, until the tofu has nicely browned on all sides, about 8 minutes. While the vegetables are cooking, clean the kale by removing the thick stems from the leaves, then tear into 1- to 2-inch (2.5- to 5-cm) pieces. Add to the pan with the tofu and sauté for just a few minutes, until wilted. Add the rinsed rice, Creole broth, beans, and salt and stir to combine. Cover the skillet with aluminum foil and a lid and transfer to the oven. Bake for 1 hour or until the rice and vegetables are completely cooked. This recipe is meant to yield a jambalaya that is on the drier side. If you'd like a saucier dish, add a bit of water or stock as desired. Divide among serving bowls, garnish with scallions, and serve.

FALL | WINTER

Wild Rice–Stuffed Portobellos

V | GF | DF | SF

At Greens, we have always loved wild rice, which is not actually a rice at all, but rather a type of aquatic grass. Since our collaboration dinner with Native American chef Crystal Wahpepah, we've come to love it and appreciate it even more. For this special dinner, she brought us a particular kind of wild rice that is still harvested by the Red Lake Nation by hand in canoes. Stories like this really put our ingredients into perspective; what may seem commonplace to some is sacred to others, and we appreciate the opportunity to understand the significance of each ingredient we use, down to a single grain of wild rice. Here, we use it with other native ingredients, such as cranberries and chestnuts.

SERVES 4

4 large portobello mushroom caps

⅓ cup (79 ml) light olive oil

2 maitake mushrooms

2 tablespoons salt

½ teaspoon freshly ground black pepper

2 medium shallots, minced

1 small carrot, minced

½ rib celery, minced

¼ cup (35 g) chopped chestnuts (see note)

2 tablespoons dried cranberries, chopped

1 sprig sage

1 sprig thyme

2 tablespoons finely chopped fresh parsley

2 cups (320 g) cooked wild rice (see note, page 25)

¼ cup (60 ml) water or Vegetable Stock (page 39)

Porcini Jus (page 39) (optional)

Preheat the oven to 400°F (200°C). On a baking sheet, break the maitake apart into small pieces and spread them out evenly. Drizzle the mushrooms with 2 tablespoons of oil, and season with 1½ teaspoons of salt and ¼ teaspoon of black pepper. Roast in the oven until the mushrooms are lightly cooked and starting to brown at the tips, about 15 to 20 minutes.

While the mushrooms roast, make the wild rice filling. Heat a medium skillet over medium-high heat with the remaining olive oil (3 tablespoons plus 1 teaspoon/50ml). Add the shallots and carrot and cook for 2 to 3 minutes, until the carrot begins to soften. Add the celery and cook for another 2 minutes. Remove from the heat and then transfer the cooked vegetables to a medium bowl. Add the chestnuts and cranberries and mix to combine.

Remove the sage and thyme leaves from the stems and finely chop. Add to the bowl along with the parsley and cooked wild rice. Once the maitakes are cooked, add them to the bowl with the wild rice and mix until combined.

Evenly divide the wild rice filling among the portobello caps, doming the filling and packing it tightly so that it doesn't fall apart. Place the stuffed portobellos in a casserole dish. Add the water or stock to the bottom of the dish and cover with foil.

Bake the mushrooms for about 30 minutes with the foil, then remove the foil and bake uncovered for another 10 to 15 minutes, until the filling forms a light crust on the top. Serve the baked portobellos with Porcini Jus (page 39), if desired.

NOTE

You can often find peeled and cooked chestnuts in stores around the holidays, or you can purchase them online.

MAIN COURSES | 183

Sustainable Greens

Greens is known for being a sustainable restaurant, probably even one of the first. Even today, sustainability in our ingredients is one of the most important considerations for all of the decisions that we make. Sustainability has become a buzzword in recent years, especially with talks of global warming, rising sea levels, and a whole slew of other issues that are coming about because of humanity's poor habits. And so, because of this, sustainability has become popularized as something we all know that we should support. However, the message behind the practice is often lost in our modern world, especially when supporting that cause often comes with a higher price tag or more hoops to jump through. To grow a more sustainable world, it's important that we remember what's at the root of living sustainably, and that's building relationships and making a commitment to maintain them.

At the beginning of our food cycle is perhaps not a farmer or a seed, but a colony of microorganisms in the dirt. We now know that monocropped agriculture is ruining our land by stripping it of its necessary nutrients, lessening diversity, and causing other unforeseen problems like erosion and less nutrient-dense food. By contrast, a farmer that practices crop rotation and natural fertilization from animals has healthier, more diverse soil, and therefore, healthier plants. In this regard, the first sustainable relationship we harbor, quite literally, is between people and the earth itself. From there, it's up to us to communicate with our farmers and support their efforts to maintain the land in a healthy way. At Greens, we work with a small army of farmers who work hard to grow the diversity of our crops on a diverse area of land. In turn, we create delicious, healthy food for consumers who want to eat the freshest vegetarian cuisine. It's a tasty game of pass the baton that ultimately helps the world.

Of course, these sustainably minded relationships transcend the kitchen, and must be maintained long term. Our dining room is an eye-catching testament to what that maintenance looks like. When the founders of Greens toured Building 308 at Fort Mason Center back in the '70s, it was a monstrous, 4,000-square-foot, oil-stained warehouse with 26-foot ceilings and a lot of empty space. But the historic building had good bones, and the sprawling windows with incredible bay views were worth investing in. The San Francisco Zen Center decided that it would be the perfect location to extend Zen practice into the workplace, and so construction began. Zen Center carpenters, led by Paul Discoe, designed and built out the interior from twelve different kinds of reclaimed wood. The tables were made using Japanese joinery techniques, and all of these tables are still in use today. Our bar and original wood structures are all still intact as well. Our redwood masterpiece *Greens*, created by JB Blunk in 1979, still stands proudly and serves as a coveted seating area. Some folks enter our dining room and still see a glimpse into the past, and we take that as a compliment. We sand and refinish the wood in the dining room ourselves, breathing new life into the old wood, hoping to preserve the simplicity and beauty of our dining room for as long as possible.

Our commitments to sustainability are ever growing. We are committed to our history and our future by maintaining what already exists and fostering new growth in sustainable ways. Like Annie says, there is always more work to be done and changes to be made, and we plan to do so sustainably for hopefully the next hundred years.

SPRING

Lemongrass Tofu & Asparagus Stir-Fry

V | GF | DF | NF

Lemongrass is a delicious flavor when utilized correctly. In the Greens kitchen, we use a metal pan to crush the stalks to "bruise" them before finely mincing. If you have a culinary mallet, you can give it a good whack with that as well. Anything heavy, really. Once all of the ingredients are prepared, this entire dish can be cooked in less than 20 minutes. What's better than a meal that's flavorful and fast? To save even more time, you can always use prepared lemongrass purée.

SERVES 2 TO 4

1 stalk lemongrass

4 cloves garlic, minced

½ Fresno chile, minced or ½ teaspoon sambal

3 tablespoons sugar

2 tablespoons rice vinegar

2 tablespoons soy sauce or tamari

¼ teaspoon kelp powder, such as Burlap & Barrel

Juice of 1 lime

½ cup (120 ml) water

1 teaspoon cornstarch

3 tablespoons grapeseed oil

1 block tofu, sliced into ¾-inch cubes

½ bunch asparagus, bottom third removed and then sliced into 1-inch (2.5-cm) chunks on a diagonal

2 spring onions, sliced thin

1 carrot, julienned

Salt

Hot steamed rice, for serving

Begin by preparing the sauce. Remove any hard, dried leaves from the lemongrass and cut it into 2- to 3-inch (5- to 7.5-cm) segments. Smash the lemongrass with the side of a knife, a mallet, or the bottom of a pan to crush and bruise the stalk. Then, slice the lemongrass crosswise into thin strips, then chop finely. Add the lemongrass to a food processor with the garlic, chile, sugar, rice vinegar, soy sauce, and kelp powder. Pulse until the mixture creates a homogenous paste. Remove from the food processor and stir in the water and cornstarch.

Next, heat a heavy-bottomed skillet over medium-high heat. Add the oil and heat for a few minutes before adding the cubed tofu. Fry the tofu, waiting several minutes before stirring each time to allow it to crisp nicely on all sides. Once the tofu has browned on all sides, add the asparagus, spring onions, and carrot. Allow to cook for 2 to 3 minutes before adding the prepared lemongrass sauce.

Cook the mixture until the sauce thickens, about 3 to 4 minutes. Adjust the salt to taste, then serve over steamed rice.

SPRING | SUMMER | FALL | WINTER

Chipotle & Lime Grilled Tofu

V | GF | DF | NF

If there was ever a tofu dish that was meant for the Grilled Peppers with Herby Corn Salsa (page 162), it would be this tofu. Add a little steamed jasmine rice to make this a full meal. The creaminess of the corn salsa mixed with the spicy, lime-forward tofu makes for the perfect balance of flavors and textures. We serve this dish only in the summer at Greens because of this magnificent pairing, but you can technically make this tofu anytime. It would be excellent in the fall with some sweet potatoes, too.

....

SERVES 4

2 blocks Hodo tofu (10 ounces/283 g) per block

Salt

⅔ cup (160 ml) grapeseed oil

⅓ cup (80 ml) fresh lime juice

⅓ cup (140 g) chipotle chiles in adobo

2 shallots, chopped

1 clove garlic

¾ teaspoon ground coriander

½ teaspoon ground cumin

⅛ teaspoon freshly ground black pepper

Grapeseed oil, for the grill

Grilled Peppers with Herby Corn Salsa (page 162), for serving

Steamed rice, for serving

Halve the tofu blocks widthwise to make 2 wide tiles from each block.

Next, add the remaining ingredients to a blender pitcher and blend until smooth. You can also add to a container and blend with an immersion blender. Pour the marinade over the cooked tofu and make sure the marinade completely covers all sides of the tofu. Allow to marinate for at least 20 minutes or up to overnight.

When ready to cook, heat the grill over high heat. Brush the grill with an oil-soaked rag to make sure the grates are clean and to prevent the tofu from sticking. Remove the tofu from the marinade and drain off any excess. Place the tofu on the grill and cook for about 5 to 6 minutes per side or until the tofu is nicely charred. Once the tofu is cooked, brush with more of the marinade and serve with Grilled Peppers with Herby Corn Salsa and steamed rice.

MAIN COURSES | 187

SPRING | SUMMER | FALL | WINTER

Shepherd's Pie

VP | GF | DFP | NF | SF

Shepherd's Pie is one of the most popular dishes we make at Greens. In fact, it's so popular that I often reserve this dish for special occasions since it causes such a frenzy that we can hardly keep up with making enough to meet the demand. Plus, it makes it even more special for when we do bring this recipe back out again. While this dish can be made in any season, it's particularly lovely in the spring, when the English peas are fresh, and the carrots are tender and sweet.

....

SERVES 4 TO 6

FOR THE FILLING

1 pound (450 g) mixed mushrooms, such as cremini, maitake, royal trumpet, oyster, etc.

Light olive oil, as needed

Salt

1 cup (185 g) peeled pearl onions

2 tablespoons brown sugar

¼ cup (60 ml) dry red wine

1 large carrot, diced

⅓ cup (50 g) shelled English peas, fresh or frozen

¼ cup (10 g) chopped fresh parsley

1 cup (240 ml) Porcini Jus (page 39)

FOR THE MASHED POTATOES

2 pounds (900 g) russet potatoes

Salt

½ cup (1 stick/113 g) stick butter

½ cup (120 ml) heavy cream
(or Cashew Cream, page 36, for vegan)

4 ounces smoked cheddar cheese
(may substitute an equal amount
of vegan cheese)

Preheat the oven to 425°F (220°C). Prepare the mushrooms by cutting them into 1-inch (2.5-cm) chunks. Then, toss them with olive oil and season lightly with salt and spread in an even layer on a baking sheet. Roast the mushrooms for about 25 minutes, or until the mushrooms are somewhat dry and are brown on the edges. Reduce the oven heat to 400°F (200°C).

Meanwhile, make the sweet-and-sour onions. If the pearl onions are very small, keep them whole. Larger onions can be halved lengthwise. Heat a heavy-bottomed skillet over medium high heat. Add a small drizzle of oil to the pan and add the onions. Let the onions cook, untouched, for at least 2 minutes before shaking the pan and continuing to cook for another several minutes untouched to allow the onions to char slightly. When the onions have slightly softened and are nicely charred, add the brown sugar, red wine, and a pinch of salt. Cook until the pan is dry and the onions are shiny and glazed. Transfer to a large clean bowl.

Next, bring a small pot of water to a boil. Add a handful of salt to the water, then drop in the carrots and cook them until just tender. Remove from the water with a slotted spoon and add to the bowl with the onions. Then, if you are using fresh peas, add them to the boiling water and cook for 1 to 2 minutes before adding to the bowl with the onions and carrots. Frozen peas can be added directly to the bowl without further cooking.

Once the mushrooms are cooked, add them to the bowl with the remaining vegetables. Add the chopped parsley and Porcini Jus and mix until combined. Add the mushroom mixture to an 8-inch square baking dish, or another baking dish with a 2-quart capacity, and set aside.

Next, make the mashed potatoes. Peel the potatoes and cut them into 1-inch (2.5-cm) chunks. Place them in a pot and top with cool water and a handful of salt. Bring to a boil, then reduce to a simmer and cook until the potatoes are fork-tender, 15 to 20 minutes.

Drain the potatoes well and set aside. In the same pot, add the butter, and cream. Cook until the edges of the mixture begin to simmer, then immediately remove from the heat and stir in the cheese, and the cooked potatoes. Mash the potatoes and adjust the seasoning to taste.

Either pipe or spread the potatoes over the top of the mushroom mixture, then bake at 400°F (200°C) uncovered for 45 minutes, or until the potatoes have browned slightly on the edges. Serve immediately.

SPRING | SUMMER | FALL | WINTER

Manicotti with Broccoli & Béchamel

NF | SF

Manicotti is one of the most magical dishes in the world, if you ask me. Similar to cannelloni, manicotti comprises crêpes that are filled and rolled, then topped with a sauce. I have fond memories of my grandmother making a stack of crêpes so high, you could hardly see the woman behind them. She would fill them with a simple mixture of ricotta, Parmesan, and some basil and then top with "gravy," our family's word for tomato sauce. This version of manicotti trades the tomato for a creamy béchamel, and the lemon-garlic broccoli filling makes for a lovely, veggie-forward entrée. If broccoli isn't your vegetable of choice, some sautéed spinach or kale, small cubes of zucchini, and even diced and steamed sunchokes would do the trick.

....

YIELDS 10 MANICOTTI

FOR THE CRÊPES

2 large eggs

1½ (360 ml) cups milk

1 teaspoon salt

1 cup (120 g) all-purpose flour

Cooking spray

Start by making the crêpe batter. Whisk the crêpe ingredients together until smooth, and no lumps remain. This can be done by hand or in a blender.

Heat an 8-inch nonstick skillet over medium-low heat. Spray the pan with cooking spray and pour a heaping ¼ cup of the batter into the center of the pan. Quickly swirl the batter out to the edges in a thin, even layer. If the batter does not spread, your pan may be too hot. Once the batter has set in an even circle, allow to cook for about 30 seconds. Then, using a rubber spatula, loosen the edges and quickly flip the crêpe, cooking for another 10 seconds. Remove from the pan and place on a clean plate. Wipe the pan out with a paper towel and repeat this process until all of the batter is used. You may stack the crêpes on top of one another—they won't stick together.

BROCCOLI

Broccoli is, hands down, my favorite vegetable. I love it roasted, steamed, grilled, and raw and I eat it almost every day. There are plenty of broccoli varieties out there that are good for different applications. Broccolini and broccoli di ciccio tend to be rather delicate and stemmy, which make them perfect for a quick pan sear, perhaps with a drizzle of Garlic Confit (page 33). Piracicaba and other head-forming broccolis are great on the grill or roasted, as their bigger stems won't get stringy or dry when cooked for longer periods of time.

190 | MAIN COURSES

FOR THE FILLING

1 tablespoon butter

2 cups (180 g) fresh or frozen broccoli, chopped

1 clove garlic, minced

2 scallions, sliced thin

¼ teaspoon freshly ground black pepper

¼ teaspoon chile flakes (optional)

1 cup (230 g) ricotta cheese

¼ cup (25 g) grated Parmesan cheese

¼ cup (30 g) shredded low-moisture mozzarella cheese

½ teaspoon salt

1 lemon

FOR THE MORNAY SAUCE

2 tablespoons butter

4 scallions, sliced thin

1 clove garlic, minced

2 tablespoons all-purpose flour

1½ cups (360 ml) milk

¼ cup (25 g) grated Parmesan cheese

Salt

Once the crêpes are cooked, make the filling. Melt the butter in a medium skillet over medium-high heat. Add the chopped broccoli and cook until the florets turn bright green. Add the garlic and cook for another 2 minutes, until fragrant. Turn off the heat and add the scallions, black pepper, and chile flakes. Continue stirring for another few seconds until fragrant, then transfer the broccoli mixture to a bowl. Allow to cool for about 10 minutes before adding the ricotta, Parmesan, mozzarella, salt, and the zest and juice of the lemon. Stir to combine.

Next, make the mornay sauce. Heat the butter over medium heat in a small saucepan. Add the scallions and garlic and cook for 30 seconds, until bubbling. Add the flour and whisk to combine. Add the milk, whisking constantly until combined. Heat the mixture, whisking frequently, until it comes to a boil and thickens. Remove from the heat and stir in the Parmesan cheese. Season with salt to taste.

To assemble the manicotti, preheat the oven to 350°F (180°C). Spoon enough béchamel into the bottom of a 9-inch by 13-inch pan to lightly coat the bottom. Next, place ¼ cup of the broccoli filling onto the center of a crêpe. Roll the crêpe up, pushing tightly against the filling as you roll so that it spreads to fill the entire crêpe. Place the filled crêpe seam-side down in the prepared pan. Repeat the process until the entire pan is filled. Do not leave any space between the manicotti—they should be pressed together snugly. You may even lay some of the manicotti horizontally in the pan to fill any small gaps.

Finally, top the filled manicotti with the remaining béchamel. At this point, the manicotti can be covered and placed in the fridge for a day or two if making ahead. If serving immediately, place the manicotti in the oven and bake for 45 minutes, uncovered, until the béchamel is lightly browned on the top. Serve immediately.

The manicotti can be placed in the oven directly from the refrigerator and baked for the same length of time, or until lightly browned on the top.

SUMMER

Chiles Rellenos

VP | GFP | DFP | NF | SF

When I started as a line cook, one of the first dishes I learned to prepare was our stuffed poblano pepper with goat cheese and quinoa. It saw various versions over the year, corn turning to pumpkin as the season grew colder. We would stuff dozens of these every day and serve them with salsas and Rancho Gordo beans. This recipe is a modernized version of our classic chile, with an option to batter and fry if desired. Be sure to serve with something bright and creamy, like the Cilantro Lime-Crema (page 37).

SERVES 4

FOR THE CHILES

4 large poblano chiles

1 cup (200 g) cooked brown rice (see note, page 25)

1 cup (180 g) cooked black beans or pinto beans (see note, page 22)

1 cup (115 g) grated Oaxaca or low-moisture mozzarella cheese (optional)

½ cup (80 g) corn kernels, cut fresh from the cob

¼ cup (30 g) toasted pepitas (see note, page 25)

¼ small red onion, minced

2 tablespoons chopped fresh cilantro

1 chipotle chile in adobo, minced

1 teaspoon salt

FOR THE BATTER (IF FRYING)

½ cup (60 g) all-purpose flour

1 cup (240 ml) sparkling water + more as needed

Oil, for frying, such as canola oil or other high-heat oil

1 teaspoon Maldon salt

Follow the instructions on page 26 to prepare the poblanos. Once cleaned, slice a slit on one side of the peppers to make a pocket for the filling, making sure to leave about ½ inch (12 mm) of space between the stem and tip so the peppers don't fall apart. Set aside.

Next, make the filling. Combine the remaining chile ingredients together in a bowl and mix until fully combined and sticky. Divide the mixture evenly among the chiles and carefully stuff them. Make sure not to rip the chiles while stuffing. At this point, the chiles can be kept in the refrigerator for up to 2 days.

To bake the chiles, preheat the oven to 400°F (200°C). Put the stuffed chiles in an 8-inch square baking dish and bake for about 35 to 40 minutes, or until the filling is fully heated through.

To fry the chiles, seal the openings of the chiles with toothpicks. Then, make the batter by whisking together all of the batter ingredients. The mixture should be somewhat loose, but still able to stick to the peppers. If it slides off or doesn't stick, it's too thin. If it is thick like pancake batter and sticks in clumps to the chiles, it's too thick. if it's too thin, add more flour; if it's too thick, thin it with more water. The mixture should be somewhere in between these textures, and it may thicken as it sits, so be sure to test the batter just before frying.

When ready to fry, heat 2 inches (5 cm) of oil in a heavy-bottomed saucepan over medium heat. Heat the oil to 350°F (180°C). Once heated, dip the chiles in the batter, holding them from the stems, let the excess batter drip back into the bowl, then immediately place in the hot oil. Fry for about 5 to 8 minutes, or until the batter is golden brown and the chiles are heated all the way through. If the chiles are darkening too much before cooking all the way though, you can remove them from the oil and finish them in a 350°F (180°C) oven.

Place the fried chiles on paper towels to drain them of excess oil and sprinkle with some Maldon sea salt. Serve immediately.

MAIN COURSES | 193

SPRING | FALL | WINTER

Sunchoke Koftas in Curry

VP | GF | DFP | SF

These tubers have a texture of potatoes with a mildly tart, artichoke-like flavor, which makes them a surprisingly fun addition to koftas.

·······························

SERVES 4

FOR THE KOFTAS

2 medium sunchokes

1 teaspoon salt + more as needed

1 large Yukon potato

¾ cup (180 g) cup paneer

1 tablespoon cashews, finely chopped

1 tablespoon raisins, finely chopped

2 tablespoons chopped fresh cilantro

½ jalapeño chile, minced

1 teaspoon grated fresh ginger

3 tablespoons cornstarch

½ teaspoon garam masala

1 quart (1l) grapeseed oil, for frying

FOR THE CURRY

3 green cardamom pods

½-inch (12-mm) piece cinnamon stick

1 bay leaf

4 cloves

2 tablespoons grapeseed oil

1 large yellow onion, sliced

3 medium Roma tomatoes, diced

½ cup (60 g) raw cashews

1 cup (240 ml) water

1 tablespoon sugar

½ teaspoon ground coriander

Pinch of cayenne pepper

2 tablespoons dry fenugreek leaves (methi)

¾ cup (180 ml) heavy cream

Cilantro, for garnish

To make the koftas, clean the sunchokes well and remove any dirt and stuck bits from the skin. Halve or quarter the sunchokes, depending on their size, and place in a saucepan with enough water to cover. Add a generous pinch of salt and bring to a boil, then reduce the heat to a simmer and cook until the sunchokes are very tender but not falling apart, 20 to 25 minutes.

Drain the sunchokes well. Finely chop the sunchokes and place in a bowl. Peel the potato and dice into large cubes. Place in a small saucepan and cover with cool water. Add a generous pinch of salt and bring to a boil, then reduce to a simmer until fork-tender. Drain well and allow to dry out for a few minutes. Add the cooked potatoes and the remaining ingredients, except for the oil, and stir until combined, mashing the potatoes as you mix to create a dough. Place in the refrigerator to chill for at least 1 hour.

After chilling, divide the mixture into 12 equal balls. Heat the grapeseed oil in a high-walled saucepan over medium heat until the oil reaches 350°F (180°C). Working in batches, fry the koftas until they are a deep golden-brown color. Drain on paper towels and set aside.

To make the curry, begin by frying the whole spices in the grapeseed oil, about 30 seconds. Add the onion, tomatoes, cashews, water, sugar, coriander, and cayenne. Cook until the onions and cashews are very tender, about 10 to 15 minutes. Once cooked, remove the bay leaf, blend the sauce with an immersion blender, and add the fenugreek leaves and heavy cream, mixing well to combine.

When ready to serve, heat the sauce back to a simmer and add the koftas. (Adding the koftas just before serving will help keep them crisp.) Warm for 3 to 5 minutes just to heat through, then divide among serving bowls. Garnish with cilantro and serve immediately.

NOTE

To make this recipe vegan, replace the paneer with firm tofu and replace the heavy cream with Cashew Cream (page 36).

SUNCHOKES

Sunchokes are funny little things. These unique vegetables are actually the tubers of a sunflower plant, and they taste something between a potato and an artichoke. Sunchokes, unlike potatoes, can be eaten raw, and their raw texture is very akin to a water chestnut, making them an ideal last-minute mix-in for stir fries. When roasted, sunchokes take on a potato-like texture and are a delicious, unique substitute for potatoes. They are excellent fried, boiled, and topped with butter, or mixed into fillings, like the koftas on this page. Look for sunchokes in the fall through the early spring and be sure to wash them thoroughly—their many knobs can trap dirt!

SUMMER | FALL

Moussaka

NF | SF

Greens loves gratins. There are many gratin recipes in our archives, and even more that have been published in our previous cookbooks. It was one of those items that I could always expect on the menu when I was a young line cook. We would make the Gratin Provençal in the summer months and our Southwestern-Style Gratin with sweet potatoes and chipotle in the fall. We still love making versions of gratins at Greens but have updated from the very '80s-esque ring molds to cozy ceramic crocks. The Moussaka is an excellent casserole to make in the late summer or early fall, when eggplants and tomatoes are at their peak excellence, and the cool weather is starting to roll in. It's a harbinger of cozier times to come and still celebrates summer all the while. I'd eat this every day if I could!

....

SERVES 8

FOR THE VEGETABLES

3 medium zucchini

2 Yukon gold potatoes

1 large globe eggplant

Salt

Olive oil, for tossing the vegetables

To prepare the vegetables, preheat the oven to 425°F (220°C). Slice the zucchini, potatoes, and eggplant to ¼-inch (6.35-mm) thick using a mandoline or a very sharp knife and keep in separate containers. Salt the eggplant and let sit for at least an hour. Toss the zucchini and potatoes separately with just enough olive oil to coat and a pinch of salt and place them on separate baking sheets in a single layer. Roast in the oven until just tender, 20 to 25 minutes. Once the eggplant has rested, pat the eggplant dry with paper towels and then toss with oil and bake until just tender, 25 minutes. Reduce the oven heat to 350°F (180°C).

To make the mushroom sauce, use a food processor or a knife to finely chop the mushrooms into small pieces about ¼ inch in size. Do not overprocess or the mushrooms will turn into a paste.

Heat the ⅓ cup (80 ml) olive oil in a heavy-bottomed saucepan over medium heat. Add the diced onion and mushrooms, and cook until the onion is translucent and the mushrooms have wilted and released their liquid. Add the red wine and reduce by half, then add the remaining sauce ingredients. Bring the sauce to a slow simmer and cook for about 20 to 25 minutes to allow the flavors to come together. Set aside.

Next, make the mornay sauce. Melt the butter in a saucepan over medium heat. Add the flour and whisk constantly until the mixture lightens in color slightly and begins bubbling rapidly and resembles pancake batter. Add the milk and continue whisking until the sauce comes to a boil and thickens. Reduce the heat to low and allow to simmer for about 20 minutes. Remove from the heat and add the cheese, nutmeg, white pepper, and salt.

FOR THE MUSHROOM SAUCE

1 pound (450 g) cremini mushrooms

⅓ cup (80 ml) olive oil + more for roasting

Salt

1 large yellow onion, diced

2 tablespoons Garlic Confit (page 33)
or 1 clove raw garlic, sliced

One 28 ounce (794 g) can crushed tomatoes

¼ cup (60 ml) dry red wine

1 bay leaf

¼ teaspoon ground cinnamon

¼ teaspoon freshly ground black pepper

FOR THE MORNAY SAUCE

½ cup (1 stick/113 g) butter

½ cup (60 g) all-purpose flour

4 cups (1 l) milk

1 cup (100 g) grated pecorino romano
or Parmesan cheese + more for layering

Pinch of freshly grated nutmeg

Pinch of freshly ground white pepper

Salt

½ bunch parsley, chopped finely

To assemble the moussaka, spoon a ¼ inch layer of the mushroom sauce to the bottom of a 9- by 13-inch (23- by 33-cm) casserole dish. Add a single layer of the potatoes, shingling them slightly so as to not leave gaps. Sprinkle this layer lightly with pecorino and the chopped parsley, then layer some zucchini on top. Sprinkle with some cheese and parsley and repeat with a layer of eggplant. After the eggplant, add another layer of the mushroom sauce.

Repeat this process until all the vegetables have been used. Top the casserole with the béchamel sauce and bake at 350°F (180°C) for 60 to 75 minutes, or until the mornay sauce has browned on the top and the casserole is bubbling on the sides. Garnish with any remaining parsley and serve immediately.

The moussaka can also be assembled ahead of time and stored in the refrigerator for up to 2 days before baking. It can be baked from the fridge for the same amount of time, or until the bechamel has browned.

FALL | WINTER

Root Vegetable Biryani

V | GF | DF | NFP | SF

Biryani is a dish I love and order frequently when I dine out, but has always been something that seemed like a bit too much work to make at home. This simplified version is weeknight approved and doesn't skimp on any of the flavor.

SERVES 4

FOR THE RICE

2 tablespoons olive oil

1 tablespoon minced garlic

1 tablespoon minced ginger

½ jalapeño, minced

2 cups (400 g) basmati rice

Pinch of saffron threads

2 teaspoons salt

2½ cups (600 ml) boiling water

FOR THE VEGETABLES

1 large yellow onion, sliced very thin

1 medium turnip, cut into ½-inch (12-mm) chunks

½ medium sweet potato, peeled and cut into ½-inch (12-mm) chunks

1 small celery root, peeled and cut into ½-inch (12-mm) chunks

2 tablespoons garam masala

Olive oil, for tossing

Salt

½ bunch lacinato kale

FOR GARNISH

1 bunch cilantro and/or parsley, chopped

½ cup (60 g) toasted cashews

Lime wedges, for squeezing

Heat the olive oil in a large sauce pot. Add the garlic, ginger, and jalapeño together over medium-high heat for 3 to 5 minutes, until fragrant and starting to stick. Add the rice and saffron threads and saute for another 3 to 5 minutes, until some rice kernels turn opaque. Add the salt and boiling water. Cover the pot, reduce the heat to low, and cook for 12 minutes until the rice is fully cooked and the pan is dry. Once the rice is cooked, fluff the rice with a fork, and allow the steam to escape.

Preheat the oven to 400°F (200°C). Toss the onion and root vegetables together in a bowl with the garam masala and enough olive oil to coat. Sprinkle lightly with salt and spread on a baking sheet and roast until fork-tender, about 25 to 30 minutes. While the vegetables are cooking, clean the kale and remove the tough stems. Chop the kale into small pieces and set aside.

Add the kale to the cooked rice and stir in to allow it to wilt. Add the roasted vegetables and stir until well distributed. Top the biryani with the cilantro and toasted cashews and serve accompanied by the lime wedges for squeezing.

CELERY ROOT

Often overlooked, celery root (aka celeriac) is another vegetable that deserves some more attention. Its mild, slightly sweet, and nutty flavor is excellent with cream and butter, and pairs well with truffles, too. For Christmas, we sometimes make a celery root cream and mix that into mashed potatoes. But it also holds up very well to spices, making it the perfect addition to dishes like this Root Vegetable Biryani.

SPRING | SUMMER | FALL | WINTER

Tofu & Vegetable Brochettes with Chimichurri

V | GF | DF | NF

If you know Greens, you know the tofu brochettes. It is one of the few dishes that has remained on the menu almost consistently for 45 years. Even one of our kid's coloring pages shows a woman making the skewers in the kitchen (which, I recently found out, is based on a real photo from the early '80s). While we cycle through other delicious grilled entrées now, the brochettes are always bound to return to the menu with a new iteration. Here, we use our Chimichurri (page 47) as both a marinade and sauce for the maximum flavor pre- and post-grilling. To make this a complete meal, serve with Grilled Sweet Potatoes with Tahini Cashew Cream (page 159) or the Couscous & Baby Artichoke Salad (page 103).

....

YIELDS 6 SKEWERS

1 block (10 ounces/283 g) Hodo tofu or extra-firm tofu

12 baby creamer potatoes

Salt

6 small pearl onions

6 seasonal vegetables, such as fennel, tomatoes, cauliflower, etc.

12 cremini mushrooms

Chimichurri (page 47)

Six 10-inch (25 cm) bamboo skewers

Cut the block of tofu into 12 equal pieces by cutting the short edge into thirds and the long edge into quarters. Set aside.

Clean the baby creamer potatoes well and add to a saucepan with a handful of salt and cover with water. Bring to a boil and cook until the potatoes are just tender, 8 to 10 minutes. Remove the potatoes from the water with a slotted spoon and set aside in a bowl. Next, add the pearl onions to the boiling water and cook until the onions are just tender and look slightly translucent, 3 to 4 minutes. Remove the onions from the water and place them in another bowl. Repeat with any tougher seasonal vegetables, boiling them in the salted water until just tender, 2 to 4 minutes, depending on the vegetable. Softer, quicker-cooking seasonal vegetables such as tomatoes do not need to be par cooked. Do not overcook any of the vegetables or they will fall off the skewer when grilling. Put each vegetable in a separate bowl as they are removed from the water.

Next, arrange all of the vegetables on a clean working surface. Have ready bamboo skewers. Start with a cremini mushroom and slide it, cap-side first, onto the skewer, leaving just enough space at the end of a skewer to grab with your fingers. Next, add a cube of tofu and slide it snugly next to the mushroom. Then, add a potato, followed by a pearl onion, and the seasonal vegetable. Next, add another potato, another tofu, and finish with a cremini mushroom, this time placing it stem side first so the two mushroom caps on either end "enclose" the vegetables on the skewer. Continue this process until all of the brochettes have been assembled.

Next, place each brochette one at a time in a long, wide casserole dish. Brush the skewer on all sides with the Chimichurri before starting on the next skewer. When all of the skewers have been brushed, pour some more Chimichurri over the top for extra flavor. Be sure to leave a little sauce for after grilling. Marinate the brochettes for at least 30 minutes, or up to overnight in a covered dish in the refrigerator.

When ready to cook, heat the grill over high heat. Place the skewers over direct heat and cook each side until nicely charred, about 8 minutes total, turning the skewers every few minutes to cook all sides evenly. Remove the skewers from the grill and top with the remaining Chimichurri.

SUMMER

Saffron Goat Cheese Risotto

GF | NF | SF

Risotto is a wonderful option for vegetarian dinners not only because it is rich and filling, but also because it is a wonderfully versatile dish that is easier to make than one might think. While it's typical to add the vegetable stock in multiple additions, I discovered that it really isn't all that necessary. As long as you stir the risotto while it slowly cooks, you can add all of your vegetable stock at once! Just be sure to add the creamy ingredients, like heavy cream, after the rice has absorbed most of the stock.

SERVES 4

4 Fairy Tale eggplants or
½ Japanese eggplant

Olive oil, for tossing and making green olive oil

Salt

1 zucchini

1 cup (150 g) cherry tomatoes

½ bulb fennel, fronds reserved for garnish

1 shallot, minced

1 clove garlic, minced

1 cup (220 g) Carnaroli or Arborio rice

¼ cup (60 ml) dry white wine

3 cups (720 ml) regular Vegetable Stock
or use the corn variation (page 39)

Pinch of saffron threads

½ cup (115 g) soft goat cheese

⅔ cup (160 ml) heavy cream

4 tablespoons (60 g) Lemon Butter (page 33)

2 tablespoons Castelvetrano olives

Preheat the oven to 400°F (200°C). Halve the Fairy Tale eggplants or slice the Japanese eggplant into diagonal wedges about 1-inch (2.5-cm) thick. Toss with olive oil and a little salt and place on a large, rimmed baking sheet. Slice the zucchini diagonally into 1-inch (2.5-cm) wedges, toss with oil and a little salt, and place next to the eggplant. Toss the tomatoes with oil and a little salt and place on the baking sheet as well. Finally, slice the fennel into ½-inch (12-mm) strips, cutting perpendicular to the core to keep the pieces intact. Toss with oil and a little salt and place on the baking sheet. Bake the vegetables for 25 to 30 minutes or until tender.

Meanwhile, make the risotto. Heat a medium skillet over high heat. Add a drizzle of olive oil to lightly coat the bottom of the pan, then add the shallot and garlic. Cook for 1 to 2 minutes or until the shallot is slightly translucent. Add the rice and cook until the rice has turned mostly opaque, 2 to 3 minutes more. Add the wine and reduce until dry. Next, add the stock in one full addition along with the saffron and a generous pinch of salt. Reduce the heat to low, stirring consistently so the rice doesn't clump.

Adjust the heat so that the stock is not bubbling at all, but there is a visible amount of steam. This is the perfect temperature to cook the risotto. Stir the risotto every few minutes to prevent sticking on the bottom of the pan as well as to release the starches in the grains. As the rice absorbs the liquid, the heat may need to be adjusted to prevent bubbling. Be sure to keep the heat consistent or the rice will cook too quickly.

Once the rice has absorbed nearly all of the stock, taste the rice for doneness. The rice should be nearly al dente at this point. If the rice is still very crunchy, add more water, a little at a time, until it reaches this point.

Once al dente, add the goat cheese, heavy cream, and Lemon Butter and stir the risotto, keeping the heat on low, until the rice has absorbed most of the cream, but is still creamy and smooth. If the rice dries out too much and looks clumpy, add more water until it becomes smooth and creamy again.

Next, make a green olive oil by combining the Castelvetrano olives with 2 tablespoons of olive oil and blending with an immersion blender until mostly smooth.

To serve, place the risotto in a large serving basin or bowl. Top with the roasted vegetables and drizzle the green olive oil over the top. Garnish with fennel fronds. Serve immediately or the risotto will become too thick.

FENNEL

For fennel, it's all about the preparation. Shaving fennel ultra-thin and serving fresh in a salad with citrus and herbs is a delightful way to enjoy. It can also be confited, which all but rids the fennel of its bright licorice qualities and instead imparts a delightful sweetness that makes for a wonderful base in pastas and soups.

SPRING | SUMMER | FALL | WINTER

Grits with Creamy Creole-Style Mushrooms

VP | GF | DFP | NF | SF

This is a dish that we served during our New Year's Eve prix fixe menu in 2022, and it was a huge hit. We like to add a bit of luck to our celebrations with some black-eyed peas (in the South, black-eyed peas are typically served on New Year's Day in order to bring good luck for the year), so this dish was a no-brainer. It's creamy, rich, and perfectly indulgent for a night like New Year's. While the Creole Broth (page 40) is necessary and takes a bit of time, the end result is worth it. If you make the broth in advance, this dish is easy enough for a weeknight dinner or can be reserved for special occasions.

....

SERVES 4

FOR THE CREOLE MUSHROOMS

1 pound (450 g) wild mushrooms, such as maitake, royal trumpet, oyster, chanterelle, etc.

2 cups (320 g) Brussels sprouts, trimmed and halved

Light olive oil, for tossing

Salt

2 cups (473 ml) Creole Broth (page 40)

¾ cup (110 g) black-eyed peas, cooked (see note, page 22)

½ cup (120 ml) heavy cream (or Cashew Cream, page 36, for vegan)

2 tablespoons chopped fresh parsley

FOR THE GRITS

1 cup (140 g) whole grits, such as Anson Mills

4 cups (1 l) water + more as needed

Salt

½ cup (120 ml) heavy cream (or Cashew Cream page 36)

4 tablespoons (60 g) butter, Miso Butter (page 33) or vegan butter

Preheat the oven to 425°F (220°C). In separate bowls, toss the wild mushrooms and Brussels sprouts with enough olive oil to coat and salt to taste. Arrange them on separate baking sheets and bake in the oven until the tops of the vegetables are crisp and golden brown, about 25 minutes.

To make the grits, sort the grits and remove any stones and debris from the grains. Bring a saucepan with the water to a boil. Add 1 tablespoon salt, then in a steady stream, add the grits, whisking constantly to avoid sticking. Continue whisking the grits until they hydrate into the water. Reduce the heat to low and allow the grits to slowly cook for about 45 minutes or until the grains are very soft and porridge-like. Add the cream and butter and then adjust the seasonings to taste.

Meanwhile, bring the Creole Broth and heavy cream to a boil in a medium saucepan, then reduce to a simmer until the sauce thickens enough to lightly coat the back of a spoon, about 10 minutes. Add the mushrooms, brussels sprouts, and black-eyed peas and cook for another minute or two until hot. Season with salt to taste.

Top the grits with the creamy mushrooms and garnish with the parsley. This dish is also fantastic when topped with Chili Crisp (page 35).

MAIN COURSES | 207

SUMMER | FALL

Stuffed Eggplants with Couscous

GFP | V | DFP | NFP | SF

There's something wonderful about serving a meal that comes all wrapped up in one flavorful package. These eggplants take a Middle Eastern approach, with floral saffron couscous, bright herbs, and nutty pine nuts.

SERVES 4

FOR THE EGGPLANT

2 medium globe eggplants

Salt

Olive oil

FOR THE FILLING

¾ cup (175 g) cooked Moroccan couscous or cooked quinoa, for gluten free

Pinch of saffron threads

Salt

1½ cups (360 ml) boiling water

2 tablespoons olive oil

½ medium yellow onion, sliced thin

2 cloves garlic, sliced thin

2 cups (300 g) grape tomatoes, halved lengthwise

½ teaspoon ground cumin

½ teaspoon ground coriander

¼ teaspoon freshly ground black pepper

½ teaspoon paprika

2 tablespoons chopped fresh dill

2 tablespoons chopped fresh parsley

2 tablespoons chopped fresh mint (optional)

Juice of ½ lemon

5 ounces (140 g) feta cheese (optional)

2 tablespoons pine nuts, for garnish (optional)

Preheat the oven to 375°F (190°C). Halve the eggplants lengthwise and diagonally score the exposed flesh several times in one direction, then rotate the eggplant 90 degrees and score across the first cuts to create a diamond pattern. Salt the eggplant well and let sit for 20 minutes.

After 20 minutes, pat the eggplant halves dry and drizzle with a generous amount of olive oil. Bake in the oven face up until fully cooked, about an hour.

While the eggplants are cooking, make the filling. Mix the couscous with the saffron and cook according to instructions on page 25. Cover immediately with plastic wrap and let sit for 15 minutes to hydrate.

In a medium saucepan, heat the olive oil over medium-high heat, then add the sliced yellow onion. Cook until the onion starts to soften, 3 to 5 minutes. Add the garlic and grape tomatoes and cook until the tomatoes begin to soften. Add the spices and continue cooking until the tomatoes are jammy and fragrant. Season with salt to taste.

Add the cooked tomatoes to a bowl and add the cooked couscous. Add the fresh herbs, lemon juice, and feta cheese (if using) and mix together until combined.

Make a well in the eggplants by pressing on the flesh and moving it aside. The eggplants can be spread out a bit but don't flatten them completely if possible. Divide the filling among the 4 eggplant halves and return to the oven for about 15 minutes. Remove from the oven and garnish with pine nuts.

208 | MAIN COURSES

SPRING | FALL | WINTER

Aloo Saag Pot Pie

VP | DFP | NF | SF

Based on the popular aloo saag curry, this pot pie boasts tons of flavor from braised greens and potatoes. Here, we also use black lentils and coconut cream for a magnificently comforting meal that will warm you to the core during the colder months.

SERVES 6 TO 8

1 large Yukon gold potato

Olive oil, for tossing

Salt

4 ounces (115 g) lacinato kale
(about 3 packed cups)

3 ounces (115 g) spinach
(about 3 packed cups)

1 cup (140 g) diced yellow onion

5 cloves garlic, minced (about 1 tablespoon)

1 knob fresh ginger, minced
(about 1 tablespoon)

1 jalapeño, minced

¼ cup (50 g) black or brown lentils,
cleaned and sorted

One 14½ ounce (430 ml) can unsweetened
coconut cream

1 teaspoon garam masala

½ teaspoon ground coriander

¼ teaspoon ground cumin

1 tablespoon dried methi leaves (optional)

1 recipe Basic Flaky Pastry (page 139)
or store-bought pie dough

Preheat the oven to 400°F (200°C). Cut the potato into a ¾-inch dice. Toss with enough olive oil to coat and a light sprinkle of salt. Roast in the oven until the potatoes are tender and started to brown on the edges, about 25 minutes.

Meanwhile, make the rest of the filling. Finely chop the kale and spinach, or pulse in a food processor until fine. Set aside. Heat about 2 tablespoons olive oil in a medium saucepan over medium-high heat. Add the onion and cook for about 5 minutes, until starting to turn translucent. Add the garlic, ginger, and jalapeño and sauté another 2 to 3 minutes, until fragrant. Then, add the chopped greens, lentils, and coconut cream.

Lower the heat to medium low and cook for about 20 minutes, allowing the coconut cream to reduce while the lentils cook. Add the potatoes and stir to combine.

Reduce the oven to 350°F (180°C). Divide the pastry in half and shape into 2 disks. Then, roll each disk out into a 13-inch (33-cm) circle, dusting lightly with flour as needed so the pastry doesn't stick. Lay one of the rounds into a 10-inch (25-cm) pie pan, pressing the dough into the edges of the pan. Next, add the vegetables to the pie pan and cover them with the second pastry round. Slice the top pastry 3 to 4 times to allow steam to escape. Bake in the oven on the bottom rack for about 60 minutes. If the crust starts to darken more than desired, cover loosely with foil to prevent further browning. Let the pot pie rest for about 10 minutes before slicing and serving.

DESSERTS

The desserts at Greens follow the same guidelines that the items on the main menu follow. Seasonality, of course, takes the forefront, meaning we enjoy citrus in the winter, rhubarb and strawberries in the spring, berries and stone fruit in the summer, and apples, pears, and persimmons in the fall. Our desserts also take a straightforward, traditional approach; it's like home baking taken to the ultimate level of deliciousness. At any given time, you can find a delicious mix of cakes, cookies, cobblers, and custards on our menu. The recipes in this chapter are a healthy mix of what you can normally find on our menus, plus some brand-new additions for you to enjoy, like the Sesame–Sugar Cookies (my personal favorite, on page 212) and a breathtaking Mocha Roulade with Hazelnut-Mocha Whipped Cream (page 225).

SPRING | SUMMER | FALL | WINTER

Sesame–Brown Sugar Cookies

NF | SF

Sesame is an ingredient that has become more common lately to use in desserts that don't usually call for it. The trend is well-deserved: sesame offers a nutty, sweet flavor and satisfying crunchy texture. In these sugar cookies, sesame is added in two ways, in the form of sesame oil and whole seeds. The cookies are made rather large, but they will have a delightful chew in the centers and a wonderful nutty flavor.

YIELDS 8 LARGE COOKIES

½ cup (1 stick/115 g) room temperature butter

¾ cup (165 g) brown sugar

1 large egg

1 teaspoon sesame oil

2 teaspoons pure vanilla extract

1 cup (120 g) all-purpose flour

½ cup (70 g) white untoasted sesame seeds

¼ teaspoon salt

1 teaspoon baking powder

¼ teaspoon baking soda

In the bowl of an electric mixer fitted with the paddle attachment, cream together the butter and sugar until light and fluffy, about 2 to 3 minutes on medium speed. Add the egg, scraping down the bowl as needed, until fully incorporated. Add the sesame oil and vanilla and mix to combine.

Next, add the flour, sesame seeds, salt, baking powder, and baking soda and stir on low speed until just combined. The dough should be sticky. Wrap the dough in plastic wrap and flatten to a disk. Refrigerate for at least 30 minutes.

After the dough has chilled, preheat the oven to 350°F (180°C). Scoop the dough into ¼ cup–sized balls. Place on a baking sheet 6 inches apart. You will need 2 baking sheets for 8 cookies.

Bake each sheet for 5 minutes, then rotate the pans, lifting them up 6 inches (15 cm) off the rack and dropping them hard to deflate the cookies. Bake for another 5 minutes, until the edges of the cookies are a light golden brown and the centers are no longer very shiny. If there is a small shiny spot in the centers of the cookies, that is OK.

Allow the cookies to cool for about 5 minutes before transferring to a cooling rack to cool. Enjoy once the cookies are mostly or completely cool. Store any extras in an airtight container at room temperature for 2 to 3 days.

FALL | WINTER

Cranberry Pistachio Almond Shortbread

VP | GFP | DFP | SF

Every year for our Thanksgiving takeout menu, we offer some kind of shortbread cookie. Some years, we make thumbprints, others we use pecans, and some years it's this cranberry pistachio almond version. I love these cookies because they are visually stunning—deep pinks and greens and pops of orange stud the dough underneath a layer of shiny, crunchy sugar. I like to save these cookies for the morning after the holiday—with a cup of tea for good measure.

YIELDS 24 COOKIES

2 cups (240 g) all-purpose flour or cup-for-cup gluten-free flour

½ cup (60 g) powdered sugar

¾ teaspoon salt

1 cup (2 sticks/230 g) butter or vegan butter, cut into ½-inch (12-mm) cubes

¼ cup (25 g) cranberries, chopped

⅓ cup (50 g) pistachios, chopped

Zest of 1 orange

¾ teaspoon almond extract

Coarse sugar, such as turbinado, for coating

In the bowl of a stand mixer fitted with the paddle attachment, combine the flour, powdered sugar, salt, and butter. Mix until the mixture resembles coarse crumbs that stick together when pressed.

Add the cranberries, pistachios, orange zest, and almond extract and mix until fully combined.

Next, form the cookies. To make rounds: Lay a sheet of parchment on a clean work surface. Spread the dough in a rough log shape across the short end of the parchment sheet. Fold the parchment paper over the dough log. While holding the parchment paper firmly, push against the dough with a bench scraper to create a neat round log.

To make rectangles: Lay a sheet of parchment on a clean work surface. Spread the dough into a rough log shape across the short end of the parchment sheet. Use your hands to form the dough into a rough rectangle. Fold the parchment paper over the dough and use a bench scraper to press the dough into a rectangle by running the bench scraper along all sides to ensure they are uniform.

Once the dough has been formed into a round log or a long rectangle, chill the dough for at least 2 hours or until the dough firms up fully.

Preheat the oven to 350°F (180°C). Remove the dough log from the refrigerator and slice into ¼-inch (6-mm) thick cookies. Pour the turbinado sugar into a bowl. Working with one at a time, coat each cookie with sugar and spread them 1 inch (2.5 cm) apart on a baking sheet. Bake until the cookies are no longer shiny on the top and are just barely starting to turn golden brown on the bottom.

Allow the cookies to cool for about 5 minutes before transferring to a tray to cool completely. Once cool, enjoy as is or with a warm mug of tea. Extra cookies can be stored for up to a week in an airtight container at room temperature.

DESSERTS | 215

FALL | WINTER

Ginger Parsnip Oatmeal Cookies

DFP | NF | SF

"Celebrating vegetables" applies to more than just our savory menu. These delightful oatmeal cookies are soft and cakey, reminiscent of carrot cake, only they're made with parsnips, carrot's more perfumed cousin. Parsnips deserve more love than they typically get, especially from a pastry perspective. They have an incredible flavor and aroma that pair with a wide array of sweet components, like ginger and warm spices. These cookies truly showcase the parsnips front and center, while being perfectly spiced with ginger in the background. Sometimes I'll zhuzh up this recipe and throw in ¼ cup (45 g) of chopped white chocolate, too. But really, they're perfect as is.

....

YIELDS 20 COOKIES

½ cup (1 stick/115 g) room-temperature butter or dairy-free butter

½ cup (110 g) brown sugar

¼ cup (55 g) granulated sugar

2 large eggs

2 teaspoons pure vanilla extract

1 cup (110 g) coarsely shredded parsnips (about 1 large parsnip)

1 cup (100 g) rolled oats

1 cup (120 g) all-purpose flour

¼ teaspoon ground allspice

¼ teaspoon salt

½ teaspoon baking soda

½ cup (85 g) chopped crystallized ginger

Preheat the oven to 350°F (180°C). Use an electric stand mixer fitted with the paddle attachment on medium speed and cream together the butter and sugar until light and fluffy, about 2 to 3 minutes. Add the eggs one at a time, scraping the bowl between each addition, until incorporated. Add the vanilla and parsnips and mix until combined.

In a separate bowl, combine the oats, flour, allspice, salt, and baking soda together. Add the oat mixture all at once to the parsnip mixture and mix on low speed until just combined. Fold in the crystallized ginger. The dough will be a bit sticky.

Scoop the cookie dough into 2 tablespoon–sized balls onto a baking sheet and bake 2 inches (5 cm) apart for about 10 minutes, until the cookies are golden brown at the edges and no longer appear wet on the tops. Remove from the oven and let cool for about 5 minutes before transferring to a cooling rack to cool completely. Serve once cool. Extra cookies can be stored for 2 to 3 days in an airtight container at room temperature.

SPRING | SUMMER | FALL | WINTER

Graham Crackers

VP | DFP | NF | SF

It's easy enough to buy a box of Graham Crackers from the store, but making them at home is almost as easy, and the resulting crackers are far superior. As always, sourcing the best ingredients makes a big difference in the final product. At Greens, we use Marshall's honey and high-quality whole wheat flour. I'd highly suggest looking for a local miller for the freshest flour, which will yield the most flavorful results. If you're making these crackers specifically to make the Chevre Cheesecake (page 233), omit the cinnamon for a more classic iteration of graham cracker crust.

....

YIELDS 24 CRACKERS

2 cups + 1 tablespoon (260 g) all-purpose flour

½ cup (75 g) whole wheat flour + more for dusting

½ teaspoon baking soda

½ teaspoon salt

3 tablespoons (45 g) sugar

¼ cup (55 g) brown sugar

Pinch of ground cinnamon (optional)

14 tablespoons (200 g) unsalted butter or vegan butter

3 tablespoons (75 g) wildflower honey, such as Marshall's or agave nectar for vegan

Combine the dry ingredients together in a bowl and whisk together. Melt the butter with the honey over a double boiler over medium heat or in the microwave, heating in 30-second increments and stirring in between until the butter is completely melted.

Add the melted butter and honey to the dry ingredients and stir until combined. The dough should be a bit sticky. Form the dough into a flattened rectangular block, wrap in plastic wrap, and refrigerate for at least 30 minutes.

Preheat the oven to 350°F (180°C). Once the dough has chilled, place it on a lightly floured work surface and dust more flour on the top. Roll out the dough, adding more flour as necessary to prevent sticking, into a rectangle approximately 12 by 18 inches (30 by 46 cm) with ⅛-inch (3-mm) thickness. Transfer the dough onto a baking sheet and, if desired, lightly score it with the back of a paring knife to create the individual crackers: To create 24 evenly sized crackers, score both the long edge of the dough in half, then divide each side into thirds for 6 equal slices. Turn the tray to the short end and slice down the center, and then cut each half in half again. Then, use a fork to create some decorative holes in each cracker. If you are making graham cracker crust, these decorative steps are not necessary as the crackers will be ground to crumbs anyway.

Bake the crackers for 10 to 12 minutes, until golden brown and slightly puffed. Remove from the oven and allow to cool completely before gently snapping the crackers apart.

Once cool, the crackers are ready to eat or grind up for graham crust. The crackers keep for up to a week in an airtight container at room temperature.

DESSERTS | 217

SPRING | SUMMER

Raspberry–White Chocolate Pound Cake

NF | SF

Everyone loves a good pound cake because there are so many that are just so-so. This one is just that—a pound cake that's so good, you'll want to close your eyes to eat it, as though minimizing your sense of sight will enhance your sense of taste. The raspberries lend a luscious sweet-tart flavor, perfectly complemented by the sweet bursts of white chocolate. As soon as raspberries return to the markets toward the end of May, I can't help but make this pound cake over and over again until they retire again at the beginning of the fall.

....

YIELDS ONE
9- BY 4-INCH (23- BY 10-CM) LOAF

½ cup (115 g) unsalted butter, room temperature + more for greasing

2¼ cups (270 g) all-purpose flour

½ teaspoon baking soda

1½ teaspoons baking powder

½ teaspoon salt

1 cup (200 g) sugar

3 large eggs

2 teaspoons pure vanilla extract

¼ teaspoon lemon extract (optional)

Zest of 1 orange

½ cup (115 g) sour cream

½ cup (120 ml) whole milk

1 cup (180 g) white chocolate chips

6 ounces (170 g) fresh raspberries

Preheat the oven to 350°F (180°C). Grease a 9- by 4-inch (23- by 10-cm) loaf pan with butter. In a medium bowl, sift together the flour, baking soda, baking powder, and salt. Set aside.

In the bowl of a stand mixer fitted with the paddle attachment, cream together the butter and sugar until light and fluffy, 2 to 3 minutes. Add the eggs one at a time, scraping down the bowl between each addition. Make sure the eggs are fully incorporated into the sugar and butter mixture before adding the next egg. Next, add both extracts and the orange zest.

Add half of the flour mixture and mix on low speed until just combined. Scrape down the sides of the bowl. Then, add the sour cream and milk. Mix to combine and scrape. Then, add the remaining flour and mix until combined. Add the white chocolate chips and fresh raspberries and fold in by hand. The raspberries should break up and streak the batter slightly. This is good—the raspberries will sink if they remain whole.

Bake for about 60 to 75 minutes, or until the cake has set and a toothpick inserted into the middle of the cake comes out clean. Allow to cool for 15 minutes, then loosen the sides with a spatula or knife and turn the pound cake out of the pan onto a cooling rack. Allow to cool completely before slicing.

Extra cake can be wrapped with plastic wrap and stored at room temperature for 2 to 3 days.

SPRING

Rye Cake with Apricot Preserves

NF | SF

A sponge cake is an excellent vessel for alternative flours like rye. While it's true that some flours may be heavier than all purpose flour, which can affect the texture, I find that you can be successful with it as long as you're thoughtful of exactly how much you're adding. In this cake, just a half cup of rye flour provides an intensely deep, nutty, caramelized flavor that pairs wonderfully with apricot preserves. This cake is also delicious with apple butter in the fall.

....

SERVES 8 TO 10

FOR THE CAKE

¼ cup (30 g) butter, melted + more for greasing

½ cup (50 g) rye flour + more for dusting

½ teaspoon baking powder

¼ teaspoon salt

4 large eggs, separated

½ cup (110 g) brown sugar

1 tablespoon pure vanilla extract

¼ cup (50 g) granulated sugar

Preheat the oven to 350°F (180°C). Grease and flour one 9-inch (25-cm) round cake pan. Combine the rye flour, baking powder, and salt together in a bowl. Whisk to combine, then set aside.

Add the egg yolks and brown sugar to the bowl of a stand mixer fitted with the whisk attachment. Beat on high speed for about 5 minutes, until the yolks are pale yellow and fluffy, and can create ribbons when the beater is lifted. Add the melted butter and vanilla extract and mix until just combined. Add the egg yolk mixture to the bowl with the flour mixture and fold together until the dry ingredients are just incorporated.

Clean the stand mixer bowl and whisk attachment and dry them well. You want to be sure that they are impeccably clean and dry in order whip the egg whites properly. Add the reserved egg whites to the bowl and beat on medium speed until the egg whites are frothy. Increase the speed to high and beat until soft peaks form, then slowly add the granulated sugar in 2 additions. Beat until stiff peaks form.

Fold one-third of the egg whites into the bowl with the egg yolk–flour mixture until no streaks remain. Then, fold in the remaining egg whites until no streaks remain. Pour the batter into the prepared cake pan and bake until golden brown and a toothpick comes out clean when inserted into the center of the cake, 15 to 20 minutes.

Remove from the oven and allow the cake to cool in its pan for 10 minutes before turning them out onto a cooling rack to cool completely.

FOR THE APRICOT PRESERVES

1 pound (454 g) apricots

½ cup (100 g) sugar

Pinch of ground cinnamon (optional)

Juice of 1 lemon

FOR THE BROWN SUGAR BUTTERCREAM

3 tablespoons brown sugar

½ cup (1 stick/113 g) butter

Pinch of salt

1 teaspoon vanilla extract

1 cup (200 g) powdered sugar

To make the apricot preserves, halve the apricots and remove the pits. For larger apricots, you may quarter them, but for smaller ones, leave them in halves. Add the prepared apricots and the remaining ingredients to a saucepan and cook over medium-low heat until the apricots have broken down and the mixture has become thick and jammy, about 30 minutes. Remove from the heat and allow to cool completely.

To make the brown sugar buttercream, add the brown sugar and butter to the bowl of a stand mixer fitted with the paddle attachment. Beat the brown sugar with the butter on medium speed until light and fluffy, about 3 to 5 minutes. Take your time beating the mixture together so the brown sugar can dissolve. Then, add the salt, heavy cream, and vanilla and beat together. Finally, add the powdered sugar and continue beating until the mixture is smooth and fluffy.

To assemble the cake, place the cake on a decorative plate. Add the buttercream to the top of the cake, spreading just to the edge, but leaving a ¼-inch (6.35-mm) rim around the cake. Leave the sides clean. Spread the buttercream so that the center of the cake has a slightly thinner layer of buttercream than the edges, as to make a well to hold the apricot preserves. Once the buttercream has been spread, add the apricot preserves to the well of buttercream and spread just shy of the edges of the buttercream.

Serve the cake immediately, or store in the fridge up to a day. If refrigerating, allow the cake to temper for at least 1 to 2 hours, or until the buttercream has softened to room temperature.

FALL | WINTER

Maple Black Walnut Baklava

VP | DFP | SF

Black walnut trees are native to North America, but unlike pecans, they don't get the attention they deserve, in my opinion. I have fond memories of harvesting black walnuts with my mom back on the East Coast, and not-so-fond memories of processing them afterward. The shells of these nuts are incredibly tough to crack, so unlike regular English walnuts, black walnuts can only be purchased in bits and pieces. But this makes them perfect for baklava, where nuts are ground finely with spices and baked between layers of buttery filo dough. Black walnuts pair wonderfully with maple, perhaps because they grow in similar regions in the United States, or perhaps by coincidence. This recipe brings them both together for a uniquely "American" baklava.

....

YIELDS 18 PIECES

FOR THE BAKLAVA

1½ cups (200 g) black walnuts, toasted (see note, page 25)

2 teaspoons ground cinnamon

1 teaspoon ground cloves

2 teaspoons flaky Maldon sea salt

1 cup (2 sticks/230 g) butter, melted + more for greasing

1 pound (450 g) package filo dough, thawed if frozen, according to package directions

FOR THE SYRUP

1 cup (240 ml) pure maple syrup

1 cup (240 ml) water

1 tablespoon apple cider vinegar

½ vanilla bean

Preheat the oven to 350°F (180°C). Begin by preparing the black walnut filling. Add the toasted nuts to a food processor with the cinnamon and cloves. Pulse the nuts until they are finely chopped, but not pasty. Stir in the Maldon salt, then set aside.

Grease the bottom and sides of a 9- by 13-inch (23- by 33-cm) baking pan with butter. Cut the filo sheets in half so that they fit the pan. Lay one single filo sheet into the greased pan and brush with a thin layer of the melted butter. Add 7 more filo sheets to the pan, brushing each layer with butter before adding the next sheet.

Next, add a generous ⅓ cup (50 g) of walnut filling to the pan and spread it evenly across the filo layer. Add a filo sheet over the nut mixture and brush it with butter. Add 4 more filo sheets to this layer, brushing with butter in between each addition. Then, repeat this process until all of the nut mixture has been used. Add one final layer of filo using 8 sheets, brushing with butter in between each layer. Brush the top of the baklava with butter.

Next, using a sharp knife, cut the baklava into thirds starting from the short end of the pan. Then, turn the pan to the long edge and cut it down the middle. Then, cut each half into thirds to make 18 pieces. Bake the baklava for 45 minutes, turning halfway through baking.

Make the syrup while the baklava bakes. Combine the maple syrup, water, sugar, and apple cider vinegar together in a small saucepan. Slice the vanilla bean in half and add to the pot. Bring to a boil over high heat, then reduce the heat to medium-low and simmer the syrup for about 15 minutes.

Once the baklava is ready to be taken out of the oven, remove the vanilla pod and immediately pour the syrup over the baklava, making sure to evenly coat the entire pan, edges and corners included.

Allow the baklava to cool completely before serving, at least 4 hours. For best results, cool the pan overnight so the syrup can properly soak into the filo. Cover the baklava with foil and store at room temperature for several days, up to a week.

DESSERTS | 223

Black Walnuts & Native Plants

What's a black walnut? A cousin of the English variety, black walnuts are a nut native to North America. Their shells are tough to crack, and their flavor pungent, with strong nutty, earthy, and funky qualities that make them a wonderful pairing with aged cheeses, and sweeter things like pumpkins and maple syrup or honey. I have fond memories of harvesting black walnuts with my mom. There are black walnut trees everywhere on the East Coast, and we'd often park in the community pool's parking lot to forage for them. The trees were always teeming with nuts come September, and we'd often pick so many that we'd have to make several trips to the car. We'd bring them home and clean them well, then dry them for a few weeks before cracking them open (not easily, mind you) to enjoy in all of our autumn baked goods.

One year, I asked Connie Green from Wineforest Wild Foods for some advice to crack them, and she joked to simply "run them over with the car." Despite the f-bombs and frustration of cracking the damn things, I have to admit that baking with something you found is an extraordinary feeling.

Our first year foraging for these walnuts piqued my interest in learning about more native plants. Of course, there are certain celebrity wild plants that we all love—ramps, mushrooms, nuts, and even maple syrup. But the truth is, there are edible and medicinal plants all around us—you just need to know what to look for. I often pass by fields of wild oats, barley, and buckwheat on my evening walks, with wild fennel poking through with their bushy fronds every so often. There are soft purple radish blooms, bright yellow mustard flowers, satellite-shaped miner's lettuce, and three-cornered leeks all over the place in the springtime. Even the impressively thorny thistle with its bright purple flowers and giant cow parsnip make appearances. It's a sight to behold once you begin to recognize just how much of what you see is edible. Better yet, it's an incredible way to connect with the land you live on, the history of that land's cuisine, and the traditions that were forged from something as simple as a walnut.

SPRING | SUMMER | FALL | WINTER

Mocha Roulade with Hazelnut-Mocha Whipped Cream

N F P | S F

This espresso-laden roulade is a coffee lover's dream. Light, fluffy mocha sponge cake is filled with a wonderfully crunchy hazelnut-mocha whipped cream, thanks to the addition of hazelnut praline. While the praline adds a lovely texture, it can be omitted for those with allergies. This cake takes a bit longer to make than some of the other desserts in this book. Temperatures are important here— make sure to roll the sponge cake while it is still warm and only unroll when it has fully cooled. The mocha whipped cream also needs to be completely cold before whipping, otherwise, it won't form stiff peaks. Despite these moments of necessary patience, this cake is definitely a worthy weekend endeavor.

....

SERVES 8

FOR THE MOCHA ROULADE CAKE

Cooking spray

⅔ cup (80 g) all-purpose flour

¼ cup (20 g) unsweetened cocoa powder + more for dusting

½ teaspoon baking powder

2 tablespoons instant espresso powder

2 shots brewed espresso or 3 tablespoons strongly brewed coffee

2 tablespoons canola oil

6 large eggs, whites and yolks separated

Pinch of cream of tartar

1¼ cups (250) sugar

Preheat the oven to 350°F (180°C). Prepare a 13- by 18-inch (33- by 46-cm) baking sheet with parchment paper and spray liberally with cooking spray. Sift together the all-purpose flour, cocoa powder, and baking powder together in a small bowl. In a separate bowl, add the espresso powder, brewed espresso, and canola oil together and mix to combine. Set both bowls aside.

Next, in the bowl of a stand mixer fitted with the whisk attachment, add the egg whites and cream of tartar. Beat the egg whites on medium speed until frothy, then increase the speed to high and beat until soft peaks form. Then, add ½ cup (50 g) of sugar in 2 quick additions. Continue to beat on high speed until the egg whites form glossy, stiff peaks, 5 to 8 minutes.

Transfer the egg whites to a clean bowl and add the egg yolks to the stand mixer bowl (there's no need to clean the bowl). Add the remaining ¾ cup (150 g) sugar and beat the egg yolks on high speed until they are thick, pale, and form thick ribbons when lifted with a spatula, 5 to 8 minutes. Then, add the dry ingredients and beat until fully incorporated, scraping the sides of the bowl as necessary (the mixture will be thick). Then, add the espresso mixture and beat until smooth.

Remove the bowl from the stand mixer and scrape the whisk clean with a rubber spatula. Next, add about one-third of the egg whites and gently fold them into the chocolate mixture until fully incorporated. Add the remaining egg whites and fold until just combined.

Spread the batter evenly on the prepared baking sheet with an offset spatula. Bake for 18 to 22 minutes or until the sponge cake is set. Remove from the oven and allow to cool until the cake is warm but able to be handled. The cake will sink a bit as it cools— this is normal.

When the cake is cool enough to handle, place a clean tea towel over the cake and invert it onto a clean surface. Peel off the parchment paper and then, using a fine-mesh strainer, dust the surface of the cake with a thin layer of cocoa powder to prevent it from sticking to the tea towel.

CONTINUES

DESSERTS | 225

MOCHA ROULADE WITH
HAZELNUT-MOCHA WHIPPED CREAM

FOR THE HAZELNUT PRALINE

Cooking spray

⅓ cup (67 g) sugar

1 tablespoon water

⅓ cup (45 g) hazelnuts, chopped

FOR THE HAZELNUT-MOCHA WHIPPED CREAM

½ cup (85 g) semisweet baking chocolate wafers

2 tablespoons instant espresso powder

1⅔ cups heavy cream

⅓ cup (70 g) powdered sugar + more for dusting (optional)

Pinch of salt

Next, starting from one of the shorter edges, roll the cake along with the tea towel until you reach the other end. Be sure to roll tightly in order to get a pretty roll, but be careful not roll so tightly so as to break the cake. Allow the cake to fully cool while rolled.

While the cake is cooling, make the filling. Start by making the praline. Prepare a clean baking sheet by spraying it liberally with cooking spray. In a clean saucepan, add the sugar and water and stir until the sugar has a sandy consistency. Heat the sugar over medium heat, stirring occasionally until it is completely melted. Once melted, continue cooking, stirring constantly until it becomes a deep caramel color.

Add the chopped hazelnuts and quickly stir to combine, then immediately spread onto the prepared baking sheet in a thin layer using an offset spatula. Allow to cool completely. Once cooled, break into small pieces, and add to a food processor. Process the praline until very finely chopped. Set aside.

To make the whipped cream, combine the chocolate and espresso powder together in a medium heatproof bowl. Then, heat ⅔ cup (160 ml) of the heavy cream in a small saucepan until it just begins to boil. Pour over the chocolate and allow it to sit for 5 minutes. After 5 minutes, whisk the mixture together until smooth and allow it to cool completely.

Once fully cooled, add the chocolate cream to the bowl of a stand mixer fitted with the whisk attachment. Add the remaining 1 cup (240 ml/120 g) cream along with the powdered sugar and salt. Beat the mixture on high speed until stiff peaks form, about 5 minutes. Be careful not to overmix. Fold in the hazelnut praline.

To assemble, carefully unroll the mocha cake and remove the tea towel. Evenly spread the whipped cream with an offset spatula along the surface of the cake. Then, roll the cake back up, starting at the same end that it was originally rolled. If desired, trim the cake ends and dust with powdered sugar for a cleaner appearance. Slice into 1-inch slices and serve. The roulade is best served fresh, but you may store leftovers in the refrigerator for up to 2 days and eat straight from the fridge—no need to temper this cake.

SUMMER

Peaches & Coconut Frangipane Tart

GFP | NF | SF

One of my fondest memories as a child is eating peaches with cream at my grandmother's house in the summer. The peaches were so juicy that they would drip down your arm, and the whipped cream was always "homemade." This tart is a grown-up version of this fond memory, featuring a marvelous coconut frangipane and a toasted coconut chip garnish.

SERVES 8 TO 10

FOR THE TART SHELL

½ cup (1 stick/115 g) butter, softened + more for greasing

⅓ cup (70 g) sugar

2 large egg yolks

¼ teaspoon vanilla bean paste or 1 teaspoon pure vanilla extract

1½ cups (180 g) all-purpose flour (see note, page 229)

¼ teaspoon salt

FOR THE COCONUT FRANGIPANE FILLING

½ cup + 2 tablespoons (1 stick + 2 tablespoons/250 g) butter, softened

⅓ cup (70 g) sugar + more for sprinkling

⅓ cup (40 g) coconut flour

¼ cup (30 g) sweetened coconut

1 egg

½ teaspoon vanilla bean paste or 2 teaspoons vanilla

¼ teaspoon salt

1 or 2 medium peaches

Start by making the tart base. Grease a 9-inch (23-cm) tart pan and set aside. Combine the butter and sugar together in a stand mixer fitted with the paddle attachment. Beat until light and fluffy, then add the egg yolks and vanilla. Mix to combine, then add the flour and salt and mix until the dough just roughly comes together. Form the dough into a flat disk, wrap in plastic wrap, and store in the refrigerator for at least 30 minutes.

Meanwhile, make the frangipane filling. Combine 2 sticks of butter and the sugar together in a stand mixer fitted with the paddle attachment. Beat the butter and sugar together until light and fluffy, 2 to 3 minutes, then add the remaining ingredients, except for the peaches, all at once and mix until combined. Set aside.

To prepare the peaches, cut them in half and remove the cores. Slice the peaches into ¼ inch (6.35 mm) slices, and set aside.

When the tart dough has chilled, remove it from the refrigerator. Preheat the oven to 350°F (180°C). Roll the tart dough into a 10-inch (25-cm) circle a bit more than ⅛-inch (3-mm) thick. Gently lift the tart dough over the prepared tart pan and press the dough into the pan, taking care to push the dough into the edges of the pan to prevent air bubbles. Use a knife to cut away the extra dough to make the rim of the tart neat.

Using an offset spatula, add the coconut frangipane filling in an even layer to the bottom of the tart shell. Arrange the peach slices on top of the frangipane closely together in a spiral pattern, starting from the center of the tart and working outward, filling as much space as possible without overlapping the peaches. Melt the remaining 2 tablespoons of butter and brush it over the peach slices. Dust with a thin layer of sugar, then place in the oven and bake for about 45 minutes, or until the frangipane is golden brown and puffy and the edges of the tart shell are golden brown. Allow to cool completely.

CONTINUES

DESSERTS | 227

PEACHES & COCONUT
FRANGIPANE TART

FOR GARNISH

1 cup (240 ml) heavy cream

2 tablespoons powdered sugar

¼ cup (15 g) toasted coconut flakes or chips

To garnish the tart, whip the cream with the powdered sugar until stiff peaks form. Slice the tart into 6 to 8 slices. Serve each slice with a big dollop of the whipped cream, then top with some toasted coconut flakes. The tart is best served the same day, but can be kept at room temperature overnight along with the coconut chips. The whipped cream should be stored in an airtight container in the refrigerator.

NOTE

To make this gluten free, substitute an equal amount of gluten-free flour for the all-purpose flour. Add ¾ teaspoon guar gum or ½ teaspoon xanthan gum if your gluten-free flour mixture does not already contain one of these ingredients.

SUMMER

Blueberry Lavender Cake with Cream Cheese Frosting

DFP | NF | SF

The delicate balance between blueberries, lavender, and lime in this recipe is as delicious as it is beautiful. The best blueberries to use are wild blueberries, as they are smaller, deeper in flavor, and won't sink in the cake. For an even more delightful cake, substitute huckleberries, which are smaller still and have a beautiful depth of flavor. If you're using regular fresh blueberries, be sure to chop them up into smaller pieces.

....

SERVES 8 TO 10

FOR THE CAKE

Butter or cooking spray, for greasing

1½ cups (330 g) sugar

1½ teaspoons lavender buds

¾ cup (1½ sticks/185 g) butter, softened

5 large eggs

1 cup (240 g) milk

2 teaspoons pure vanilla extract

2⅓ cups (293 g) flour

1 teaspoon salt

1½ cups (225 g) wild blueberries, huckleberries, or chopped blueberries + more for garnish (optional)

FOR THE CREAM CHEESE FROSTING

8 ounces (225 g) cream cheese

½ cup (1 stick/115 g) butter, softened

2 cups (230 g) powdered sugar

1 teaspoon pure vanilla extract

Pinch of salt

Lime zest, for garnish (optional)

Preheat the oven to 350°F (180°C). Grease with butter or cooking spray and flour the bottom and sides of two 9-inch (23-cm) round cake pans. Place the sugar and lavender buds in the bowl of a stand mixer. Using your hands, massage the lavender into the sugar until it is fragrant, about 30 seconds. Add the softened butter to the bowl, affix the paddle attachment and beat on medium speed for about 3 minutes, until light and fluffy.

Next, separate the egg yolks from the whites and reserve the whites for later. Add the yolks to the bowl and beat on high speed until the mixture is pale and fluffy. Add the milk and vanilla, a little at a time, until fully incorporated.

Next, add the flour and salt and fold in to combine. Transfer the mixture to another bowl and wash the bowl to the stand mixer thoroughly and dry it well. Add the egg whites to the clean mixer bowl and fit it with the whisk attachment. Beat the egg whites on medium speed until frothy, then increase the speed and whip the egg whites to stiff peaks.

Using a rubber spatula, gently fold one-third of the egg whites into the cake batter until no streaks remain. Then, gently fold in the remaining egg whites and the blueberries until mostly incorporated (some streaking is OK).

Divide the batter between the prepared cake pans and bake for about 35 minutes, or until a toothpick inserted in the center of the cake comes out clean. Cool the cakes in the pans for about 10 minutes before turning out onto a wire rack to cool completely.

Next, make the Cream Cheese Frosting. Add the cream cheese to the bowl of a stand mixer fitted with the paddle attachment. Beat the cream cheese on high speed, scraping down the sides of the bowl as needed, until it is very smooth, and no lumps remain. Add the softened butter and beat until smooth. Add the remaining ingredients and mix on medium-low speed until combined, scraping down the bowl as needed.

When the cakes are completely cooled, add a thin layer of cream cheese frosting to the top of one of the cakes. Add the second cake on top of the buttercream lining up the edges, then top the second layer with a generous amount of the buttercream. Leave the sides of the cake unfrosted. Use the back of a spoon to smooth the buttercream into a scalloped texture. If desired, garnish with more blueberries and some freshly grated lime zest.

SUMMER

Chevre Cheesecake with Fresh Berries

NF | SF

For a cheesecake that is creamy, perfectly tangy, and light enough to serve in the summer, look no further than this chevre cheesecake. While adding goat cheese may sound a bit unconventional, the balance and texture it provides is perfect, without a trace of that strong "goaty" flavor that you get from eating it raw. Because this cheesecake is very silky and custardy in texture when compared to a New York style–cheesecake, it's nice to enjoy it in the summer months with berries that are just bursting with juicy goodness. You can really enjoy this cheesecake year-round though, swapping out the berries for other seasonal fruits like cherries in the spring or citrus in the winter.

....

SERVES 8 TO 10

Butter or cooking spray, for greasing

10 ounces (285 g) Graham Crackers (page 217) or store-bought

3 tablespoons butter, melted

¼ cup (55 g) brown sugar

Pinch of salt

1 pound (450 g) fresh goat cheese

1 pound (450 g) cream cheese, softened

¾ cup (150 g) sugar

¾ cup (175 ml) heavy cream

6 large egg yolks

Zest and juice of 1 lemon

2 cups (280 g) berries, such as raspberries, tayberries, mulberries, blackberries, or strawberries

Preheat the oven to 350°F (180°C). Lightly grease a 9-inch (23-cm) springform pan with butter or cooking spray, and cover the outside of the pan with foil to prevent leakage.

Prepare the graham cracker crust. Using a food processor, pulse the graham crackers into fine crumbs. You can also put the crackers into a locking plastic bag and smash them with a rolling pin. Transfer the crumbs to a bowl and add the melted butter, brown sugar, and salt. Mix well until combined. The graham cracker crumbs should stick together when pressed.

Add the crust mixture to the bottom of the prepared springform pan and press the crust halfway up the sides of the sides of the pan and evenly over the bottom. Bake for 8 to 10 minutes, or until the crust is lightly browned. Remove from the oven and let cool for 10 to 15 minutes while you prepare the filling.

While the crust bakes, prepare the cheesecake filling. In the bowl of a stand mixer fitted with the paddle attachment, mix the goat cheese and cream cheese with the sugar until it is very smooth and soft, scraping down the edges and bottom of the bowl to ensure there are no lumps. In a separate bowl, add the cream, egg yolks, and lemon zest and whisk together until combined. With the mixer running, slowly pour the cream mixture into the goat cheese mixture in 3 additions, scraping down the bowl in between additions, until it is completely combined and there are no lumps.

Pour the cheesecake filling into cooled crust. Place the cheesecake in a casserole dish or a larger baking pan and fill the dish halfway with water. Bake the cheesecake for about an hour, until the edges have set, but the center still has a slight jiggle to it when shaken.

Remove the cheesecake from the oven and carefully remove it from the water bath. Check the foil to make sure no water has seeped into the cheesecake. Allow the cheesecake to cool to room temperature in the pan, then cover loosely with plastic wrap before placing in the fridge to chill, for at least 4 to 6 hours.

When you are ready to serve, slice the cake into 8 to 10 slices, making sure to get some berries with each slice. Serve directly from the refrigerator. Extra cheesecake can be covered with plastic wrap and keeps for 3 to 4 days in the fridge.

DESSERTS | 233

FALL | WINTER

Vanilla-Poached Apple Cake

V | DF | NF

One of the first signs of autumn in the Bay Area is the emergence of apples. Gravensteins and Pink Pearls are the first varieties to pop up in the market, reminding chefs and patrons alike that it's time to start thinking of the cooler days to come. I like to use a tart apple for this cake because of how well it balances the flavor of the vanilla beans. Gravensteins or Lady apples would be my first choices for local varieties of apples, but Granny Smith or Honeycrisp would also be wonderful options too. As an extra treat, serve this warm with a scoop of vanilla ice cream.

SERVES 8 TO 10

FOR THE POACHED APPLES

2¼ cups (500 ml) water

¾ cup (150 g) sugar

½ vanilla bean

1 large tart apple (about 8 ounces), peeled and diced small

FOR THE CAKE

Cooking spray

1¾ cups (220 g) all-purpose flour

1 cup (200 g) sugar

1 teaspoon baking soda

1 teaspoon salt

7 ounces (210 ml) soy milk

5 tablespoons (74 ml) olive oil

1 tablespoon apple cider vinegar

2 teaspoons pure vanilla extract

Begin by poaching the apples. Add the water and sugar to a saucepan. Slice the vanilla bean lengthwise with a small paring knife to expose the seeds and use your fingers to press the pod open the pod so that it lays flat. Use the side of the knife to scrape across the open pod and gather the vanilla seeds inside. Add the seeds and the pod to the pot with the sugar and water. Bring the mixture to a simmer, then add the apple pieces and simmer slowly until the apples are just tender, about 5 to 7 minutes. Strain the poaching liquid and reserve the apples for the cake.

Preheat the oven to 375°F (190°C). Lightly grease with cooking spray, and flour a 9-inch (23-cm) round cake pan. To make the cake, combine the flour, sugar, baking soda, and salt together in a bowl. In a separate bowl, combine the soy milk, olive oil, vinegar, and vanilla and whisk together until combined. Allow the mixture to sit for about 5 minutes so that the vinegar and soy milk mixture can "curdle." Then, add the flour mixture to the soy milk mixture and whisk to combine. Finally, using a rubber spatula, gently fold half of the poached apples into the batter.

Pour the batter into the prepared cake pan and smooth the top. Top the cake with the remaining poached apples and bake for about 25 to 30 minutes, until the cake springs back when touched in the middle or a toothpick comes out clean. Allow the cake to completely cool before slicing and serving. The cake keeps for up to 2 days at room temperature when wrapped in plastic wrap.

SPRING

Vegan Lemon Mousse with Cherry Compote

V | GF | DF | NF

For the longest time, we have struggled with finding a vegan mousse recipe that doesn't include chocolate. Chocolate has a lot of structure to it, plus tons of bold flavor, that allows it to work well with silken tofu to make a creamy, luscious mousse. Unfortunately, white chocolate isn't usually vegan, and the vegan varieties that we've seen are overly processed and low quality. I had a "eureka!" moment one day when I realized that the main ingredient in chocolate that gives it that lovely texture is cocoa butter, which is widely available online and in health food stores. We tried it out as a base for mousses, and it works like a charm! This lemon version is our absolute favorite and is terrific with the bright cherry compote.

SERVES 4

FOR THE MOUSSE

6 ounces (170 g) food-grade cocoa butter

1¾ tablespoons (25 g) coconut oil

1 block (8 ounces) silken tofu

½ cup (150 g) agave nectar

¼ cup (55 g) soy milk

Zest and juice of 1 lemon

¼ teaspoon apple cider vinegar

1 teaspoon pure vanilla extract

1 teaspoon salt

FOR THE CHERRY COMPOTE

2 cups (300 g) pitted red or black cherries, such as Bing

⅔ cup (70 g) sugar

Zest and juice of 1 lemon

1 teaspoon cornstarch

Melt the cocoa butter and coconut oil together over simmering water in a double boiler. While the cocoa butter melts, add the remaining ingredients to a blender pitcher. You may also place everything in a bowl and use an immersion blender. Once the cocoa butter is completely melted, add the mixture to the blender pitcher or bowl and blend until smooth. The mixture should be quite loose. Split the mousse among into four 1 cup (240 ml) ramekins or jars and cover with plastic wrap. Refrigerate the mousse overnight until firm.

To make the compote, combine the pitted cherries, sugar, lemon zest and juice, and cornstarch in a small saucepan. Bring the mixture to a boil slowly over medium-low heat. The cherries should release their juices and start to break down. Continue cooking until the cherry juice has thickened slightly and appears glossy. Remove from the heat and allow to cool completely. Store in the refrigerator overnight.

The following day when the lemon mousse has set, top each ramekin with the cherry compote, and serve. This mousse is also delicious with the addition of crushed Graham Crackers (page 217).

DESSERTS | 237

SPRING | SUMMER | FALL | WINTER

Makrut Lime Granita

V | GF | DF | NF | SF

The Italian cousin of a snow cone, granita is a delicious and easy dessert that only takes a blender, fork, and patience. While great to eat on its own, I also like using granita on the menu in creative ways, like a topping for ice cream or sorbet for a nice texture variation, or even putting it over savory dishes like heirloom tomato salads for a cold pop of sweetness. This recipe utilizes the leaves of the makrut lime, a funky little citrus whose fruit zest and floral leaves are often used in Thai cooking. I'd suggest trying this granita on top of the Coconut Tapioca (page 239) for a wonderful summer treat.

....

SERVES 2 TO 4

1⅔ cups (400 ml) water

¼ cup (60 ml) fresh lime juice

¾ cup (150 g) sugar

¼ cup packed (8 g) makrut lime leaves

Pinch of salt

Combine all the ingredients in a blender pitcher and blend for at least 2 minutes. The mixture should warm up a little and darken in color.

Once blended, strain the mixture through a fine-mesh sieve into a clean metal baking pan. The wider the pan the better for faster freezing. Place the granita in the freezer and freeze for 1 hour.

After an hour, remove the granita from the freezer and scrape with the tines of a fork to break up the freezing crystals. Once the mixture has been fully broken up and looks like a slushy, return it to the freezer. Repeat this process every hour until the granita has a snow-cone-like texture, 2 to 4 hours, depending on your freezer. hours.

Enjoy the granita immediately or keep it frozen until ready to eat. If you're not eating immediately, cover the container with plastic or an airtight lid. You will have to break the ice crystals up again and the texture will not be quite as smooth.

SPRING | SUMMER | FALL | WINTER

Coconut Tapioca

V | GF | DF | NF | SF

We love this tapioca pudding because it's light, creamy, and naturally vegan and gluten free. It pairs well with fruits from all seasons, such as oranges, strawberries, kiwi, or persimmons, but for an extra-special summery treat, top this with the Makrut Lime Granita (page 238) for a delightful variance in both texture and temperature.

SERVES 4

6 cups (1.5 l) water

½ cup small pearl tapioca

One 14-ounce (400-g) can coconut milk

¼ cup (50 g) sugar

½ teaspoon pure vanilla extract

½ teaspoon salt

Sliced seasonal fruits, such as oranges, strawberries, kiwi, or persimmons, for serving

Add the water to a saucepan and bring to a boil over medium-high heat. Add the tapioca and whisk to prevent the pearls from sticking together. Reduce to a strong simmer and cook the tapioca, stirring occasionally, until it is mostly translucent. It is OK if some of the pearls have a white spot at the center, but the majority of the pearls should be mostly clear. Strain the tapioca through a fine-mesh sieve and add back to the pot.

Add the coconut milk, sugar, vanilla, and salt to the saucepan and bring to a simmer. Cook until the mixture thickens, about 5 minutes. Remove from the heat and transfer to a bowl set over an ice bath to cool completely.

Once cool, serve with seasonal fruits of your choice.

SPRING

Strawberry Rhubarb Squares

NF | SF

Somewhere between a lemon square and a custard tart, these strawberry rhubarb bars are both custardy and buttery—the ideal bar for the spring, if you ask me. Rhubarb is actually the first sign of spring in "pastry land," as we like to call it. We scour our farm lists to find rhubarb, knowing that once we find it, it's only a matter of time before strawberries, apricots, and cherries follow. The classic combination of strawberries and rhubarb is one that we look forward to every year.

....

YIELDS 15 BARS

FOR THE CRUST

1 cup (2 sticks/230 g) cold butter + more for greasing

2¼ cups (270 g) all-purpose flour

¼ cup (50 g) sugar

¼ teaspoon salt

FOR THE FILLING

½ cup (120 ml) buttermilk

1 cup (200 g) sugar

¼ cup (55 g) brown sugar

4 large eggs

Zest and juice of 1 lemon

1 tablespoon pure vanilla extract

½ cup (60 g) all-purpose flour

½ teaspoon salt

3 cups (510 g) small diced strawberries

1 cup (130 g) small diced rhubarb

Preheat the oven to 350°F (180°C). Cut each stick of butter into 8 equal pieces and place in the bowl of a stand mixer fitted with the paddle attachment. Add the flour, sugar, and salt and mix until the butter is broken up into pea-sized lumps and the mixture sticks together when pressed.

Press the dough into the bottom of a greased 9- by 13-inch (23- by 33-cm) baking dish and bake in the oven until the edges begin to turn golden brown and the top of the crust is no longer shiny, about 7 minutes. Remove from the oven and set aside.

While the crust is baking, make the filling. Combine the buttermilk, sugars, eggs, lemon zest, lemon juice, and vanilla together in a bowl. Whisk until smooth, then whisk in the flour and salt. Fold in the strawberries and rhubarb.

Once the crust is baked, add the filling on top of the crust and return to the oven for another 20 to 25 minutes, until the custard topping has set and is still slightly soft in the center.

Remove from the heat and allow to cool completely before slicing. The bars will keep at room temperature in an airtight container for up to 3 days.

SUMMER | FALL

Fig Preserves Tart with Pistachio Crust

VP | GFP | DFP | SF

Here, a salty, nutty pistachio crust combines with fresh fig jam to create a tart perfect for fall. With notes of vanilla and orange, it's ideal for the final days of summer. Serve with Chantilly cream mixed with a touch of orange zest for an extra-special treat.

....

SERVES 4

FOR THE PISTACHIO CRUST

8 ounces (about 2 cups/227 g) raw shelled pistachios

¼ cup (30 g) flour

1 teaspoon vanilla extract

¼ teaspoon salt

6 tablespoons (85 g) melted butter

⅓ cup (70 g) sugar

FOR THE FIG PRESERVE FILLING

4 cups (330 g) fresh figs, divided (2 cups for filling, 2 cups for garnish)

⅔ cup (140 g) sugar

½ vanilla bean

Pinch salt

¾ cup (6 fl oz) water

Zest and juice of ½ orange

Preheat the oven to 350F. To make the crust, in a food processor, pulse the pistachios until very finely chopped, but do not over process into a paste. Add the chopped pistachios to a bowl and add the remaining crust ingredients and mix together until the crust holds together when pressed.

Transfer the mixture to a 9-inch tart pan. Press the mixture evenly into the sides and bottom of the pan. Bake the crust for about 7 minutes, until the pistachios begin to show a hint of color. Remove from the oven and set aside to cool.

Next, make the filling. Combine 2 cups of the figs and the remaining filling ingredients together in a saucepan. Bring to a simmer over medium heat, and cook slowly for about 20 to 25 minutes, until the liquid thickens slightly and is a dark, rich purple color. Purée the preserve, vanilla bean included, with an immersion blender until smooth.

Pour the hot fig preserves on the prepared crust and return to the oven on the bottom rack for about 25 minutes, until the preserves have set and the crust is a golden brown.

Remove from the oven and allow to completely cool. Quarter the remaining figs and garnish the tart with them in an even layer, starting from the center and working your way out to the crust.

The tart is best served fresh, but will keep in the refrigerator for up to 2 days.

NOTE

To make this gluten free, add ⅓ cup (40 g) gluten-free flour in crust + ¼ teaspoon xanthan gum if the 1:1 flour mix does not already have it.

FALL | WINTER

Almond Cardamom Persimmon Pudding

GFP | SF

Persimmon pudding is less a pudding as it is a rich, moist cake. It's also one of the most deliciou treats of autumn. I look forward to this cake every year, when the markets are brimming with end-of-summer fruits and vegetables, and hachiya persimmons are displayed proudly in the market for the first time since last autumn. Hachiya persimmons, in particular, are one of fall's delicacies, and if you are patient enough to ripen them well, you're rewarded with a luscious jammy pulp that is as delicious in this cake as it is to scoop out and eat with a spoon. In this version, I've traded the traditional cinnamon for cardamom and ginger, which makes for a lovely pair with the almond flour.

SERVES 9

Butter, for greasing

1½ cups (360 g) very ripe hachiya persimmon pulp

2 large eggs

½ cup (110 g) granulated sugar

¼ cup (55 g) brown sugar

¾ cup (185 g) whole milk

2 tablespoons butter, melted

1 teaspoon pure vanilla extract

½ teaspoon almond extract (optional)

1 cup (90 g) almond flour

1 cup (120 g) all-purpose flour (see note)

1½ teaspoons baking powder

½ teaspoon baking soda

¾ teaspoon freshly ground cardamom seeds

½ teaspoon ground ginger

½ teaspoon salt

Preheat the oven to 325˚F (160° C). Grease with butter or cooking spray, an 8-inch (20-cm) square baking pan and set aside. In a large bowl, combine the persimmon pulp, eggs, both sugars, milk, butter, and extracts together. For the smoothest texture, blend together using an immersion blender. Otherwise, whisk together until combined. Mix the dry ingredients together in a separate bowl and whisk to evenly distribute the spices. Add the dry ingredients to the wet ingredients and mix until just combined. The batter should be on the thinner side.

Pour the batter into the prepared baking pan and bake for 40 to 55 minutes, until the center has set, and the edges of the pudding are golden brown. The cake will rise in the oven and then deflate when cool. Serve warm with vanilla ice cream for a real treat. Store extra cake in the refrigerator for up to 3 to 4 days.

NOTE

To make this gluten free, substitute the all-purpose flour with an all-purpose gluten-free alternative, such as Bob's Red Mill, plus ¼ teaspoon xanthan gum if your gluten-free flour does not already have it mixed in. Be sure to use an all-purpose flour substitute, because using 100% almond flour creates a texture that is not ideal.

Acknowledgments

It takes a village to write a book such as *Seasons of Greens*, and I am incredibly grateful to all those who have supported this journey. I feel privileged to share a new Greens cookbook with the world after 20+ years, and I couldn't have done it without the help of the many folks who share my passion.

The kitchen team at Greens is a buzzing hive of energy and enthusiasm, and their hard work every day inspires me to continue creating and pushing the boundaries of vegetarian cuisine. Thank you to each and every one of you who make my job the very best. An extra-special thank-you to the sous chef team: Sergio Galdamez who not only drives our team toward success, but was also instrumental in helping me to test the recipes in this book, Nicole Edwards who leads the kitchen as my right hand, and Mariano Osario who takes on the vigor of dinner service with grace. Bri Walter, our pastry chef, is a force of nature whose understanding of flavor is sensational and inspirational, and her willingness to jump into any project, including testing a few of the pastry recipes in this book, is greatly appreciated.

A special thanks to the directors of Greens who are the driving force behind the entire restaurant operation. Seth Corr who runs the beverage program at Greens, embracing our ethos of "farmers first" to create a stellar wine list, seasonal cocktails, and an all-new non-alcoholic menu that reflects our Zen values. Gloria Elias who runs our events program, planning immaculate experiences for all those who celebrate with us. Clare Nisbett who directs our service, embodying generosity, and hospitality in all that she does. Thanks also to Natalie Sergeeva, Isabella Dito, Muna Munit, Ted Verdi, and the entire front of house staff.

Carmita Falcon Santana is the heart and soul of Greens and has been for nearly 20 years. Her selfless acts of love and kindness for Greens are why we have a functional space and a cohesive team. We are incredibly lucky to have Carmita as the "mom" of Greens.

Speaking of moms, I of course owe an enormous thank-you to my mom, Nadine, who raised me in a garden bed and taught me to love traditions and subsequently the seasons. She is the most important woman in my life,

and I would not be the same woman today without her unyielding support. Thank you to my other mom, my mother-in-law, Edie, who is my biggest cheerleader and my number one confidant for all that I do. My grandmothers, Josephine and Betty, taught me to love through food, and for that I am eternally grateful, and I hope they continue to watch over me along with my grandpas Bob and George.

My dad is the fun one, and I owe my energetic spirit and can-do attitude to him. Thanks, Dad! My little brother Bobby is the ultimate foodie and makes cooking fun. My husband Jesse has been there for me through thick and thin over the last near decade and I owe so much to him. I couldn't have asked for a better life partner. My entire family is so large it would take a whole book to name them all, but I am so lucky to have grown up in a great big family that loves one another and really loves food.

To our farmers and makers, thank you for your commitment to the land and to our bellies. I am ever inspired by your work. Eleana Hsu and Kevin Gondo, your friendship means the world to me and your hard work at Shared Cultures is awe-inspiring, and your misos make the food world a better place.

Deepest bows to the Everyday board of directors who oversee Greens, and who instill the spirit of the Zen Center in our daily lives. Thank you to Annie Somerville, who taught me so much about Greens and vegetables, especially to hold onto summer produce as long as possible. Min Kim, my mentor, has believed in me from the very beginning and helped create a brighter future for Greens.

Finally, I would like to thank those who helped bring this book to life. My agent, Michele Crim, for her expertise, unwavering support, and trust in me as a new author. Edward Ash-Milby, my editor, for his mountain of support and encouragement throughout this entire process, and for producing such a magnificent book. Thank you to Erin Scott, my photographer, and Lillian Kang, food stylist, for the mouthwatering representations of my recipes. Thanks also to Olga Katsnelson and the Postcard PR team for promoting my work. I cannot thank the entire team at Weldon Owen enough for their tireless efforts to make my dream a reality.

Index

A

agave nectar, 19
aged balsamic, 16
Aioli, 35–36
alliums, 35–36
all-purpose oil, 15
Almond Cardamom Persimmon Pudding, 243
almonds, 214–215
Aloo Saag Pot Pie, 209
appetizers, 60–83
apples, 96, 234–235
apricot preserves, 220–221
Arancini, 74–75
arrabiata
    Arrabiata Roasted Cherry Tomato Sauce, 59
    Stewed Romano Beans in Arrabiata, 160–161
artichokes, 64
    Couscous & Baby Artichoke Salad, 102–103
    Fried Baby Artichokes, 62–63
asiago cheese, 74–75
Asian vegetable stock, 39
asparagus
    Asparagus with Cannellini Beans, Creamy Tarragon Vinaigrette & Pickled Mustard Seeds, 170–717
    Lemongrass Tofu & Asparagus Stir-Fry, 186
"Au Poivre," 181
autumn recipes. See fall recipes
Autumn Vegetable Jambalaya, 182
avocados
    Avocado & Citrus Salad with Chimichurri, 98–100
    Green Goddess Hummus, 44

B

Baby Lettuces with Snap Peas & Extra-Herby Ranch, 97
baby potatoes, 101
baklava, 222–223
balsamic vinegar, 16, 68–69
barley, 150–151
Basic Cut Pasta, 134
Basic Flaky Pastry, 139
beans
    Asparagus with Cannellini Beans, Creamy Tarragon Vinaigrette & Pickled Mustard Seeds, 170–717

Berebere Spiced Lentils, 172
Black Lentil Mulligatawny, 111
cooking procedures for, 22
Escarole & Fagioli Pasta, 131
Fava Bean & Green Garlic Fattoush, 90
Gigante Beans with Mint Pesto & Barley, 150–151
Grilled Baby Fava Beans, 66
Grits with Creamy Creole-Style Mushrooms, 206–207
Mayocoba Beans with Urfa Biber, 167
pantry staples, 19
Pappardelle with Peperonata & Shell Beans, 135
Smashed Cannellini Bean Toasts, 70
Stewed Romano Beans in Arrabiata, 160–161
Summer's Bounty Salad, 86–87
Turmeric Chickpea Soup, 106
using when fresh, 86
béchamel, 190–191, 199
beets, 98, 148–149
Berebere Spiced Lentils, 172
berries
    Blueberry Lavender Cake with Cream Cheese Frosting, 230–231
    Chevre Cheesecake with Fresh Berries, 232–233
    huckleberries, 230
    Mara des Bois strawberries, 129
    Strawberry Rhubarb Squares, 240–241
    Strawberry Tatsoi Salad, 94–95
biryani, 200–201
Black Lentil Mulligatawny, 111
black walnuts, 222–223, 224
black-eyed peas, 207
Blistered Shishito Peppers, 166
Blueberry Lavender Cake with Cream Cheese Frosting, 230–231
boxed wine, 16
Brait, Andrew, 220
bread crumbs, 16
brine, for pickles, 32
broccoli, 190–191
brochettes, 202–203
broth, 40, 182
brown butter, 128
brown rice, 25
brown sugar buttercream, 220–221

Brussels sprouts, 144
    Brussels Sprouts, Caramelized Shallot & Taleggio Galette, 145
    Steamed Brussels Sprouts with "Cali" Kosho, 168–169
burrata
    Burrata Toasts with Balsamic Cherries, 68–69
    Fettuccine with Herb-Marinated Tomatoes & Burrata, 130
butter, 15
    Basic Flaky Pastry, 139
    compound butters, 32–33
    Honeynut Squash Gnocchi with Brown Butter, 128
    keeping stocked, 19
butterbeans, 70
buttercream, 220–221
Butternut Squash Soup, 115

C

cabbage
    Ethiopian Cabbage & Potato Puffs, 143–144
    Grilled Cabbage with Makrut Lime Sambal, 152
    Quick Kimchi, 29
    Roasted Cabbage & Farro Salad, 91
cakes
    Blueberry Lavender Cake with Cream Cheese Frosting, 230–231
    Chevre Cheesecake with Fresh Berries, 232–233
    Mocha Roulade with Hazelnut-Mocha Whipped Cream, 225–226
    Raspberry–White Chocolate Pound Cake, 218–219
    Rye Cake with Apricot Preserves, 220–221
    Vanilla-Poached Apple Cake, 234–235
Calabrian chile paste, 59, 153
Cali kosho, 168–169
California artichokes, 103
canned chiles, 19
cannellini beans, 70, 150–151
capers, 19
Caramelized Mushroom & Onion Pasta, 126–127
cardamom, 242
Carolina Gold rice, 182

carrot hummus, 48

cashew cream, 35–36, 159

cassava, 148

cauliflower, 132–133

Celery & Peanut Noodle Salad, 92–93

celery root, 200

Chanterelle Shumai with Mirin Sauce, 79–81

cheese, 19
- Blueberry Lavender Cake with Cream Cheese Frosting, 230–231
- Brussels Sprouts, Caramelized Shallot & Taleggio Galette, 145
- Butternut Squash Soup, 115
- Chevre Cheesecake with Fresh Berries, 232–233
- Corn & Asiago Arancini, 74–75
- Macadamia Nut Ricotta, 36
- Manicotti with Broccoli & Béchamel, 190–191
- Pierogi with Peas & Feta, 136–138
- Saffron Goat Cheese Risotto, 204–205
- Spinach & Ricotta Dumplings, 124–125
- Taleggio, 91
- Whipped Garlic Ricotta, 52

Chef Somerville, 10

cherries
- Burrata Toasts with Balsamic Cherries, 68–69
- Vegan Lemon Mousse with Cherry Compote, 236–237

Cherry Bomb chiles, 67

chestnuts, 183

Chevre Cheesecake with Fresh Berries, 232–233

chickpeas, 106

chile powder, 167

chiles
- Calabrian chile paste, 59, 153
- Cherry Bomb chiles, 67
- Chiles Rellenos, 192–193
- Chipotle & Lime Grilled Tofu, 187
- Corn & Poblano Empanadas, 140–142
- dried and canned, 19
- Goat Cheese–Stuffed Cherry Bomb Chiles, 67
- Mayocoba Beans with Urfa Biber, 167
- Sautéed Pea Tendrils with Calabrian Chile, 153

Slow Roasted Chile-Orange Pecans, 65

chili crisp, 35

Chimichurri, 47, 98–100

Chipotle & Lime Grilled Tofu, 187

chocolate, 218–219

chowder, 110

Cilantro-Lime Crema, 36

citrus juice, 26

cocoa butter, 237

coconuts
- Coconut Tapioca, 239
- milk of, 19
- Peaches & Coconut Cream Pie, 227–229

collard greens, 104–105

compote, 236–237

compound butters, 32–33

confit, garlic, 33

cookies
- Ginger Parsnip Oatmeal Cookies Graham Crackers, 216
- Sesame–Brown Sugar Cookies, 212–213

cooking methods/procedures, 22–26

cooking wine, 16

Coral Lentil Dal, 112–113

corn
- Corn & Asiago Arancini, 74–75
- Corn & Poblano Empanadas, 140–142
- Creamy Corn Chowder, 110
- Grilled Peppers with Herby Corn Salsa, 162–163
- Pozole Verde, 118
- vegetable stock, 39

couscous
- cooking methods for, 25
- Couscous & Baby Artichoke Salad, 102–103
- Stuffed Eggplants with Couscous, 208

crackers, 217

Cranberry Pistachio Almond Shortbread, 214–215

cream cheese, 115, 230–231

creams, 35–36

Creamy Corn Chowder, 110

Creamy Garlic & Herb Polenta, 173

Creamy Sesame Vinaigrette, 94–95

Creamy Tarragon Vinaigrette, 170–717

Creole Broth, 40, 182, 206–207

Creole Pumpkin & Collard Greens Soup, 104–105

cucumbers, 121

curry, 112, 194–195

D

dairy free, acronym for, 26

dal, 112–113

deep fryers, 34

desserts, 212–243

Diamond Crystal Kosher Salt, 15–16

dill, 172–173

doughs, 123

dried chiles, 19

dry wine, 16

dumplings, 79–81, 124–125

E

edamame, 92

eggplant
- Eggplant Caponata, 49
- Roasted Eggplant & Pepper Soup, 107
- Stuffed Eggplants with Couscous, 208

eggs, 19, 134

empanadas, 140–142

Escarole & Fagioli Pasta, 131

Escarole & Potato Salad, 101

espresso-laden roulade, 225

Ethiopian Cabbage & Potato Puffs, 143–144

Ethiopian spiced red lentils, 172

Extra-Herby Ranch, 97

extra-virgin olive oil, 15

F

fall recipes
- Almond Cardamom Persimmon Pudding, 242
- Aloo Saag Pot Pie, 209
- Autumn Vegetable Jambalaya, 182
- Basic Cut Pasta, 134
- Basic Flaky Pastry, 139
- Berebere Spiced Lentils, 172
- Black Lentil Mulligatawny, 111
- Blistered Shishito Peppers, 166
- Brussels Sprouts, Caramelized Shallot & Taleggio Galette, 145
- Butternut Squash Soup, 115

247

Caramelized Mushroom & Onion Pasta, 126–127
Celery & Peanut Noodle Salad, 92–93
Chanterelle Shumai with Mirin Sauce, 79–81
Chimichurri, 47
Chipotle & Lime Grilled Tofu, 187
Coconut Tapioca, 239
Coral Lentil Dal, 112–113
Cranberry Pistachio Almond Shortbread, 214–215
Creamy Corn Chowder, 110
Creamy Garlic & Herb Polenta, 173
Creole Pumpkin & Collard Greens Soup, 104–105
Eggplant Caponata, 49
Escarole & Fagioli Pasta, 131
Escarole & Potato Salad, 101
Ethiopian Cabbage & Potato Puffs, 143–144
Fig Preserves Tart with Tapioca Crust, 242
Fried Baby Artichokes, 62–63
Gigante Beans With Mint Pesto & Barley, 150–151
Ginger Parsnip Oatmeal Cookies Graham Crackers, 216
Graham Crackers, 217
Grilled Cabbage with Makrut Lime Sambal, 152
Grilled Romesco Sauce, 58
Grilled Sweet Potatoes with Tahini Cashew Cream, 159
Grits with Creamy Creole-Style Mushrooms, 206–207
Honeynut Squash Gnocchi with Brown Butter, 128
Kale & Apple Salad, 96
Linguine with Cauliflower & Chard, 132–133
Makrut Lime Granita, 238
Maple Black Walnut Baklava, 222–223
Masala Roasted Winter Squash, 164–165
Mayocoba Beans with Urfa Biber, 167
Mint Pesto, 54–55
Mocha Roulade with Hazelnut-Mocha Whipped Cream, 225–226

Peanut Hoisin Sauce, 57
Portobello Tamarind Soup, 114
Roasted Cabbage & Farro Salad, 91
Roasted Carrot Hummus, 48
Roasted Eggplant & Pepper Soup, 107
Roasted Pepper Panzanella, 88–89
Roasted Potatoes with Dill & Garlic, 172–173
Root Vegetable Biryani, 200–201
Sesame–Brown Sugar Cookies, 212–213
Shepherd's Pie, 188–189
Slow Roasted Chile-Orange Pecans, 65
Smashed Cannellini Bean Toasts, 70
Souvlaki-Style Tofu Brochettes, 202–203
Stuffed Eggplants with Couscous, 208
Sunchoke Koftas in Curry, 194–195
Sun-dried Tomato Harissa, 53
Sweet Potato Summer Rolls with Peanut Hoisin Sauce, 76–78
Turmeric Chickpea Soup, 106
Vanilla-Poached Apple Cake, 234–235
Whipped Garlic Ricotta, 52
Wild Mushrooms "Au Poivre," 181
Wild Rice–Stuffed Portobellos, 183
Yuca "Fries" with Beet Slaw, 148–149
farro, 25, 91
fats, 15
fattoush, 90
fava beans
Fava Bean & Green Garlic Fattoush, 90
Grilled Baby Fava Beans, 66
fazool, 131
fennel, 205
feta cheese, 136–138
Fettuccine with Herb-Marinated Tomatoes & Burrata, 130
Fig Preserves Tart with Tapioca Crust, 242
filo rolls, 82

flour, 19
fork-tender, 48
Frantoi Cutrera tomatoes, 53
fresh beans, 86
Fried Baby Artichokes, 62–63
fried bread salad, 90
fries, 148–149
frosting, 220–221, 230–231
fruit, 120–121
fryers, 34
frying oil, 15
Full Belly Farm, 220

G

galette, 145
garlic
confit, 33
Creamy Garlic & Herb Polenta, 173
Roasted Potatoes with Dill & Garlic, 172–173
Whipped Garlic Ricotta, 52
gazpacho, 120–121
Ginger Parsnip Oatmeal Cookies Graham Crackers, 216
gluten-free recipes
acronym for, 26
Almond Cardamom Persimmon Pudding, 243
Coconut Tapioca, 239
Fig Preserves Tart with Tapioca Crust, 242
Peaches & Coconut Cream Pie, 227–229
gluten-free flour, 19
gnocchi, 128
goat cheese
Chevre Cheesecake with Fresh Berries, 233
Goat Cheese–Stuffed Cherry Bomb Chiles, 67
Nettle & Goat Cheese Filo Rolls, 82
Saffron Goat Cheese Risotto, 204–205
gochujang, 29
golden balsamic, 16
Graham Crackers, 217
grains, 25
granita, 238
Gratin Provençal, 198–199
gratins, 198–199

Gravensteins apples, 234
Green Dragon Temple. *See* Green
  Gulch Farm
green garlic, 44, 46, 90
Green Goddess Hummus, 44–45
Green Gulch apples, 96
Green Gulch Farm, 154–157
green olives, 132
Green Restaurant, 10–13
griddle cakes, 71
Grilled Baby Fava Beans, 66
Grilled Cabbage with Makrut Lime
  Sambal, 152
Grilled Peppers with Herby Corn
  Salsa, 162–163
Grilled Romesco Sauce, 58
Grilled Sweet Potatoes with Tahini
  Cashew Cream, 159
Grilled Zucchini with Mint Pesto, 158
Grits with Creamy Creole-Style
  Mushrooms, 206–207
Gypsy pepper, 89

H

hachiya persimmons, 243
harissa, 53
hazelnuts, 225–226
Heirloom Tomato & Stone Fruit
  Gazpacho, 120–121
Heller, Emila, 155
herb butter, 33
hoe cakes, 71–73
hoisin sauce, 57, 76–78
honey, 19
honey-dijon vinaigrette, 86
Honeynut Squash Gnocchi
  with Brown Butter, 128
huckleberries, 230
hummus, 44–45, 48

I

instant couscous, 25

J

Jambalaya, 182
jarred capers, 19
johnny cakes, 71–73
juicing, 26
Juliet tomatoes, 59

K

Kale & Apple Salad, 96
kimchi
    Kimchi Noodle Soup, 116–117
    Quick Kimchi, 28–29
koftas, 194–195
kosher salt, 15–16

L

Lady apples, 234
lavender, 230–231
Legacy Business Registry of
  San Francisco, 12
lemon butter, 33
Lemon Chive Aioli, 36
Lemongrass Tofu & Asparagus
  Stir-Fries, 186
lentils
    Aloo Saag Pot Pie, 209
    Berebere Spiced Lentils, 172
    Black Lentil Mulligatawny, 111
    cooking procedures for, 22
    Coral Lentil Dal, 112–113
    pantry staples, 19
lettuce, 97
limes
    Chipotle & Lime Grilled Tofu, 187
    Grilled Cabbage with Makrut
      Lime Sambal, 152
    Makrut Lime Granita, 238
Linguine with Cauliflower & Chard,
  132–133

M

Macadamia Nut Ricotta, 36
makrut lime
    Grilled Cabbage with Makrut
      Lime Sambal, 152
    Makrut Lime Granita, 238
Maldon sea salt, 16
Manicotti with Broccoli & Béchamel,
  190–191
Maple Black Walnut Baklava,
  222–223
Mara des Bois strawberries, 129
Marshall's honey, 217
Masala Roasted Winter Squash,
  164–165
Matthiasson Winery, 220
Mayocoba Beans with Urfa Biber, 167
microclimates, 129

milk, 19. *See also* coconuts, milk of
minestrone, 108–109
Mint Pesto
    Gigante Beans With Mint Pesto &
      Barley, 150–151
    Grilled Zucchini with Mint Pesto,
      158
    Mint Pesto, 54–55
mirin sauce, 79–81
misir wat, 172
miso, 16
    Aioli, 35
    butter, 33
    Caramelized Mushroom & Onion
      Pasta, 126–127
    in kimchi, 29
    in vegan Aioli, 36
Mocha Roulade with Hazelnut-
  Mocha Whipped Cream, 225–226
Moussaka, 198–199
mousse, 236–237
muhammar, 56
mulligatawny, 111
mushrooms, 180
    Caramelized Mushroom & Onion
      Pasta, 126–127
    Grits with Creamy Creole-Style
      Mushrooms, 206–207
    Portobello Tamarind Soup, 114
    sauces, 199
    Wild Mushrooms "Au Poivre," 181
    Wild Rice–Stuffed Portobellos,
      183
mustard seeds, pickled, 29, 170–717

N

Nettle & Goat Cheese Filo Rolls, 82
nettles, 82–83
new potatoes, 101
nut free, acronym for, 26
nuts, 25

O

oatmeal cookies, 216
oil, for frying, 15
olive oil, 15
olives, 19, 132
onions, 126–127
oranges, 65

P

panko bread crumbs, 16
pantries, 15–19
panzanella, 88–89
Pappardelle with Peperonata & Shell Beans, 135
parsnips, 216
pasta
  Basic Cut Pasta, 134
  Caramelized Mushroom & Onion Pasta, 126–127
  Celery & Peanut Noodle Salad, 92–93
  dry, cooking, 19
  Escarole & Fagioli Pasta, 131
  Fettuccine with Herb-Marinated Tomatoes & Burrata, 130
  Kimchi Noodle Soup, 116–117
  Linguine with Cauliflower & Chard, 132–133
  Manicotti with Broccoli & Béchamel, 190–191
  Pappardelle with Peperonata & Shell Beans, 135
pastry, 139
pea tendrils, 153
Peaches & Coconut Cream Pie, 227–229
Peanut Hoisin Sauce, 57, 76–78
peanuts, 92–93
peas, 207
  Baby Lettuces with Snap Peas & Extra-Herby Ranch, 97
  Pierogi with Peas & Feta, 136–138
pecans, 65, 96
Peperonata, 50–51, 135
peppers, 50
  Blistered Shishito Peppers, 166
  broiling, 58
  Chiles Rellenos, 192–193
  Goat Cheese–Stuffed Cherry Bomb Chiles, 59
  Grilled Peppers with Herby Corn Salsa, 162–163
  Pappardelle with Peperonata & Shell Beans, 135
  Peperonata, 50–51
  Roasted Eggplant & Pepper Soup, 107
  Roasted Pepper Panzanella, 88–89
  roasting and peeling, 26

persimmon, 242
pesto
  Gigante Beans With Mint Pesto & Barley, 150–151
  Grilled Zucchini with Mint Pesto, 158
  Mint Pesto, 54–55, 150–151, 158
piccata, 178–179
pickled mustard seeds, 29
pickles, 32
pie, 227–229
Pierogi with Peas & Feta, 136–138
pistachio, 214–215, 242
plant protein, 15
plant-based milks, 19, 152, 209
poblano chiles, 140–142, 192–193
polenta, 173
Porcini Jus stock, 39–40
Portobello Tamarind Soup, 114
portobellos, 183
pot pie, 209
potatoes
  Escarole & Potato Salad, 101
  Ethiopian Cabbage & Potato Puffs, 143–144
  Grilled Sweet Potatoes with Tahini Cashew Cream, 159
  Roasted Potatoes with Dill & Garlic, 172–173
  Shepherd's Pie, 188–189
  Sweet Potato Summer Rolls with Peanut Hoisin Sauce, 76–78
pound cake, 218–219
Pozole Verde, 118–119
praline, hazelnut, 226
proteins, 15
pudding, 242
puff pastry, 139
pumpkins, 104–105, 165
puréeing, 26

Q

Quick Kimchi, 28–41
quinoa, 25

R

raisins, 132
ramen noodles, 117
ranch dressing, 97
rasam, 111
Raspberry–White Chocolate Pound Cake, 218–219

refrigerator, supplies for, 19
rhubarb
  Rhubarb Muhammar, 56
  Strawberry Rhubarb Squares, 240–241
rice
  Autumn Vegetable Jambalaya, 182
  cooking methods for, 25
  Root Vegetable Biryani, 200–201
  Wild Rice–Stuffed Portobellos, 183
rice paper, 76
ricotta
  macadamia nut, 36
  Spinach & Ricotta Dumplings, 124–125
  Whipped Garlic Ricotta, 52
risotto, 74–75, 204–205
Roasted Cabbage & Farro Salad, 91
Roasted Carrot Hummus, 48
Roasted Cherry Tomato Sauce, 59
Roasted Eggplant & Pepper Soup, 107
Roasted Pepper Panzanella, 88–89
roasted peppers, 26
Roasted Potatoes with Dill & Garlic, 172–173
romanesco, 178
romano beans, 160–161
romesco sauce, 58
Root Vegetable Biryani, 200–201
rough puff, 139
Russian roulette peppers, 166
Rusyn people, 137
Rye Cake with Apricot Preserves, 220–221

S

Saffron Goat Cheese Risotto, 204–205
salads, 86–103
salt, 15–16
salted capers, 19
Sambal, 152
sauces
  Chanterelle Shumai with Mirin Sauce, 81
  Mint Pesto, 54–59, 150–151, 158
  mushrooms, 199
  Wild Mushrooms "Au Poivre," 181

Sautéed Pea Tendrils with Calabrian Chile, 153
Savory Johnny Cakes with Marinated Tomatoes, 71–73
seasonality, 22, 129. *See also* fall recipes; spring recipes; summer recipes; winter recipes
seeds, 25
sesame vinaigrette, 94–95
Sesame–Brown Sugar Cookies, 212–213
shallot, 145
Shared Cultures, 127
Shepherd's Pie, 188–189
Shishito peppers, 50, 166
shortbread, 214–215
shumai, 79–81
slaw, 148–149
Slow Roasted Chile-Orange Pecans, 65
Smashed Cannellini Bean Toasts, 70
snap peas, 97
soup, 104–121
Southwestern Style Gratin, 198–199
Souvlaki-Style Tofu Brochettes, 202–203
soy free, acronym for, 26
soy sauce, 16
Spinach & Ricotta Dumplings, 124–125
spreads, 47–53
spring garlic, 46
Spring Minestrone, 108–109
spring recipes
    Aloo Saag Pot Pie, 209
    Asparagus with Cannellini Beans, Creamy Tarragon Vinaigrette & Pickled Mustard Seeds, 170–717
    Autumn Vegetable Jambalaya, 182
    Avocado & Citrus Salad with Chimichurri, 98–100
    Baby Lettuces with Snap Peas & Extra-Herby Ranch, 97
    Basic Cut Pasta, 134
    Basic Flaky Pastry, 139
    Berebere Spiced Lentils, 172
    Blistered Shishito Peppers, 166
    Burrata Toasts with Balsamic Cherries, 68–69
    Celery & Peanut Noodle Salad, 92–93
    Chimichurri, 47

Chipotle & Lime Grilled Tofu, 187
Coconut Tapioca, 239
Coral Lentil Dal, 112–113
Couscous & Baby Artichoke Salad, 102–103
Creamy Garlic & Herb Polenta, 173
Escarole & Fagioli Pasta, 131
Ethiopian Cabbage & Potato Puffs, 143–144
Fava Bean & Green Garlic Fattoush, 90
Fig Preserves Tart with Tapioca Crust, 242
Fried Baby Artichokes, 62–63
Gigante Beans With Mint Pesto & Barley, 150–151
Graham Crackers, 217
Green Goddess Hummus, 44–45
Grilled Baby Fava Beans, 66
Grilled Cabbage with Makrut Lime Sambal, 152
Grilled Sweet Potatoes with Tahini Cashew Cream, 159
Grits with Creamy Creole-Style Mushrooms, 206–207
Kimchi Noodle Soup, 116–117
Lemongrass Tofu & Asparagus Stir-Fries, 186
Linguine with Cauliflower & Chard, 132–133
Makrut Lime Granita, 238
Mayocoba Beans with Urfa Biber, 167
Mint Pesto, 54–55
Mocha Roulade with Hazelnut-Mocha Whipped Cream, 225–226
Nettle & Goat Cheese Filo Rolls, 82
Peanut Hoisin Sauce, 57
Pierogi with Peas & Feta, 136–138
Raspberry–White Chocolate Pound Cake, 218–219
Rhubarb Muhammar, 56
Roasted Carrot Hummus, 48
Roasted Pepper Panzanella, 88–89
Roasted Potatoes with Dill & Garlic, 172–173
Rye Cake with Apricot Preserves, 220–221
Sautéed Pea Tendrils with Calabrian Chile, 153

Sesame–Brown Sugar Cookies, 212–213
Shepherd's Pie, 188–189
Slow Roasted Chile-Orange Pecans, 65
Smashed Cannellini Bean Toasts, 70
Souvlaki-Style Tofu Brochettes, 202–203
Spinach & Ricotta Dumplings, 124–125
Spring Minestrone, 108–109
Spring Vegetable Piccata, 178–179
Spring Yellow Curry, 196–197
Strawberry Rhubarb Squares, 240–241
Stuffed Eggplants with Couscous, 208
Sunchoke Koftas in Curry, 194–195
Sun-dried Tomato Harissa, 53
Sweet Potato Summer Rolls with Peanut Hoisin Sauce, 76–78
Turmeric Chickpea Soup, 106
Vegan Lemon Mousse with Cherry Compote, 236–237
Whipped Garlic Ricotta, 52
Wild Mushrooms "Au Poivre," 181
Yuca "Fries" with Beet Slaw, 148–149
squash
    Butternut Squash Soup, 115
    Honeynut Squash Gnocchi with Brown Butter, 128
    Masala Roasted Winter Squash, 164–165
    summer, 118
Star Canyon Ranch, 92, 95
Steamed Brussels Sprouts with "Cali" Kosho, 168–169
Stewed Romano Beans in Arrabiata, 160–161
stir-fries, 186
stock, Asian vegetable, 39
strawberries
    Mara des Bois strawberries, 129
    Strawberry Rhubarb Squares, 240–241
    Strawberry Tatsoi Salad, 94–95
Stuffed Eggplants with Couscous, 208
sugar, 19
sugar cookies, 212–213

summer recipes
    Autumn Vegetable Jambalaya, 182
    Basic Cut Pasta, 134
    Basic Flaky Pastry, 139
    Berebere Spiced Lentils, 172
    Blistered Shishito Peppers, 166
    Blueberry Lavender Cake with Cream Cheese Frosting, 230–231
    Celery & Peanut Noodle Salad, 92–93
    Chanterelle Shumai with Mirin Sauce, 79–81
    Chevre Cheesecake with Fresh Berries, 232–233
    Chiles Rellenos, 192–193
    Chimichurri, 47
    Chipotle & Lime Grilled Tofu, 187
    Coconut Tapioca, 239
    Coral Lentil Dal, 112–113
    Corn & Asiago Arancini, 74–75
    Corn & Poblano Empanadas, 140–142
    Creamy Corn Chowder, 110
    Creamy Garlic & Herb Polenta, 173
    Eggplant Caponata, 49
    Ethiopian Cabbage & Potato Puffs, 143–144
    Fettuccine with Herb-Marinated Tomatoes & Burrata, 130
    Fig Preserves Tart with Tapioca Crust, 242
    Gigante Beans With Mint Pesto & Barley, 150–151
    Goat Cheese–Stuffed Cherry Bomb Chiles, 67
    Graham Crackers, 217
    Grilled Cabbage with Makrut Lime Sambal, 152
    Grilled Peppers with Herby Corn Salsa, 162–163
    Grilled Romesco Sauce, 58
    Grilled Sweet Potatoes with Tahini Cashew Cream, 159
    Grilled Zucchini with Mint Pesto, 158
    Grits with Creamy Creole-Style Mushrooms, 206–207
    Heirloom Tomato & Stone Fruit Gazpacho, 120–121
    Linguine with Cauliflower & Chard, 132–133
    Makrut Lime Granita, 238
    Mayocoba Beans with Urfa Biber, 167
    Mint Pesto, 54–55
    Mocha Roulade with Hazelnut-Mocha Whipped Cream, 225–226
    Pappardelle with Peperonata & Shell Beans, 135
    Peaches & Coconut Cream Pie, 227–229
    Peanut Hoisin Sauce, 57
    Peperonata, 50–51
    Portobello Tamarind Soup, 114
    Pozole Verde, 118–119
    Roasted Cherry Tomato Sauce, 59
    Roasted Eggplant & Pepper Soup, 107
    Roasted Pepper Panzanella, 88–89
    Roasted Potatoes with Dill & Garlic, 172–173
    Rye Cake with Apricot Preserves, 220–221
    Saffron Goat Cheese Risotto, 204–205
    Savory Johnny Cakes with Marinated Tomatoes, 71–73
    Sesame–Brown Sugar Cookies, 212–213
    Shepherd's Pie, 188–189
    Slow Roasted Chile-Orange Pecans, 65
    Smashed Cannellini Bean Toasts, 70
    Souvlaki-Style Tofu Brochettes, 202–203
    Spinach & Ricotta Dumplings, 124–125
    Stewed Romano Beans in Arrabiata, 160–161
    Stuffed Eggplants with Couscous, 208
    Summer's Bounty Salad, 86–87
    Sun-dried Tomato Harissa, 53
    Sweet Potato Summer Rolls with Peanut Hoisin Sauce, 76–78
    Turmeric Chickpea Soup, 106
    Whipped Garlic Ricotta, 52
    Wild Mushrooms "Au Poivre," 181
    Yuca "Fries" with Beet Slaw, 148–149
summer rolls, 76–78

summer squash, 118
Summer's Bounty Salad, 86–87
Sunchoke Koftas in Curry, 194–195
Sun-dried Tomato Harissa, 53
sun-dried tomatoes, 16
sustainable greens, 184–185
sweet pickles, 32
sweet potatoes
    Grilled Sweet Potatoes with Tahini Cashew Cream, 159
    Sweet Potato Summer Rolls with Peanut Hoisin Sauce, 76–78
Swiss chard, 132–133

T

Tahini Cashew Cream, 159
Tahini Garlic Cashew Cream, 36
Taleggio cheese, 91, 145
tamarind, 114
tapioca, 239, 242
tarragon, 170–717
tarts, 242
Tashker, Sara, 155
tatsoi, 94–95
tenderness, 48
Thai curry, 197
tikil gomen, 143
toasts, 70
tofu
    Chipotle & Lime Grilled Tofu, 187
    Lemongrass Tofu & Asparagus Stir-Fries, 186
    Souvlaki-Style Tofu Brochettes, 202–203
tomatillos, 118
tomatoes, 88
    broiling, 58
    canned, 19
    Fettuccine with Herb-Marinated Tomatoes & Burrata, 130
    Heirloom Tomato & Stone Fruit Gazpacho, 120–121
    Roasted Cherry Tomato Sauce, 59
    Savory Johnny Cakes with Marinated Tomatoes, 71–73
    Sun-dried Tomato Harissa, 53
    when sweet or acidic, 89
Tsegaye, Adiam, 172
Turkish chili powder, 167
Turmeric Chickpea Soup, 106
Turmeric Ginger Cashew Cream, 36

U

urfa biber chile, 167

V

Vanilla-Poached Apple Cake, 234–235

vegan
    acronym for, 26
    Aioli, 35
    butter, 139
    Lemon Chive Aioli, 36

Vegan Lemon Mousse with Cherry Compote, 236–237

vegetables. *See also* specific types of vegetables
    Autumn Vegetable Jambalaya, 182
    pantries for, 15–19
    peeling, 26
    preparing, 26
    Root Vegetable Biryani, 200–201
    stock, 38–39
    vinaigrette
    Asparagus with Cannellini Beans, Creamy Tarragon Vinaigrette & Pickled Mustard Seeds, 170–717
    Creamy Sesame Vinaigrette, 94–95
    honey-dijon vinaigrette, 86
    peanut, 92
    pecans, 96

vinegars, 16

W

Wahpepah, Crystal, 183
walnuts, 222–223, 224
Waters, Alice, 47
Weinstein, Sidney, 95
Whipped Garlic Ricotta, 52
    white balsamic, 16
white chocolate, 218–219
white rice, 25
whole wheat flour, 217
Wild Mushrooms "Au Poivre," 181
wild rice
    cooking methods for, 25
    Wild Rice–Stuffed Portobellos, 183
wine, 16, 129

winter recipes
    Almond Cardamom Persimmon Pudding, 242
    Aloo Saag Pot Pie, 209
    Autumn Vegetable Jambalaya, 182
    Avocado & Citrus Salad with Chimichurri, 98–100
    Basic Cut Pasta, 134
    Basic Flaky Pastry, 139
    Berebere Spiced Lentils, 172
    Black Lentil Mulligatawny, 111
    Blistered Shishito Peppers, 166
    Brussels Sprouts, Caramelized Shallot & Taleggio Galette, 145
    Butternut Squash Soup, 115
    Chimichurri, 47
    Chipotle & Lime Grilled Tofu, 187
    Coconut Tapioca, 239
    Coral Lentil Dal, 112–113
    Cranberry Pistachio Almond Shortbread, 214–215
    Creamy Garlic & Herb Polenta, 173
    Creole Pumpkin & Collard Greens Soup, 104–105
    Escarole & Fagioli Pasta, 131
    Escarole & Potato Salad, 101
    Ethiopian Cabbage & Potato Puffs, 143–144
    Fig Preserves Tart with Tapioca Crust, 242
    Gigante Beans With Mint Pesto & Barley, 150–151
    Ginger Parsnip Oatmeal Cookies Graham Crackers, 216
    Graham Crackers, 217
    Grilled Cabbage with Makrut Lime Sambal, 152
    Grilled Sweet Potatoes with Tahini Cashew Cream, 159
    Grits with Creamy Creole-Style Mushrooms, 206–207
    Honeynut Squash Gnocchi with Brown Butter, 128
    Kimchi Noodle Soup, 116–117
    Linguine with Cauliflower & Chard, 132–133
    Makrut Lime Granita, 238
    Maple Black Walnut Baklava, 222–223
    Masala Roasted Winter Squash, 164–165
    Mayocoba Beans with Urfa Biber, 167
    Mint Pesto, 54–55
    Mocha Roulade with Hazelnut-Mocha Whipped Cream, 225–226
    Peanut Hoisin Sauce, 57
    Roasted Cabbage & Farro Salad, 91
    Roasted Carrot Hummus, 48
    Roasted Pepper Panzanella, 88–89
    Roasted Potatoes with Dill & Garlic, 172–173
    Root Vegetable Biryani, 200–201
    Sesame–Brown Sugar Cookies, 212–213
    Shepherd's Pie, 188–189
    Slow Roasted Chile-Orange Pecans, 65
    Smashed Cannellini Bean Toasts, 70
    Souvlaki-Style Tofu Brochettes, 202–203
    Stuffed Eggplants with Couscous, 208
    Sunchoke Koftas in Curry, 194–195
    Sun-dried Tomato Harissa, 53
    Sweet Potato Summer Rolls with Peanut Hoisin Sauce, 76–78
    Turmeric Chickpea Soup, 106
    Vanilla-Poached Apple Cake, 234–235
    Whipped Garlic Ricotta, 52
    Wild Mushrooms "Au Poivre," 181
    Wild Rice–Stuffed Portobellos, 183
    Yuca "Fries" with Beet Slaw, 148–149

winter squash, 115, 164–165

Y

yellow curry, 196–197
Yuca "Fries" with Beet Slaw, 148–149
yuzu kosho, 168–169

Z

zucchini, 118, 158

About the Author

KATIE REICHER, executive chef of San Francisco's renowned Greens Restaurant, brings a unique blend of family culinary traditions, formal training, and personal philosophy to her role. Raised in New York with influences from both Italian American and Ukrainian heritage, Katie developed a deep appreciation for seasonal, comforting cuisine from an early age. After studying at Cornell University and the Culinary Institute of America, she gained invaluable experience at Greens through an externship. Katie worked her way up through various positions at the restaurant before being named executive chef in 2020, continuing its legacy of female culinary leadership. Her approach to vegetarian cuisine is both traditional and innovative, focusing on seasonal ingredients and local sourcing. Katie aims to nourish guests physically, spiritually, and emotionally through her cooking. Her media appearances include NBC California Live and Forbes, and she actively collaborates with other renowned chefs, hosts dinner series, and participates in culinary summits and charitable events.

About the Photographer

ERIN SCOTT is a food and lifestyle photographer based in the San Francisco Bay Area. She's inspired by honest food, real people, and the magic of light. Erin comes to food photography as a passionate eater, gardener, and cook. She has been a fan of Greens for decades—Erin even had her prom dinner at the restaurant.

weldon**owen**

an imprint of Insight Editions
P.O. Box 3088
San Rafael, CA 94912
www.weldonowen.com

CEO Raoul Goff
SVP Group Publisher Jeff McLaughlin
VP Publisher Roger Shaw
Executive Editor Edward Ash-Milby
Assistant Editor Kayla Belser
VP Creative Chrissy Kwasnik
Art Director and Designer Megan Sinead Bingham
Production Designer Jean Hwang
VP Manufacturing Alix Nicholaeff
Senior Production Manager Joshua Smith
Strategic Production Planner Lina s Palma-Temena

Photographer Erin Scott
Food Stylist Lillian Kang
Food Stylist Assistant Paige Arnett
Photography Assistant Mark Davis

Weldon Owen would also like to thank the following people for their work and support in producing this book: Karen Levy , Jennifer Newens, Crystal Erickson, and Kevin Broccoli

Text © 2025 Katie Reicher
Photography (pages 4–5) © Chris Michel; Photography (pages 20–21) © Nader Khouri, Photography (page 23) © Nader Khouri

All rights reserved. No part of this book may be reproduced in any form without written permission from the publisher.

ISBN: 979-8-88674-143-8

Manufactured in China by Insight Editions
10 9 8 7 6 5 4 3 2 1

The information in this book is provided as a resource for inspiration and education. Author and Publisher expressly disclaim any responsibility for any adverse effects from the use or application of the information contained in this book. Neither the Publisher nor Author shall be liable for any losses suffered by any reader of this book.

Insight Editions, in association with Roots of Peace, will plant two trees for each tree used in the manufacturing of this book. Roots of Peace is an internationally renowned humanitarian organization dedicated to eradicating land mines worldwide and converting war-torn lands into productive farms and wildlife habitats. Roots of Peace will plant two million fruit and nut trees in Afghanistan and provide farmers there with the skills and support necessary for sustainable land use.